Privatization
in Bangladesh

Privatization in Bangladesh

Economic Transition in a Poor Country

Clare E. Humphrey

Westview Press
BOULDER, SAN FRANCISCO, & OXFORD

To Nizam Uddin Ahmed,
friend, colleague, and trail guide
along a treacherous path

Westview Special Studies on South and Southeast Asia

Published in 1990 in the United States of America by Westview Press, Inc., 5500 Central Avenue, Boulder, Colorado 80301, and in the United Kingdom by Westview Press, Inc., 36 Lonsdale Road, Summertown, Oxford OX2 7EW

Library of Congress Cataloging-in-Publication Data
Humphrey, Clare E.
    Privatization in Bangladesh : economic transition in a poor
country / by Clare E. Humphrey.
    p.   cm.—(Westview Special Studies on South and Southeast
Asia)
    Includes bibliographical references.
    ISBN 0-8133-7980-6
    1. Privatization—Bangladesh.   2. Government business enterprises—
Bangladesh.   I. Title.   II. Series: Westview special studies on
South and Southeast Asia.
    HD4295.6.H86   1990
    338.95492—dc20   90-34394
                                                                              CIP

Printed and bound in the United States of America

         The paper used in this publication meets the requirements
  (∞)   of the American National Standard for Permanence of Paper
         for Printed Library Materials Z39.48-1984.

10   9   8   7   6   5   4   3   2   1

Contents

Acknowledgments   ix

1 Introduction   1

Notes, 6

2 Privatization—An Overview   7

How to Approach Privatization: Ten Propositions
and Caveats, 8
Why Privatize? 9
Privatization in Traditional Societies, 13
Types of SOEs Suitable for Privatization, 15
Types of Privatization, 15
Notes, 18

**3 The Prelude—Colonialism, Partition,
Liberation, and Nationalization**   19

The British Period (1757–1947), 20
The Pakistan Period (1947–1971), 21
Liberation and Nationalization—the Mujib Period
(1971–1975), 28
Notes, 39

4 The First Phase (1975–1981)   46

The Zia Government, 46
Revised Investment Policy of 1975, 47
"Privatization" of the Commercial Sector, 50
The Industrial Sector and the Public/Private Mix, 52
Summary of the Zia Period (1975–1981), 56
Notes, 59

5 **The Second Phase (1982–1988)** 63

New Industrial Policy of 1982, 65
Reorganization and Revitalization of the Public
Enterprise System, 74
Privatization and Private Sector Development Since
NIP-'82, 77
Industrial Policy of 1986 and the "51-49 Plan," 85
Privatization in Bangladesh—A Recap, 91
Notes, 92

6 **The Private Sector's Performance** 98

Notes on the Bangladesh Business Community, 100
Interaction With the Government and the Public
Enterprises, 106
The Volatile Labor Question—The Dilemma of
Unemployment in a Poor Country, 113
The Traditional Tests—Management and the
Bottom Line, 118
Profit and Loss in Jute and Textiles, 124
Privatization of Fertilizer Distribution, 127
Summary, 129
Notes, 131

7 **The Public Sector's Performance** 136

Politics and the Decision-making Process, 137
Comparison With Taiwan's Privatization
Program, 141
Implementation of Privatization Policy, 144
The Public/Private Mix, 145
Foreign Investment, 147
Donor Agencies and Private Sector Development, 148
Improvement of the Public Enterprise System, 150
Selling Shares of Public Enterprises—
the 51-49 Plan, 152
The Future of Privatization in Bangladesh, 155
Notes, 157

8 **Conclusions and Recommendations** 160

Conclusions, 160
Recommendations, 163
Notes, 178

List of Acronyms and Abbreviations 179
Bibliography 183
Appendix A: Divested Industrial Enterprises 205
Appendix B: State-Owned Enterprises 252
Appendix C: Survey Questionnaire for
    Privatized Enterprises 258
Appendix D: Terms and Conditions for
    Transfer of Ownership of Privatized Jute Mills 261
Index 267
About the Author 275

Acknowledgments

The original study from which this book evolved was done under a contract with the Center for Privatization, a project of the U.S. Agency for International Development (USAID). It was designed to be USAID's first in-depth policy-oriented analysis of a country's privatization program.

The field research in Bangladesh was carried out in two phases, August-December 1986 and February-March 1987. The first draft of the study was written in Washington, D.C., over several months in the spring and early summer of 1987. After a lengthy review by the Center and USAID, in Washington and Dhaka, comments were sent to me in mid-October in Accra, Ghana, where I was serving on another assignment. Some revisions were made in Washington in late 1987, and a specially tailored executive summary with recommendations was submitted for the consideration of the government of Bangladesh in December 1987.

Several professional friends and colleagues, who had read and commented on the original study, urged me to consider publication. A two-month consulting assignment in Nepal intervened. That consultancy involved advising the cabinet and the King on the privatization of the state tea corporation. The intriguing experience of the Nepal assignment, coupled with my earlier study on Taiwan's pioneering divestiture of several large state enterprises, prompted me to take another look at the Bangladesh report as a useful case study. The job of collecting additional material and editing, revising, and updating the original study was accomplished in the spring and summer of 1988.

In the course of the field research in Bangladesh, I met with more than one hundred government and business leaders. Particular appreciation is expressed to His Excellency Vice President Moudud Ahmed (who at that time was Deputy Prime Minister and Minister of Industries) for a lengthy interview and assistance in obtaining important data on the government's privatization program.

Special thanks are also due to Shamsul Haque Chishty, Secretary, Ministry of Establishment, to whom anyone studying privatization in Bangladesh is indebted for the landmark paper he wrote on the subject for an Asian Development Bank conference in 1985. I also wish to thank Dr. Tawfique Chowdhury, Joint Secretary, Ministry of Finance, Mr. Azizul Haque, Additional Secretary, Ministry of Industries, Dr. Shahadat Ullah of the Planning Commission, and Mr. Shafiul Azam, former Minister of Industries. Dr. Surrinder Malik, Chief Economist of the World Bank office in Dhaka, was most accommodating in sharing economic data, World Bank analyses, and his own formidable knowledge of Bangladesh's economy.

I especially wish to express my profound appreciation and respect to Mr. Shafiqur Rahman, retired Joint Secretary, Ministry of Industries. Shafiqur Rahman, Bangladesh's leading authority on privatization, was most generous in sharing his knowledge and insights during eight lengthy meetings with me.

Innumerable business leaders were unsparing of their time and thoughts. I honor their requests for anonymity, but acknowledge the value of their contributions.

The staff of USAID/Dhaka could not have been more cooperative and supportive during the lengthy periods of field research. I want particularly to thank Mission Director John Westley and Howard "Bob" Kramer, Director of the Programs Office.

My wife, Rosalie, spent countless hours reading drafts, smoothing out stylistic rough spots, questioning questionable logic, and patiently explaining the complexities of our computer. She several times received telephone calls at her office from a thoroughly panicked spouse, after I had perpetrated some error on that unfathomable yet indispensable electronic marvel. She was always able to come to my rescue. A special thanks is due our daughter, Linda, a professional editor, for venturing into that sensitive area of suggesting improvements to the parental prose (which definitely benefitted in the process) and for formatting the manuscript for publication.

Above all, I wish to express my appreciation for the dedication and competence of my chief collaborator on this project, Mr. Nizam Uddin

Ahmed of the USAID/Dhaka staff. The study could not have been completed without his unparalleled contacts and his keen insights into the functioning of the Bangladesh bureaucracy and Bengali society. Therefore, it is my great pleasure to dedicate this study to him. However, I assume sole responsibility for the material and views expressed in this study.

Clare E. Humphrey
Washington, D.C.

1

Introduction

This study of privatization in Bangladesh has been undertaken for two reasons. First, privatization is increasingly recognized as a legitimate and effective tool for economic transformation and development. In fact, some observers believe that privatization may be one of the most important trends in economic development in the coming decade.

Second, Bangladesh has been chosen for this study both because it is a country with monumental social and economic development problems, and because it has divested more state-owned enterprises (SOEs) than any other less developed country (LDC). The convergence of these factors makes a study of privatization in Bangladesh appropriate and, hopefully, valuable to observers and practitioners concerned with economic development, social change, and modernization in the Third World.

Country after country has come to the conclusion, albeit some reluctantly and belatedly, that the private sector functions more effectively than the public sector. At the minimum, privatization is a way to tap the energy and resourcefulness of the private sector, while reducing government losses and budget drains.

As a consequence, there has been a gradual, but widespread movement to transfer government assets and functions to the private sector, thereby dismantling some of the state enterprises and state control systems so painstakingly constructed during the 1950s, '60s, and early '70s.

Privatization transactions have covered a wide spectrum of geo-

graphic and economic sectors in a variety of countries at vastly different stages of development. A representative sampling could include:[1]

- telecommunications in the United Kingdom and Italy
- airlines in Singapore, Niger, and Malaysia
- banks in Chile, Bangladesh, and the Philippines
- fisheries in Kenya and Somalia
- mining in Taiwan and Togo
- aluminum in Costa Rica
- hotels in Mexico, Sierra Leone, and Jamaica
- oil and petrochemicals in South Korea and the United Kingdom
- fertilizer and seed distribution in Senegal
- paper manufacturing in Thailand and Taiwan
- tool manufacturing in the Ivory Coast
- rice and flour milling in Pakistan
- cement in Turkey and Taiwan
- jute and textile mills in Bangladesh
- port authority and container terminal in Malaysia
- sugar in Uganda and Jamaica
- bus systems in Sri Lanka and Argentina
- holding companies in Brazil
- auto manufacture/assembly in Spain, Mozambique, and Mexico
- road supervision and construction in India and Bolivia
- prisons in the United States
- food processing in Mali, Zaire, and Turkey
- bicycle and scooter manufacturing in India
- forestry in Ecuador

This listing is illustrative, but not all-inclusive; it has been included
to provide some sense of the diversity of privatization activities. The
procedural approaches and privatization techniques employed in these
transactions have been equally varied.

One of the more encouraging aspects of the privatization picture in
the Third World is that the impetus for much of the activity has
originated from the LDCs themselves, rather than from aid-donor
countries attempting to shove western free-enterprise down their
throats.

Of course, there has been some donor pressure to which aid-dependent countries have prudently responded. But in many instances,
beleaguered LDC governments have come to officials of developed
countries and said in effect, "We've got a problem. Our state enterprises are floundering; but we don't know what to do about it. Please
give us some guidance on how to extricate ourselves from this di-

lemma." While such a scenario indicates the presence of problems, it demonstrates a healthier attitude and greater commitment than mendicancy.

Considering the great amount of privatization activity that has taken place, it is surprising that no in-depth study of one country's privatization effort has been carried out. There have been a number of worldwide surveys of privatization transactions and several procedural "how to" manuals. However, most existing studies (with a few outstanding exceptions) have been concerned with technical rather than policy issues.

Additionally, most studies have been transaction-oriented, aimed at the enterprises being privatized. Less attention has been given to analyzing the overall national scene and the underlying forces and factors—social, historical, political, and cultural, as well as economic— that influence development, government decisions and privatization programs. Some observers believe that useful lessons can be gleaned from a comprehensive study of one country's overall experience with privatization and the conditions and issues surrounding it. What is needed is one country's privatization story, as completely as it is possible to tell it, and this is the prime motivation behind the present study.

Why Bangladesh? Partly because more public enterprises have been divested there than in any other country—a total of 1,076. The 609 of these that were in the industrial sector will be the focal point of our investigations. This stupendous statistical record prompted such a recognized authority as Elliot Berg to rhapsodically refer to Bangladesh as one of two "champion performers in the world of privatization or divestiture."[2] One of the main thrusts of this study will be to determine if this accolade is deserved.

But it is not only the sheer number of Bangladesh's privatization transactions that provides useful insights into the complexities of privatization there or anywhere else. I shall leave to the concluding chapter an evaluation of whether quantity equates with quality. Other statistics and features are equally compelling for drawing the thoughtful observer to Bangladesh.

For one thing, Bangladesh is somewhat atypical in that the majority of its many privatization transactions have been divestitures. In contrast to the popular conception, divestiture is not the most often used method of privatization. It is, on the contrary, one of the least often used, mainly because of the financial and political complexities and pitfalls involved in implementing it. On the other hand, analysis of these very difficulties in the Bangladesh context can provide meaningful insights.

Most readers who pick up this study are probably already familiar with Bangladesh's situation. But for those who are approaching this study because of their interest in privatization, rather than any particular knowledge of Bangladesh, a few notes might be in order.[3]

Bangladesh covers an area of 55,598 square miles. This is slightly smaller than Iowa, which ranks 25th among American states. But instead of Iowa's comfortable population of about 3 million, Bangladesh is jammed with 107 million souls, most of whom live in abject poverty and squalor.

The average per capita income is $150 per year, and perhaps 80 percent of the population live below that. Even the lowest cost of living framework cannot make that into a living wage. Annual population increase is averaging 2.5 percent. Life expectancy is improving, but is still only around age 50. Health and nutrition figures are sobering. Literacy is estimated at 24 percent, but only 10 percent for women.

Although blessed with a rich cultural heritage that has produced some of South Asia's greatest poets and writers, the area we now call Bangladesh has had a checkered history. It has suffered in debilitating succession from British colonialism and exploitation; an unequal partnership with Pakistan resulting in a bloody fratricidal war of liberation, followed by two coups complete with presidential assassinations; an unsuccessful experiment with socialism which featured nationalization of the industrial sector; and political and economic instability that has continued to the present day.

In addition, the Bengalis have been plagued with the disruption and factionalism normally associated with an impoverished, conservative society in the throes of traumatic change. Traditional ways appear inadequate for the challenges of late twentieth century society, but no new system of values and practices has arisen to replace them. Islam is the only cultural shield and solace against an otherwise hostile environment.

Economically, East Bengal cum East Pakistan cum Bangladesh has always been a backwater area, dominated, alternately, by Calcutta, London, or Karachi. Bangladesh has been called an "international basket case" for more than a decade. It is the poorest large country in the world. The economy is heavily agricultural, and the population is rural and conservative. Agricultural output and productivity are increasing, but relatively inelastic. Natural gas is the only plentiful natural resource.

Infrastructure is inadequate. Topography dictates transportation. More produce and people are transported on the many rivers than on roads and railroads combined. The extensive river system and the agricultural economy as a whole are vulnerable to annual flooding during the monsoon season. Rampant deforestation has increased erosion and the danger of flooding. A few years ago, a tidal wave and consequent flooding wiped out 300,000 people at a single stroke.

Industry, while currently only about 15 percent of gross domestic product (GDP), is increasing. It offers the best hope for economic progress, employment expansion and better income distribution. One of the many tragedies of Bangladesh's situation is that its leading industry and foreign exchange earner, jute, is an industry that is slowly dying due to competition from synthetic fibers.

The work force is unskilled and unmotivated except for survival. The fledgling management group, while expanding and improving professionally, is still more attuned to trade and commerce than industry and to the demands of familial rather than corporate enterprise.

In view of all of the adverse factors present in Bangladesh, it is amazing that any progress has been made, but it has. Almost all of the gains have been registered in the private sector. The pervasive but inertial state enterprise system continues to lose money. A mixed, broader-based, more diverse and balanced economy is emerging, but the process is agonizingly slow and painful.

Privatization has been at the center of the process and the accompanying controversy. The recent economic history of Bangladesh cannot be analyzed properly without an understanding of the issues surrounding privatization. Conversely, Bangladesh has had to confront, at one time or another, and in one form or another, almost every problem faced by LDCs trying to get out of the bog of economic stagnation. The fact that Bangladesh's circumstances have been especially stark only makes it a more suitable case study. If privatization can assist in generating positive and substantial benefits to Bangladesh's troubled economy, the lessons can be adapted and applied elsewhere.

With this in mind, the approach throughout this study has been to consider several basic questions related to the process of privatization.

These basic questions fall into two categories: six questions designed to analyze the Bangladesh experience; and six which stress self-analysis for those concerned with development problems of other lands.

Questions to Ponder About the Bangladesh Case

- What did they do?
- What were the conditions that prompted them to do it?

- What were their short-range objectives and strategies?
- What were their long-range objectives and strategies?
- What did they accomplish, and how?
- Where did they fail, and why?

Questions for Other Countries to Ponder About Their Own Situations

- What do we want to accomplish in the long run?
- What do we want to accomplish in the short run?
- What is our plan of action?
- What factors will most affect our efforts, both positively and negatively?
- What can we adapt from the Bangladesh experience?
- What must we do differently, and why?

This approach may seem simplistic to some, but it strikes to the core of our purpose. Each factor, each step in the process of privatization, should be scrutinized through the prism of these and similar questions. Such application, done with thoughtfulness, candor, and consistency can transform this study from a document to be read into a tool to be used.

We shall come back to these questions at the end of the study as a reflective exercise during our final evaluation.

Notes

1. This listing has been compiled from a variety of periodical, scholarly and official sources. In a number of the economic categories listed here, there has been activity in other countries besides the ones mentioned.

2. Stated in a speech presented at a Conference on Privatization, held in Washington, D.C., in February 1986 under the sponsorship of the U.S. Agency for International Development (USAID). The other country is Chile. Berg further stated that they "are far and away the leaders of the divestiture parade in the less developed world." ibid.

3. The figures that follow came from a number of sources, but mainly from *Statistical Pocket Book of Bangladesh—1986* (Dhaka, Bangladesh Bureau of Statistics, 12/2/86), and from several publications of the World Bank.

2

Privatization—An Overview

The principal purpose of this study is to document and analyze Bangladesh's extraordinary experiment with privatization of the industrial sector of its "modern" economy and, to a lesser extent, of commercial, financial, and agri-business institutions and activities as well. The preoccupation of the study will, therefore, be with what has actually been taking place in Bangladesh. But if this exercise is to be useful to those both inside and outside of Bangladesh who are grappling with the complexities, potentialities, and pitfalls of privatization, we should first devote some attention to certain salient features of and basic questions related to the privatization process. Chapter 1 offered a few descriptive notes on the scope of privatization around the world. This chapter attempts to provide some understanding of the nature of the phenomenon.

This chapter will present a brief overview of some distinctive aspects of privatization, which, while a relatively new phenomenon on the development scene, has attracted worldwide attention and occasioned heated debate in recent years. This overview is not intended to be an in-depth theoretical or technical discourse on privatization, but rather a brief exposition of a few important, practical issues that one should bear in mind when approaching the study of any country's privatization situation. This overview can serve as a logical framework for my analysis of Bangladesh's privatization policies and programs.

The reader will not be burdened with the usual pedantic, meticulous "definition of privatization." We will assume that the audience

7

to which this study is addressed already has a relatively well-developed perception of what privatization amounts to and what it involves. Therefore, it will suffice to say that the term "privatization" will be used in this study in its widest possible sense, i.e., the replacement of government institutions or activities with those of the private sector.

How to Approach Privatization: Ten Propositions and Caveats

The following is a set of general thoughts to keep in mind while reading this study. These thoughts do not constitute a comprehensive conceptual framework for the subject, but they have influenced how this study was approached and structured. They do represent the author's viewpoint or bias, but should be taken as a point of departure rather than a subjective, ideological argument. They will be analyzed, clarified, and elaborated upon in various ways in subsequent sections of this chapter and throughout the rest of the study.

1. Privatization is often more influenced by political issues than by strictly economic considerations.

2. Privatization and divestiture are not synonymous. Divestiture is only one type of privatization, and is perhaps one of the least attractive and least utilized methods. There are "many roads to privatization," just as there are to its counterpart, socialism.

3. Privatization is too often associated primarily with questions of equity, particularly in developed countries; but privatization of a *function* or *service* can, at times, be just as important. A good illustration of this has been the privatization of fertilizer distribution in Bangladesh.

4. One should approach this subject from the standpoint of privatization of an *economy*, not merely the unloading of inefficient, money-losing state enterprises. Privatization should be undertaken to develop viable enterprises and a more vibrant economy, not simply to cut state-owned enterprise (SOE) losses or reduce government deficits.

5. A government's privatization policy will be ineffective unless it is preceded by a well thought-out plan with clearly defined long-range objectives, backed up with will and commitment, and implemented through an effort that is comprehensive, coordinated, and consistent.

6. Privatization of state enterprises will accomplish little without parallel government-sponsored policies and programs to en-

courage, assist, and cooperate with the private sector. The private sector must be viewed by the government as an economic partner, not a competitor. Establishing conditions that generally promote the benefits of competitive market forces is crucial to the success of privatization.

7. Privatization should be approached as a policy-oriented subject, not a bookkeeping problem. Zeroing in initially on the individual state enterprise often obscures this basic fact. It also places the cart before the horse. Analyzing the policy framework and regulatory environment within which privatization and the private sector must operate is infinitely more productive than "calling in the investment bankers" or "looking into the books" of public enterprises that are likely candidates for unloading.

8. The approach to privatization should be pragmatic, rather than ideological, with the emphasis on "what will work in this society, this bureaucracy, this situation." Fortunately, pragmatism has been more displayed by LDC governments than by some of their privatization mentors from developed nations.

9. There is no standard formula for privatization. Conditions, problems, strategies and solutions will vary from country to country, although many of the more basic privatization issues appear almost everywhere, transcending cultural barriers. Innovators should empathetically tailor privatization efforts to local situations, while guarding against the tendency of traditional societies undergoing painful transition to use distinctive circumstances and sociocultural patterns as a shield to avoid taking action on needed change.

10. Privatization is a means, not an end; and it is not a panacea for solving all the ills of a sick economy. Privatization is fraught with political, social, and economic problems and risks; its implementation is characterized by nagging uncertainties and few short-term victories; it is an untidy business.

If all this is true, why would any government leader in his right mind opt to follow a course of privatization? They are doing so in increasing numbers for the same reason that people choose democracy or surgical operations—while not completely reassuring or satisfying, they (and privatization) are preferable to the alternative.

Why Privatize?

Very few governments have embarked on a program of privatization because they wanted to. Most have done so because they felt they had to. It has largely been a negative, reluctant act undertaken because the existing method of building the economy and doing business through state-operated enterprises and state control systems was not working well. Because privatizing is usually tried because something else has failed, it is seldom approached with the same positive attitude or amount of planning accorded the preceding system. Emphasis is placed on getting rid of something rather than building up something else. As a consequence, LDC governments frequently have not thought out the subject thoroughly, have not anticipated the implications of their actions, prepared solutions or countermeasures, or even coped with situations that arose out of privatization policy moves.

Not infrequently, privatization has been viewed as the lesser of two evils. At times, it has actually been regarded as the greater evil, but one that at least held out the hope (often a forlorn one) of greater "efficiency" and "profitability." But deep down in their hearts, most LDC governments still feel more comfortable with the economy largely concentrated in the public sector (the so-called "controlling the commanding heights" syndrome), rather than in the hands of what some in the government view as the unpredictable, hard to control, unscrupulous, and selfish private sector.

This is still the belief in many LDCs, despite the growing body of evidence that the countries with the most rapid and balanced economic development are those that have opted for a mixed economy led by a strong, vibrant private sector. Perhaps the fear of foraging into the unknown and the distrust with which the business community has been held in most traditional societies partially explain why the mythology of privatization has spread more widely than its actual application. Nevertheless, it does appear that "the era of wholesale expansion of public sector enterprises . . . is drawing to a close, replaced by encouragement for private development and, in many cases, a drive to privatize existing parastatals."[1]

One might ask what prompted the establishment and expansion of state enterprise systems that so characterized Third World economic development in the nineteen fifties, sixties, and even into the mid-seventies. A representative sampling of reasons includes:

- Most LDCs were ill-prepared to operate in the modern, competitive economic scene that emerged after World War II. At independence, most LDCs inherited economic systems that had been controlled by the interests of the former colonial power. Therefore, there was a tradition of direct government participation in and control of the economy.

- LDC economies were generally quite elementary and fragile, heavily agricultural, and oriented toward production of raw, or at best, processed materials. The economy and such supporting infrastructure as existed had been designed to serve the interests of the former colonial system rather than the more comprehensive needs of an independent nation.
- The few indigenous persons with a modicum of management experience were established in the bureaucracy, not the business community. The civil service contained the educated elite.
- The business sector was essentially commercial in nature, not industrial. The business community was largely composed of traders, retailers, and a few service people, with ethnic minorities or foreigners often controlling whatever distribution and financial systems existed.
- Political and economic instability and consequent feelings of insecurity inhibited private investment, both foreign and domestic.
- In almost all traditional societies, the business sector was regarded with distrust, even disdain, and placed at the lower end of the social ladder. In many countries there was a rich tradition of exploitation by self-serving, clannish monopoly capital.

Under these and other circumstances, it is small wonder that LDC governments decided that the interests of the people as a whole would best be served if the economy were placed firmly in the hands of the government, not just for planning and oversight, but operationally as well. Government enterprises and companion control systems were seen as the most effective way to:

- generate revenue for the treasury;
- implement policy—economic, political, and social;
- protect national security through direct intervention in strategic areas;
- expand the economy and control the directions it takes and the way it functions;
- encourage foreign investment in cooperation with large, stable government institutions;
- ensure equitable distribution of products, services, and benefits to all segments of society.

These various motives are often found mixed together, inseparably, in an ill-defined policy mish-mash.[2] They are often blunted or cancelled out by contradictory economic and social aims. "Unrecognized or unresolved conflicts within these aims and between them and prevailing market conditions have been an important underlying factor when parastatals have failed to discharge their (assigned) duties efficiently."[3]

The ability of state enterprises to perform productively is affected when they are manipulated for political reasons to weaken political opposition or pay off political cronies (for instance, after independence or after a coup) or for purposes of personal gain. A state enterprise offers enormous possibilities for in-house corruption, another reason some "public servants" resist moves toward privatization. Many observers have come to wonder if the government sector is, after all, the champion of the general welfare.

In many LDCs during the first euphoric years after independence, overly ambitious plans were launched, impossible tasks undertaken, and extravagant promises made. Given the nature and magnitude of the challenges, and the thin human and financial resources available to meet them, it was inevitable that underachievement would result in most LDCs, with consequent disillusionment and cynicism.

It soon became obvious that state enterprise systems were inefficient, unimaginative, inertial, overblown bureaucracies, unable to understand and respond to the economic forces of national and international marketplaces. They were obviously incapable of providing the dynamic leadership and operational performance required for the growth and progress the nation wanted. Though some government enterprises were well managed and operated at a profit, most lost money (some heavily); and the entire state-controlled system created a tremendous and ever-increasing drain on an already tight national budget and strained resources.

By the mid-seventies, the economic situation in many LDCs was not only not improving, it was deteriorating, due to both internal shortcomings and adverse conditions in the world economy over which struggling LDCs had little or no control.

In the search for solutions, the role of the private sector in developing a more varied, dynamic economy was given increased attention, at least in policy circles. The impetus for this stemmed from four sources.

First was the striking example of how some formerly less-developed countries had achieved remarkable economic growth, essentially through the medium of private sector development. Countries such as Korea, Taiwan, Malaysia, and Singapore were seen as models.

Second, private sectors in many LDCs had, over the years, gradually developed greater capacities for handling a wider range of more sophisticated economic activities. Financial and human resources, while still in short supply, were at least more plentiful and professional than before.

Third, dissatisfaction with the performance of enterprises directly operated by the state prompted officials to look at the advantages of a changed role for government, that of a planner, pump primer and watchdog, but no longer a factory manager.

Fourth, bilateral and multilateral donor agencies, who had formerly been just as eager as recipient governments to entrust new ventures to government operations (it was easier for both sides), began exerting subtle and not so subtle pressures to encourage private sector initiatives and to limit or reduce public enterprise activities. Although the accusation of foreign donor pressure is often overstressed by critics of privatization, there is no doubt that donors must bear appropriate responsibility for both the problem and the solution. Additionally, donor representations on the issue have at times been more ideological than the inclinations of LDC recipients, who have tended to wrestle with economic problems on more pragmatic terms.

Of course, there have been other motivations for privatization beyond the four just listed. They have been as varied as the conditions that created the particular country's situation. The issues, problems, and possible solutions vary with each country. As stated previously, there are no "formula" solutions or universal models; there are only broad principles and unifying threads for guidance. Conversely, while each country is in many ways unique, many have similar developmental problems.

Privatization in Traditional Societies

One aspect of the process of social change and modernization that is all too frequently (and conveniently) overlooked is that much of the problem is deeply imbedded in the nature and contemporary problems of traditional societies undergoing rapid, traumatic transition with which they cannot comfortably cope. Most LDC societies are faction-ridden and basically inequitous, with strong antagonisms between rural and urban populations, between military and civilian factions, educated and illiterate, rich and poor, and family and "outsiders." Such societies are also burdened with tribal rivalries, linguistic and religious barriers with political overtones, and ethnic animosities and discrimination. Traditional values and institutions are being seriously questioned, but new, satisfying value systems that would enable people to cope better with the challenges of late 20th century life have not been developed to replace them.

Viewed in this context, the public versus private sector debate takes on a different coloration, one that owes less to any foreign political or economic ideology, but is more illuminated by indigenous behavioral and organizational patterns. These are especially pertinent features to analyze when one bears in mind that in most traditional societies there has usually been a special relationship between the rulers and the commercial sector. Despite the social distance that was rigidly maintained between the two groups, the merchants depended on the rulers for patronage and the elite needed the traders' money. One is led to wonder whether the corrupt official and the avaricious businessman are aberrations or typical representatives of troubled, transitional societies and their value systems?

Critics of privatization abound. Intellectuals and academics are among the most vocal, usually along ideological lines related to distribution of income, protection of the poor, and service to society as a whole. The bureaucracy resists it as a threat to cherished and deeply entrenched prerogatives to job security, power, and carefully cultivated patterns of graft. Workers and unions fight privatization out of fear that increased efficiency will be achieved by laying off workers. Even some well-placed members of the economic oligarchy use their influence to curtail privatization and any broadening of the base of private sector activity for fear of losing their dominance over the economy.

All of these groups are able to influence the general public through their own constituencies and control over the media. About the only constituencies on the side of privatization are the rest of the business community (including the Chamber of Commerce and Industry and other trade associations) and a few economic planners and political leaders (who also wield influence over the media in most LDCs). The battle lines are drawn; and only a consistent, long-term effort with measurable, visible results will tip the scales one way or the other.

Many of the motives underlying the drive for privatization are, ironically but predictably, similar to the reasons that prompted nationalization in the first place. The two phenomena merely reflect vastly different approaches to accomplishing the same goals, such as reduction of fiscal drain, replenishment of the exchequer, attraction of private investment, response to donor pressure, ideological commitment, efficiency, and economic expansion.

It is essential that governments contemplating a shift in the public-private mix develop a privatization strategy with clearly defined objectives and goals. Such a strategy will keep them aware of where they should be heading. Otherwise, they are just trying to reduce deficits by unloading unsuccessful public enterprises on a private sector that doesn't want them.

Types of SOEs Suitable for Privatization

After the goals and objectives of privatization are planned out, one of the primary tasks is to select which SOEs are suitable for privatization. There are four types to consider. They are SOEs that are:

1. sound and profitable
2. basically sound, but not presently profitable
3. profitable, but basically unsound
4. neither profitable nor sound

Only the first two are good candidates for privatization. The first choice of most governments is usually number four. Unloading of such "dogs" is a mistake. The basic purpose of privatization should be to strengthen an economy, not just relieve the government budget. The third is not a good choice. Such SOEs have probably avoided losses mainly because of subsidies or preferential treatment that would not be provided to a private company.

Even the second type is a marginal choice, to be implemented only if it appears that through more efficient management, trimmed staff, improved marketing and the like, the firm can perform better in a competitive market. Most countries have not learned from Malaysia or Taiwan that greater long-range benefits for all concerned will result from transferring profitable properties that will contribute to the economy and breed confidence in the business community that the government is serious about promoting economic growth through privatization and private sector activity.

Proper handling of the privatization transaction is another key step in this complex process. The negotiations must be conducted with scrupulous attention to fairness, impartiality, and honesty. The valuation of assets and setting of a sales price that is mutually advantageous are most important. The tendency of government auditors is to set the price too high in order to avoid accusations that the government is giving away the country's patrimony to rich cronies and power brokers. The treasury deserves a fair return, but the buyer must not be burdened with obligations that put survival of the enterprise in doubt from the outset.

Types of Privatization

As we have pointed out, divestiture by selling the entire enterprise by open tender or to selected buyers is not the only way to transfer government assets or functions to the private sector. Some of the other methods are:

1. *Partial divestiture.* Partial divestiture can involve sale of a particular unit of a particular SOE, but is usually concerned with sale of a percentage of the SOE's shares. Sale of minority shares is sometimes criticized as not really being privatization, but merely a way to raise money from the private sector. But if it is used to help build a capital market where none previously existed and is aimed at eventual majority private ownership, this method can be productive, up to a point.

2. *Break-up.* Break-up usually involves selling or spinning off sections of large SOEs, i.e., units that can be viable on their own. Marketing arms are frequently good candidates, because sales and marketing are areas where governments are usually fairly inept. Splitting of commercial and policy or promotional functions is increasingly favored. Additionally, SOEs are often umbrella organizations for a variety of disparate units that have little relation to one another.

3. *Liquidation or close-down.* To liquidate is a difficult decision for a government, because it involves admitting a failure. Sometimes, this tactic involves the establishment of a new private counterpart. It also necessitates unloading government assets at fire sale prices, with inevitable public criticism. Liquidation does, however, have the one saving grace of putting an end to continuing losses, while putting some cash in the till.

4. *Marginalization.* This is sometimes called "quiet liquidation." It involves freezing or gradual reduction of an SOE's budget or operations, while slowly building up a replacement in the private sector. This method is proving useful in many cases. It is politically less volatile than outright divestiture. The long-term returns are greater, though short-range costs can be higher, since two entities must be supported during the early stages of the process.

The proper method of privatization will vary from case to case and country to country. Much will depend on the sophistication and condition of the local economy in general, and of the private sector in particular. The goal is to build up a broader, more varied, and more dynamic economic base, which will do a better job of reaping the benefits of a more competitive market economy. The goal is definitely not to replace a public monopoly with a private monopoly.

The government should make every effort to make clear to the public that it is trying to create new jobs and generate wider ownership and more equitable income distribution, not wittingly or unwittingly concentrating wealth under the guise of "privatization."

It is inevitable that interests opposed to privatization will recommend that the public sector and its SOEs should be given the "three Rs treatment," that is Reorganization, Reform, and Rehabilitation. This is an attractive alternative for insecure governments. It is an approach with which they are familiar and comfortable. It is usually an unproductive approach as well, perpetuating, even enhancing, inherent weaknesses and vested interests.

This approach is sometimes combined with recommendations for contract management, franchising, or leasing arrangements for SOE operations. Such mechanisms can improve SOE efficiency and profitability to a certain extent, depending on the degree of autonomy given to the management contractor. But the results will usually be limited, because the basic bureaucratic environment within which public sector enterprises must exist will still be the prevailing, even pervasive influence. Also, such methods do not address the question of the link between efficiency and survival in a competitive market.[4]

Leasing or franchising shift the focus of the enterprise a bit more toward a market-driven mode, because the lessee or franchise operator is usually given a freer hand in running the enterprise on a businesslike basis, even though the government maintains a modicum of influence and certain residual rights.

Governments frequently justify management contracts as a "stepping stone" to eventual privatization. The stated rationale is that if the troubled SOE is first reorganized and then run more efficiently by private sector personnel and methods, its value will increase and it can eventually be sold at a better price. While this has happened in some instances, the management contract has more often been used as a ploy to keep the SOE within the government. Additionally, if contract management does whip the SOE into shape and it starts making money, the likelihood is greater that the government will then decide to keep it, despite having been shown evidence that private operation may be the way to go.

Drives to improve the performance of the public sector mesh with legitimate desires to further the social goals and programs of the government. Public enterprises, by their very nature are better suited to address such questions than are private companies. In a developing country with a subsistence economy, this is a matter which must be studied carefully and sympathetically. There are other fields in which national security is directly involved. Some SOE operations and functions should remain in government hands.

A variety of financial methods and arrangements are employed to carry out privatization transactions. While it is not the purpose of this overview section to investigate such mechanisms thoroughly, a list of a few of the more important ones might prove useful. Such methods include obtaining loans from official banks or development finance institutions (DFIs), establishing loan guarantee programs in cooperation with private commercial banks, floating shares or convertible bonds, creating debt-equity swaps, forgiving liabilities or allowing flexibility in valuation of SOEs being unloaded, making changes in the regulatory environment, establishing trusts for employee stock option programs (ESOP), encouraging private investment, setting up joint ventures involving international or domestic partners, and obtaining multilateral or binational donor financing. These and several other mechanisms will be discussed in some detail at appropriate points throughout the study.

The issues mentioned in this brief overview, along with many other complex pressures and problems, bedevil beleaguered governments as they try to promote economic progress and well-being for their people. The following chapters investigate how the government of Bangladesh has addressed these issues while carrying out the Third World's most extensive program of privatization.[5]

Notes

1. Bremer, Jennifer: *Options for Privatizing Agricultural Parastatals in Developing Countries* (abstract of unpublished paper, Washington, D.C., Robert R. Nathan Associates, 1986), p. 2. For much of the content of this chapter, I am indebted to Ms. Bremer through her excellent paper and numerous conversations with her. I have also been influenced in more general terms by the fine pioneering work in privatization of Elliot Berg and L. Gray Cowan, several of whose works are listed in the Bibliography.

2. ibid, p. 7.

3. ibid, pp. 7-8.

4. ibid, p. 5.

5. This introductory "overview" was written independently from the body of the study and the field research conducted in Bangladesh. Naturally, I hope the reader will detect a correlation between the content of this overview and the rest of the study. However, I want to make it clear that one was not written to either pre-ordain or document the other.

3

The Prelude—Colonialism, Partition, Liberation, and Nationalization

Useful insights for unravelling the complexities of Bangladesh's extensive privatization effort, and for gaining some understanding of how and why events evolved in the ways they have, can be gleaned from studying the three periods that preceded the emergence of a comprehensive privatization policy in 1975 under the regime of President Ziaur Rahman. Those three periods cover British colonial rule (1757-1947), union with Pakistan (1947-1971), and the first post-liberation government of independent Bangladesh under Sheikh Mujibur Rahman (1971-1975).

Conditions, patterns, and attitudes shaped during those epochs have directly and profoundly affected not only policies and practices of subsequent Bangladesh governments, but also the way Bengali society itself functions. Some of this is, of course, predictable in the evolution of any country or society; but the way the process has manifested itself in Bangladesh is often surprising.

The persistence of problems related to both the design and implementation of economic development and privatization policies makes one wonder whether the question is less one of public versus private sector dominance than it is a matter of the traits of Bengali society itself, its values, standards, and behavioral patterns, and its capacity to accept change and orderly modernization.

The continuity of problems and approaches to them is striking, even when conditions and successive regimes have been of different colorations. It reminds one of the French expression, "The more things change, the more they stay the same."

A look, albeit briefly, into the British, Pakistan, and Mujib periods sets the stage for our analysis of subsequent privatization by providing historical setting and economic precedent. It also helps to elucidate the genesis, the roots, and the distinctive character of privatization in Bangladesh.

The British Period (1757-1947)

What is now Bangladesh was known as East Bengal under the days of British colonial rule over the Indian subcontinent, in contrast to West Bengal, which centered around Calcutta. The British treated Bangladesh as a backwater area whose main value was two-fold: (a) to provide raw materials for British and Scottish factories, particularly in textiles and jute, and (b) as a market into which to dump cheap British manufactured goods.

In the 18th century, muslin made in Dhaka (formerly spelled Dacca) was popular in Europe until cheaper, machine-made British cloth drove it off the market. Handwoven jute goods began to take up the slack, but the British built jute mills in Scotland in the early 19th century; and once again, Bengali goods lost their market.

Within a few decades, the prosperous weaving industry developed in the Bangladesh area under the moghuls was destroyed; and the large artisan class (estimated at one-third of the work force) lost its livelihood. East Bengal's native industry and commerce collapsed.[1] After the opening of the Suez Canal in 1869, a flood of British goods finished the job. The East Bengal economy effectively became a colonial agricultural arm of British industry.[2]

A parallel, but in some ways even more disastrous British policy was the Permanent Settlement Act of 1793, which destroyed the traditional landholding system and created a new landlord class, called "zamindars." Most of these zamindars were Hindus, while most of the dispossessed tenants were Muslims, a circumstance that hampered the material progress of the Bengali Muslims and added more tension to ancient Hindu-Muslim rivalry.

Therefore, as a consequence of British economic and mercantile policies, "agriculture became the only occupation available to an overwhelming majority of the population, and for many has meant a life of poverty as a tenant or landless laborer."[3]

The Hindus became an economic power in Bangladesh. The Hindus apparently adapted more quickly to changing socioeconomic conditions. The Muslims remained more aloof from the modern sector, disdaining, for example, the western-oriented education system. While they zealously maintained their intellectual prominence in the subcontinent's cultural, literary, and philosophical circles, this aloofness cut the Bengali Muslims off from the new avenues opening up for the subcontinent's gradually emerging middle class.

Bangladesh's remoteness from the center of government, coupled with poor lines of communication, intensified this isolation. Additionally, the British tended to prefer recruiting Hindus for the civil service and the army. All of this combined to gradually create a minority status for the Bengalis and, perhaps most importantly, an acute awareness of their minority status.[4]

East Bengal did not share equitably in the economic infrastructure and market systems constructed by the British. Even though those systems and tariff policies were designed to favor British interests and economic institutions, a fairly solid framework was gradually built up that eventually paid dividends in terms of development of indigenous industry in much of India. But this did not happen in Bangladesh, where local participation in the economy was essentially limited to real estate speculation and petty trading. The climate was not favorable for the emergence of a Bengali capital market in industrial sectors.

It is appropriate for this study of privatization to point out that the public sector in Bangladesh under British rule was essentially limited to administrative and regulatory functions and to providing services such as communications, health, and education.[5] The colonial administration also operated a few arsenals. Activity in the marketplace, however, was left in the hands of the private sector. It must be kept firmly in mind, however, that economic activity and governmental systems were dedicated only to serving the interests of the colonial power.

The Pakistan Period (1947-1971)

After the British left and Pakistan was formed, East Bengal became East Pakistan. Unfortunately, many of the same attitudes and policies that had held East Bengal's economic development in check persisted under the flag of Pakistan. The Bengalis gradually came to the conclusion that their fate was still being governed from afar. Karachi replaced London as the seat of political and economic power, even though East Pakistan contained by far the greatest percentage of the new country's population. The factories of England and Scotland were superseded by the interests of the Western Wing's burgeoning industrial complex.

Calcutta and its environs in India maintained their immense influence over the economic life of East Pakistan (as they have continued to do to the present day Bangladesh). Even this economic fact of life had about it one of those ironic twists of fate that seem to perpetually plague Bangladesh as it struggles to arise from the economic mire. Trade across the border between Bangladesh and India continued, much of it via the black market, most of which was composed of cheap Indian manufactured goods. But partition meant that the agricultural hinterland (Bangladesh) was in various ways cut off from its traditional industrial and banking center (Calcutta). It was necessary to develop new markets and mechanisms, and West Pakistan was not an ideal partner,[6] particularly in regard to jute, the crop and troubled industry that dominated and, unfortunately, still dominates Bangladesh's economy.

The record of how badly East Pakistan fared economically and politically under union with West Pakistan is so well documented that we need only touch on a few points that bear directly on the primary investigations of this study.

The two salient features of the period from the standpoint of my investigations were: (1) Pakistan, like Britain, pursued a policy emphasizing the preeminent role of the private sector in industrial development, with government playing a catalytic, supportive, and regulatory role; and (2) priority was given to West Pakistan's development, with East Pakistan providing raw materials and a captive market for West Pakistan's industrial products, a similar role to that it had played in the days of the British Raj. During most of its 24 years under the flag of Pakistan, the indigenous economy of the Eastern Wing languished.

Successive five-year plans were clearly oriented toward private enterprise. By the Third Five-Year Plan (1965-1970), government policy was quite explicit, essentially limiting the public sector to providing infrastructure and performing service and regulatory functions, leaving "productive" investment to the private sector. It was not until the Fourth Five-Year Plan (1970-1975), promulgated shortly before the dissolution of Pakistan and the "liberation" of Bangladesh in 1971, that the government appeared to be backing off somewhat from this stance by advocating a more prominent role for the public sector in major industries involving large sums and high technology.[7]

The principal instrument for providing economic growth was the Pakistan Industrial Development Corporation (PIDC), created in 1952. PIDC used many methods for achieving its purposes. It pioneered development of industries lacking at the time but needed by the new country, often by putting up the initial capital and then floating shares for private sector participation. Frequently, PIDC covered the foreign exchange component of the venture start-up. Capital markets were not highly developed in Pakistan at the time, especially in the East Wing, and foreign exchange was severely controlled. PIDC's intention was to eventually divest itself of these enterprises it had launched; but its record in this respect was spotty at best, for reasons we will see below.

The government also encouraged indigenous entrepreneurs through liberalization of controls and imports, exchange rate manipulation, tariff and tax breaks, use of a drove of foreign advisers and technicians, price controls, and a very successful subsidy/bonus scheme to encourage exports.

In addition to PIDC, the Karachi government established such public and quasi-public bodies as the State Bank of Pakistan (the Central Bank), Industrial Finance Corporation, National Bank of Pakistan, Agricultural Development Bank, Small Industries Corporation, Port Trust, and other institutions with the priority objective to promote or facilitate private sector development.[8]

At the time of partition in 1947, the industrial sector throughout Pakistan was small, and negligible in the East Wing. In 1945, only 252 of the 13,163 industrial establishments of undivided India were located in East Bengal. That is just under 2 percent, whereas what became West Pakistan had 1,154 (9 percent).[9] Through the institutions and measures mentioned above, Pakistan developed a quite respectable industrial sector. But progress was not equal in the East and the West, essentially because the assistance given them was unequal.

From 1950 to 1970, West Pakistan received more than double the expenditure made on East Pakistan. It is also interesting to note that roughly 70 percent of the money spent over that period in the East was earmarked for the public sector, whereas in the West the ratio was almost 50 percent. Thus, in total assistance West Pakistan's private sector received more than three times the assistance accorded the East's private sector.[10]

The disparity becomes even more striking when one realizes that by far the greatest portion of funds that did go into industrial development in East Pakistan went into the enterprise activity of West Pakistanis, Marwaris, and Biharis doing business there, not Bengalis. Exact percentages are almost impossible to determine because of the tangled partnership relationships among the various groups and because of the general inadequacies of Bangladesh's statistical gathering methods and institutions.

One source states, however, that "available data relating to the manufacturing section indicates that at liberation (1971), non-Bengali business houses controlled 47 percent of fixed assets and 72 percent of private industrial assets if we exclude the public sector assets."[11]

The PIDC was reconstituted in 1962, with the EPIDC taking care of the industrial sector of the East Wing, and the WPIDC responsible for the West. This was done in recognition of past disparities, current needs, and political pressures. The reform proved beneficial to the East. "The EPIDC became the major instrument of government policy to create a class of entrepreneurs from amongst the Bengali small trading class."[12]

In following the pattern of the PIDC, the EPIDC encountered difficulty because of the lack of Bengalis with either industrial management experience or sufficient capital for large-scale joint ventures. Adequate financial assistance was provided by other government funding institutions, who even relaxed the normal debt/equity requirement of 70:30 to as low as 7.5 percent equity. In some cases, they even permitted the entrepreneur to go to local commercial banks to obtain a guarantee to cover his part of the equity. The banks did not hesitate when the investor was going to manage a 250-loom jute mill worth about rupees (Rs) 20 million.[13]

The EPIDC, during the decade of its existence, helped establish 74 manufacturing units in East Pakistan in such industrial fields as jute (39 enterprises), textiles (1), paper products (4), cement (3), fertilizer (2), chemicals (5), pharmaceuticals (2), shipbuilding (2), sugar (11), steel (1), electrical machinery and equipment (2), machine tools (1), and diesel engines (1).[14] This was a substantial step forward for East Pakistan but EPIDC's programs were designed and implemented in such a way that they did not encourage productivity as much as they did investment.[15]

EPIDC also assisted a very large number of small-and medium-scale businesses, both commercial and industrial. It is estimated that 85-90 percent of those investments were controlled by East Pakistanis.[16] It is also reported that the repayment record on these smaller loans (i.e., below Rs150,000) was very poor.[17]

Repayment of larger loans for industrial enterprises did not appear to have been a major problem until 1970, when war increased feelings of insecurity, particularly among West Pakistanis operating in the East. Repayment is, however, one of Bangladesh's gravest problems in the eighties. Government Development Finance Institutions (DFIs) have been brought to the brink of insolvency because of this problem. It is interesting to note that even in the Pakistan days, there was a drastic fall-off between DFI approvals and projects actually implemented.[18] During the Third Five-Year Plan (1965-1970), implementation was only slightly over 50 percent of sanctions in all three of the leading financial institutions. This roadblock persists to the present. EPIDC's major investment in East Pakistan's industrial development was in jute. Even then, the region we now know as Bangladesh produced 50 percent of the world's jute; and its export accounted for 80 percent of Pakistan's foreign exchange earnings.

Even though the country's Eastern Wing produced 80 percent of the jute sold on the international market, Pakistan did not possess a single jute mill in 1947. Between 1952 and 1958, PIDC assisted the private sector in establishing 12 jute mill companies, the first being the world's largest, Adamjee Jute Mills. The 12 were built in East Pakistan, but the PIDC's private sector partners were, in all cases, West Pakistanis. Eventually, all 12 were divested before liberation at prices favorable to the private investors.

EPIDC engaged in the promotion of another 27 jute processing mills,[19] many in conjunction with East Pakistanis. Disinvestment of these units up to 1970 was unsuccessful. The EPIDC had a difficult time finding Bengalis with the requisite finances, industrial experience, and long-term entrepreneurial interests. Rehman Sobhan, the leading exponent of nationalization and foe of privatization in Bangladesh, implies, probably with some justice, that public opinion in Dhaka did not favor further divestitures if the mills would fall into the hands of West Pakistani capitalists.[20]

On the export side, by 1969-70, 32.7 percent of the jute was being exported by 91 Bengali firms, 30.0 percent by 3 public enterprises, 12.5 percent by 2 foreign firms, and 24.8 percent by 10 non-Bengali companies.[21]

Aside from the 12 jute mills, EPIDC was only able to carry through on its privatization plans by 1969-1970 on one cotton mill, one sugar mill, and two large paper mills. In addition to the lack of Bengali entrepreneurs and local capital, and the fears of West Pakistani takeovers, an important reason behind the reticence to buy big industrial enterprises in the late sixties was growing unrest and political instability leading up to open civil war by the end of the decade.

A USAID-sponsored study published in early 1970 commented on the area's other important industry, textiles. It said,

> Cotton textiles, which are the next largest group of loans in East Pakistan, account for more than 10 percent of total investment impact. Seventy-five percent of the total value of all cotton textile projects sanctioned in East Pakistan from 1958 through 1968 are reportedly East Pakistan-controlled. Since 1964, only one West Pakistani-originated cotton textile project was mounted in East Pakistan. Eighty-five percent of the total investment value of all East Pakistan cotton textile mill

projects financed by the institution were sanctioned from 1966-67 through the first half of FY 1968-69. Of these, 90 percent (by value) were reportedly controlled by East Pakistani interests.[22]

In large-scale industrial production, Bengali entrepreneurs were mainly confined to jute and cotton textiles. At liberation, Bengalis owned about one-third of the fixed assets in the jute industry, and just over half in cotton textiles. However, outside these two industries, there were only six Bengali-owned enterprises with assets of more than taka (Tk)2.5 million (US$318,000 at an exchange rate then of 7.6 to 1). Bengalis were more interested in small and medium industries, where they owned approximately 20 percent of fixed assets by the time of independence from Pakistan.[23]

As we approach the time Bangladesh had to face its economic problems as an independent nation, let us take a look at a few figures and questions to see just where she stood at the end of the Pakistan period.

Through the direct effort of the EPIDC and other government agencies, the following groups of Bengali-owned enterprises were launched in key economic fields:

Field	No. of Enterprises
Jute Mills	36
Major jute exporting	16
Textiles	25
Sugar	1
Inland water transport	12
Bank	1

Beyond this, a number of Bengali firms became prominent, if not dominating, in import-export and trade generally; and a significant number did well in the contracting business or as commission agents of various types.[24]

According to Rehman Sobhan, Bengalis in sizable numbers "graduated to the ranks of the upper bourgeoisie" through the professions, academia, and especially, the civil service. In the provincial secretariats, almost all the top ranks were manned by Bengalis. In the central government, four Bengalis were Secretaries by 1970; and fourteen were Joint Secretaries. Further, he states,

Bengali professionals suddenly found themselves on the boards of foreign and non-Bengali companies operating in East Pakistan and in positions of responsibility in management. Lawyers, engineers, and accountants were much in demand by non-Bengali and government clients. Contractors flourished; indentors found their tenders being more readily accepted, even at Islamabad. This last phase was something of a golden age for the Bengali upper bourgeoisie, and reflects the political compulsions of the Pakistan rulers to influence the course of the impending elections and to moderate the character of Bengali nationalism. This phase, in turn, colored the hopes and fears of the Bengali bourgeoisie for their future in an independent Bangladesh.[25]

In 1947, there had been only a handful of large-scale industrial units—a few cotton mills with 99,000 spindles and 2,583 looms, a few sugar mills with a capacity of 39,000 tons, one cement factory with a capacity of 100,000 tons, and some jute baling presses. The bulk of activity was in a variety of small cottage industries. In 1949-50, the entire manufacturing sector accounted for only 3 percent of GDP, large-scale industry for just over 0.5 percent, and small-scale manufacturing for 2.4 percent.

By the end of the 1960s, the percentages attained somewhat more substantial levels. In 1969-70, the manufacturing sector was up to 7.8 percent of GDP; and the contribution of large-scale industries was 3.7 percent and small-scale manufacturing 4.1 percent. While this was mildly encouraging, it was not much to show for twenty years of hope and expectation, especially when West Pakistan had progressed much more rapidly.[26]

The number of registered "factories" in 1968-69 was 3,130, of which 791 units worked in textiles, 576 in chemicals, and 406 in food manufacturing.

Since the present study is preoccupied with questions of public-private balance, we will conclude this brief survey of Bengali fortunes under the Pakistan flag with some general data showing the public-private mix at the end of the Pakistan period.[27]

Type Ownership	Number of Units	Value Fixed Assets (in Tk millions)	Percent Share Fixed Assets
Under EPIDC ownership	53	2,097.0	34
Under private, non-Bengali ownership	725	2,885.7	47
Under private, Bengali ownership	2,253	1,118.8	18
Under private, foreign ownership	20	36.0	1
Total	3,051	6,137.5	100

While these figures are useful for indicating how the major players shared or, perhaps more correctly, "controlled" the industrial sector, they are somewhat misleading in that they imply 100 percent owner-ship of each unit, whereas there was a great deal of partial ownership and co-venturing.

Most of the economic activity of Bangladesh in 1969-70 was to be found in agriculture and in the 330,000 "industrial" enterprises in rural areas, most of which were really cottage industries located within the homestead. Only 3,500 of these enterprises employed more than 10 persons and, therefore, were placed under the Factories Act.[28] Unfortunately, no similar statistics exist for small and micro-enter-prises in urban areas; but there is no doubt that the domestic economy was dominated by such small-scale activity, both in rural and urban locales, as independence came to Bangladesh.

Liberation and Nationalization—the Mujib Period (1971-1975)

Bangladesh became an independent nation on December 16, 1971,[29] after a brutal civil war with Pakistan that left the population ex-hausted, the countryside devastated, and the economy shattered. The new country's leaders, few of whom possessed high-level govern-mental experience, were overwhelmed with problems of monumental dimensions. Only the exhilaration of independence or, as the Ban-gladeshis prefer to say, "liberation" sustained the beleaguered leader-ship and the general population.

Of immediate concern was the absolute necessity of getting the economy functioning again. Economic activity on a national scale had come to a virtual standstill, due to the dislocations and ravages of war and the traumatic flight of the Pakistanis who had dominated much of the economy.

During the first few months after liberation, the government en-gaged in a flurry of reorganizing activity on a number of fronts. They were preoccupied with reconstituting and restaffing the various for-mer Pakistan government agencies and autonomous bodies. Even though, as we have seen, Bengalis had been gradually creeping into the upper echelons of the bureaucracy, too few had experience at senior administrative and policy levels.

One of the most pressing problems was how to restart the many former West Pakistani-owned or managed industrial enterprises that were standing idle and vulnerable to vandalism and scavenging.

On January 2, 1972, the government passed the Abandoned Proper-ties Ordinance,[30] and took possession of not only factories and commercial establishments, but also houses and income property, and even vehicles of all types.

The government frantically searched the country for managers for these enterprises and properties. Experienced managers were in short supply in Bangladesh, especially among Bengali Muslims. To run the enterprises, the government recruited from the ranks of civil servants, merchants, union leaders, supervisory employees of the firms themselves, and even outsiders.

Some of the appointments were temporary and most were ad hoc. As might be expected, the search campaign was also used to reward supporters of the recently-established ruling party, the Awami League. Equally predictable, the performance of many appointees was poor. Most were inexperienced and inept. Not a few were unscrupulous, using the opportunity for personal financial gain by systematically stripping the resources of the industrial enterprises entrusted to them. In some cases, this was done for the legitimate purpose of paying staff and workers' salaries; but more often, it was to line the pockets of board members and managers. Credit, however, should be given to managements in those companies that "took great pains to keep the enterprises running as efficiently as resource and manpower constraints permitted."[31]

Outright plundering was even more rampant in the case of several thousand abandoned commercial firms, the majority of which were small, structurally uncomplicated companies. Many were nothing more than small family-run operations. Large numbers were so plundered by appointed managers, other employees, or even the general public that they for all practical purposes ceased to exist as functioning businesses. In the case of smaller commercial firms, these depredations often took place very quickly. In more sophisticated enterprises, the process proceeded over a period of years, as we will see in later sections.

On March 26, 1972, the landmark President's Order (P.O.) No. 27 was issued. It effectively nationalized the industrial sector, fulfilling an Awami League promise made in a highly successful election campaign in mid-1970. The party's "Manifesto" had received widespread support from the public, who had seen nationalization of financial and industrial sectors as a way to forestall concentration of wealth in a few hands. This had been the general public sentiment even before the break with Pakistan. At that time, the concern had been domination by the notorious 22 leading families of West Pakistan. In 1972, it was directed at Bangladesh's own fledgling industrial capitalist community. P.O. No. 27 had a good measure of public support and was heartily endorsed in academic and intellectual circles.[32]

As a consequence of P.O. Nos. 16, 26 and 27, the proportion of the fixed assets of the industrial sector under government control shot up overnight from the 34 percent it had been in EPIDC days to 92 percent. Of the 725 units that were taken over, 392 were brought into the public sector as state-owned enterprises. The remaining 462, while brought into the public sector, were tentatively earmarked for early or eventual disinvestment. About 160 of these were, according to some sources, released to former owners rather quickly. The remaining 300, mostly small units, were turned over to government-appointed management boards. Many of them actually remained on the government rolls, but some were gradually returned or sold to the private sector. Although these firms are listed as "industrial enterprises" or "factories," most were little more than industrial shops, employing few people. We will take another look at this group of firms later in the study.

For the moment, let us keep our attention on major enterprises. In addition to the 263 large abandoned enterprises, major enterprises included 53 enterprises operated under EPIDC, one foreign firm, and 75 *Bengali-owned* industrial enterprises, bringing the total of substantial entities to 392. [33]

While the number of SOEs was small in relation to the total number of businesses in Bangladesh (there were an estimated 2,700 small Bengali "industrial" firms), they dominated the major industries, represented 7.3 percent of GDP (but 20 percent of the non-agricultural GDP), 58 percent of the value added, 92 percent of the fixed assets, and 80 percent of the country's exports.[34] The expanded public sector was said to account for 85 percent of government revenues,[35] which says quite a bit about the tax structure.

Besides the industrial sector, the banking and insurance fields were completely nationalized under P.O. No. 26, also of March 26, 1972. Following that, several thousand commercial and trading establishments were taken over, although under no particular order.

Several of the specifics and technical provisions of the Nationalization Act warrant attention in order to comprehend the Act's scope and ramifications. Some more general questions dealing with the intent and socio-political philosophy of the framers, will then be addressed, with particular scrutiny of ideas regarding the relative roles for the public and private sectors. This chapter will end with an evaluation of the Mujib government's policies and the performance of the nationalized enterprises. By this exercise, we will attempt to show how policies and actions in the immediate post-liberation period not only influenced future developments, but made them inevitable, for better or worse.

President's Order No. 27, in addition to nationalizing certain industries and enterprises, established a number of sectoral corporations to ensure coordination of government control and to supervise management of the various nationalized enterprises placed under each of them. The following table provides an idea of the scope, industry by industry, of the Corporation network, as of December 1972.[36]

Sectoral Corporation	Number of Enterprises
Bangladesh Jute Industries Corporation	77
Bangladesh Textile Industries Corporation	72
Bangladesh Sugar Mills Corporation	16
Bangladesh Food and Allied Products Corporation	54
Bangladesh Fertilizer Chemical and Pharmaceutical Corporation	13
Bangladesh Paper and Board Corporation	9
Bangladesh Tanneries Corporation	30
Bangladesh Steel Mills Corporation	20
Bangladesh Engineering and Shipbuilding Corporation	34
Bangladesh Minerals, Oil, and Gas Corporation	7
Bangladesh Forest Products Corporation	20
Total	352

The intent of the Planning Commission (where the nationalization was hatched) was that the Corporations would be the predominant authority over the operations of the individual enterprises rather than the regular governmental ministries, under which the Corporations themselves were grouped according to industrial sector. The thought was that the Corporations would run the individual enterprises more along business lines than would the more bureaucratically-oriented line ministries.

The validity of that assumption can be challenged. While the Corporations were ostensibly designed to dispense guidance along more businesslike lines, many observers regarded the Corporations and the ministries as so similar as to be indistinguishable. The designers were, after all, academics and bureaucrats, not businessmen.

This bureaucratic struggle has never been resolved. The ministries and the Corporations are still fighting over control, and the enterprises continue to suffer for it. The ministries, in traditional bureaucratic fashion, still interfere unduly in the day to day operations of

SOEs. The Corporations continue to issue policy statements and conduct their affairs (and the affairs of the enterprises under their jurisdiction) in ways that have little relevance to market forces that govern the business world.

In the early days, this problem was supposed to be resolved by issuance of a set of Rules of Business, which would clearly stipulate "the limits of powers and responsibilities" of the government (i.e., of the ministries), the Corporation, and the enterprises under the Corporation. The Rules, which were intended to favor the role of the Corporations over the ministries and to give a semblance of autonomy to the enterprises, were never issued during the Mujib period. Long-time advocates of the pro-Corporation position maintain that the bureaucracy scuttled the draft copies of the Rules, thereby maintaining its domination over SOEs and the industrial scene.[37]

As stated in Chishty's landmark paper on privatization in Bangladesh, "The nationalization policy of 1972 did not clearly define the role of the private sector, except by implication. It specifically excluded private sector enterprises from the jute, textile, and sugar industries, raw jute export trade, insurance, and banking."[38]

We do know, however, that there was considerable, heated debate within the government on this question. Initially, the debate centered around the management and disposition of abandoned properties. Among other things, it had become "clear that the ad hoc arrangements made for running the abandoned enterprises were not proving adequate."[39]

As early as February 1972 (that is, even before P.O. No. 27), the Ministry of Industries had prepared a working paper proposing that large units be run by the state, medium-sized units be considered for joint ownership with the private sector, and small units be sold to the highest bidder. Even the idea of joint ventures with the private sector was proposed.[40]

These and similar proposals led to the full blossoming of a wider debate: should the new country follow the socialist pattern of development which would involve inhibiting the growth of a Bengali capitalist class, or should it opt for the "mixed economy" approach being pursued by a number of Asian countries.

As we have noted earlier, there was widespread support for government control of the economy among workers and academics. Within the government, however, sentiment was more evenly divided. As a matter of fact, the bureaucracy appears to have been largely in favor of a mixed economy, or at least an active private sector along the general lines pursued by the EPIDC. The political leadership was split. The principal advocates of the socialist approach were four key advisors in the Planning Commission.[41]

The issuance of P.O. Nos. 26 and 27 demonstrated rather clearly that the Planning Commission had won the day. They evidently convinced Sheikh Mujib (who was a populist rather than a socialist) and others in the core of the political leadership, that the socialist path was the one to follow and, most importantly, a course that would receive general public support. Any plans for a mixed economy or joint public-private enterprises were rejected.

The fact that 462 of the abandoned enterprises were tentatively earmarked for divestiture of one type or another would make it appear, at least on the surface, that the decision was not categoric. In fact, it was categoric. As Rehman Sobhan, one of the principal architects of the nationalization policy, has written,

> We have seen that the ideological premise of the nationalization policies was to prevent the growth of the upper bourgeoisie and to treat the private sector as merely a temporary phase whilst the public sector and socialist cadres developed their managerial resources and ideological commitment.[42]

He has written that they planned for a "phased transition to socialism,"[43] adding:

> At that original stage, it was realized that a nationalization policy which did not spell out the role of the private sector could in the future lead to contradictions in the conduct of state policy. The issue was, however, not pressed, largely for tactical reasons. It was felt that the nationalization package was itself sufficiently drastic for the upper bourgeoisie and their backers. If they realized that this was, itself, part of a policy to completely preempt the development of their class, their resistance may have become sufficiently implacable to prejudice the nationalization policy itself.[44]

In other words, the private sector was to be tolerated only until the public sector was strong enough to take over. What about the 462 abandoned enterprises? Almost all of those selected for release were small, losing money, and not considered potentially viable. Most stayed on the government rolls. Only 52 were eventually sold to private investors, and 30 were turned over to former owners.

Total private investment in these transactions did not exceed Tk50 million (approximately US$4 million), which indicates that these "industrial enterprises" were actually little more than shops and cottage industries.[45] Reasons for the reticence of the private sector to invest in such enterprises included (a) the units were too small, (b) the condition of equipment was uncertain, (c) the evaluation process of the Disinvestment Board was too slow, (d) title was unclear in many cases, and (e) workers were in firm control of a number of enterprises, and potential investors feared they would not be able to take over. A proposed scheme to enable workers' cooperatives to buy and operate some enterprises was never clarified or carried out.

The limits on private sector investment and growth were officially clarified in January 1973. Private investment was limited to Tk1.5 million (US$197,000) with growth allowed up to assets of Tk2.5 million (US$330,000), or ultimately to Tk3.5 million (US$460,000) through reinvestment of profits.[46]

The government did promise a moratorium on further nationalization for 10 years on firms of that size; but reserved the right to take over any private firm consistently losing money or running below capacity "due to mismanagement." Paradoxically, the nationalization plan placed no obligation on public enterprises to generate profits.[47]

Severe restrictions were placed on foreign investment, and collaboration with the private sector was confined to licenses and patents without equity participation. Foreign venture investment was allowed only in joint ventures with the government, with the government holding at least 51 percent of the shares.[48]

When taken together, these and other limitations amounted to virtual strangulation of the private sector. Already prohibited from participation in the key jute, textile, and sugar industries (and 15 more industries were to be added to the prohibited list), the private sector was not even permitted to grow in the few areas left to them. The black market was, in reality, the major business activity left to the private sector.

As Sobhan mentioned above, there were contradictions in the program; however, they turned out to be somewhat different from the ones he posited. First, the Awami League, while mouthing socialist slogans, was essentially quite middle class in makeup and inclination. As one senior official recently put it, "The expansion of state ownership took place under a political leadership which had traditionally followed a middle-of-the-road policy, and neither had an ideological conviction and training, nor a cadre and an organization to politically oversee implementation."[49]

Second, the socialist program of the Mujib regime did not serve all equally. The system created an atmosphere in which wealth became increasingly concentrated in the hands of a few greedy leaders. Observers have called it "State Capitalism" or "Capitalist Nationalization."[50] After liberation, the political elites jockeyed to consolidate their power base and employed the resources of the nationalized enterprises toward that end.[51]

Some analysts have regarded the left of center Awami League actions "as nothing more than a sudden spurt of enthusiasm of middle class vague ideas of social justice."[52]

Third, even though large-scale industrial production was in government hands, the marketing and distribution systems were firmly in the hands of the private sector. Each frustrated the other.[53]

It would have been difficult to achieve growth in a subsistence economy like Bangladesh's under the best of circumstances, none of which existed to help this troubled country. Externally, 1973 was a year of great instability and rising energy prices. Bangladesh, like many agriculture-based economies, was particularly vulnerable to such fluctuations. Sugar prices were plummeting. Also, increasing competition from synthetic fibers was reducing demand for Bangladesh's major export commodity, jute. Finally, in 1947 East Pakistan had been forced to realign its economy by virtue of having lost its principal trading partner (which, by no random circumstance, had also been the seat of economic policy making)—Calcutta and West Bengal. Newly independent Bangladesh faced a similar situation with the cutting of ties with Karachi and West Pakistan.

But as adverse as international factors were, internal forces were damaging the country even more. The war had shattered and devastated the country's infrastructure. To top it off, a confused, impoverished, and fractured society turned upon itself once the euphoria over liberation subsided and the new nation had to face stark reality and the possibility of unfulfilled dreams. Faction fought faction, and the problems multiplied. It was about this time that Bangladesh was labeled "the international basket case."

The hope of the Planning Commission zealots was that nationalization would be the mechanism for leading Bangladesh out of the wilderness. It was a false hope, a cruel delusion for a number of reasons.

For one thing, there weren't enough qualified people to run the government, much less take on management of all facets of the economy, including even the segment already run by Bengali industrialists. The leadership did not see, or would not see that "entrepreneurial talent, extremely scarce after independence, was concentrated in the private sector, not in the government."[54]

Anyone studying Bangladesh affairs of the period is constantly told that a main reason for nationalization was that half of the managerial talent fled to West Pakistan. There was no recourse, so the argument goes, but to have the government take over. There is a certain logic to a heavy public presence in a subsistence economy,[55] and there was certainly some justification for a high profile in Bangladesh. But the government overreached itself by assuming responsibility for 92 percent of the economy and deliberately adopting politically-oriented policies which ensured that the private sector would stagnate and could not play a supportive, collaborative role. I have come to the conclusion, through considerable reading and conversation with a great number of people in all sectors, that there were more Bengalis available for running medium-sized businesses than is often recognized.[56]

One cannot escape the thought that the principal advocates of the socialist solution were more motivated by ideology than economics. They constantly spoke and wrote about the danger to *socialism* posed by the bourgeoisie rather than centering on pragmatic considerations related to economic development.[57] The academic economists did not understand reality; they misled the Mujib government, and few saw the private sector as the only real hope for growth.[58] The obsession with ideological triumph is the only reason one can discover for taking over the Bengali-owned industrial enterprises, along with the abandoned properties. This rash and economically unsound act was eventually instrumental in solidifying the opposition.

Nationalization was a hasty act launched without any discernible long-term strategy or well-conceived plan. Everything was swallowed in one big gulp. There was no coherent policy to determine proper roles and functions allowing the public and the private sectors to work in unison.[59] The planners, while demonstrating great interest in grandiose policy, showed a parallel tendency to ignore more mundane aspects (i.e., implementation), a trait that, unfortunately, has persisted to the present. A leader of the business community later put it rather succinctly when he reminisced, "Nobody knew how to run a country."[60]

It soon became evident to even the most casual observer that the economy was not moving. The public sector was not performing up to expectations. Most of the umbrella Corporations were losing money, some (such as jute, paper, and chemicals) quite heavily. Only textiles, steel, and engineering were earning consistent profits;[61] and suspicions were raised that government accountants were engaged in "creative bookkeeping," making the situation look rosier that it actually was.[62]

The level of public subsidy was staggering, yet apparently ineffective. Savings indicators were actually negative. Inflation was rising, as were prices. The government resorted to deficit financing. Production declined, while smuggling increased. High rates of unemployment, chronic underemployment, and abysmally low per capita income pushed most of the population below the subsistence level and kept them there.[63]

The brave but unrealistic First Five-Year Plan (1973-1978) was little more than a rhetorical exercise. Manufacturing was 7.3 percent of the GDP in 1972, but only 7.4 percent by 1975.[64] Output in 1975 was only 75 percent of 1969 levels.[65]

It was obvious that some new approaches had to be tried. By July 1974, it was decided that the economy might be stimulated by giving a somewhat expanded role to the private sector. The previous ceiling on investment was raised from Tk3.5 million (US$452,000) to Tk30 million (US$3,873,000). This was partly due to a hope for infusion of capital, and also reflected the increase in the cost of land and machinery needed to set up any sizable industrial establishment.[66] Emphasis was given to labor-intensive industries.

Presidential Order No. 27 had, as we mentioned earlier, lacked specificity regarding private sector participation, except to exclude it from jute, textiles, and sugar. An early 1973 law, however, had reserved 18 industries for the public sector. They were:[67]

- arms, and ammunition, and allied defense equipment
- jute industry (sacking, hessian, and carpet backing)
- textiles (excluding handlooms and specialized textiles)
- sugar
- paper and newsprint
- iron and steel (excluding re-rolling mills)
- ship-building and heavy engineering (including machine tools and assembly/manufacture of cars, buses, trucks, tractors, and power tillers)
- heavy electrical industry
- minerals, oil, and gas
- cement
- petro-chemicals (fertilizers, PVC ethylene, and synthetic fibres)
- heavy and basic chemicals and basic pharmaceuticals
- air transport
- shipping (including coastal ships and tankers above 2000 DWT)
- telephone, telephone cables, telegraph, and wireless apparatus (excluding radio receiving sets)
- generation and distribution of electricity
- forest extraction (mechanized)

This did not leave much for the private sector. The 1974 law did not change those restrictions, but it did at least recognize that the private sector had a more definite role to play in the economy. Limited interplay between foreign investors and the private sector was permitted, mainly because of pressure from foreign business.[68] The moratorium on nationalization was extended from 10 to 15 years. The rights and interests of foreign equity investors were reconstituted. The 19 foreign firms in Bangladesh (mainly British) received preferential treatment.

Despite its shortcomings, the 1974 action was the first breach in the nationalization wall. Even though the President regarded the policy revision as just a "sop to the capitalists" that would not yield significant results, the 1974 act was, in reality, the first of several actions that led to the gradual dismantling of the state enterprise system. A senior official noted late in 1987 that the government's halting, initial effort "to woo the private sector ... lacked credibility when most of the modern sector remained under state control—even those interests which were once owned by Bangladeshis." Therefore, "steps to encourage the private sector to participate in industrial development did not bear much fruit."[69]

It comes as a surprise to most that there were approximately 120 divestitures consummated during the Mujib period.[70] Most of the units were "disinvested"[71] because they were small and unprofitable, and a certain number represented corrections of mistakes made during the chaos following liberation.

Of the 120 divestitures, 10 were former Indian properties taken over in 1965 during the Indo-Pakistan War. Most were rice mills. The others were small Pakistani-owned enterprises in a variety of fields including printing and paper (8), flour and rice mills (10), engineering (12), textiles (11), metal works (7), vegetable oils (5), chemicals (4), wood products (3), and a scattering of other activities.[72] Most of these were apparently little more than shops.

A few significant transactions were put through in recognition of the fact that the public sector was not performing adequately and private initiative was needed. For example, Bangladesh Re-Rolling Mills, Ltd., one of the steel companies of a Chittagong-based Pakistani family, which was taken over as abandoned property, was returned to the owners as early as August 1972 *at the government's request*. There were several reasons for this remarkable transfer. First, two government-appointed managers had not only proved inept, but had engaged in such outrageous corruption that a very profitable enterprise was in jeopardy. Second, the Akberali family, though West Pakistani, were respected for their integrity, business acumen, and genuine interest in the development of East Pakistan cum Bangladesh. Third, the family had been close to Sheikh Mujib himself.[73]

While the Akberali case is not typical, there were other instances of discreet moves by practical politicians and bureaucrats to back away from total dependence on the socialist model. A carefully-orchestrated campaign to discredit the performance of the public enterprises was led by dispossessed Bengali jute and textile groups. The clamor grew as SOE failures and more general inadequacies became increasingly apparent, and as political instability and dissatisfaction increased during the months before Sheikh Mujib's assassination in August 1975. One cannot fully explain the emotionalism of the campaign in purely business terms. As Klaus Lorche pointed out in his study of divestiture in the textile industry, "For many, to repossess 'their' mill was less important as an investment deal than as an exercise of a moral right; justice was done, not business."[74]

In many ways, the Mujib period is the most fascinating in the turbulent recent history of the Bengalis. The policies, issues, and patterns that surfaced during this short period have had a profound influence on the shape of events that followed.

Notes

1. Nyrop, Richard F., et al: *Area Handbook for Bangladesh* (Washington, D.C., Foreign Area Studies, American University, 1975), p. 2, 10, 20, 263. Printed and distributed through the U. S. Government Printing Office.

2. ibid, pp. 22-23.

3. ibid, pp. 1-2.

4. ibid, p. 16, 23.

5. Chishty, Shamsul Haque: *Privatization in Developing Countries: The Experience of Bangladesh* (a paper presented at the Conference on Privatization Policies, Methods and Procedures sponsored by the Asian Development Bank, held in Manila, Jan. 31-Feb. 1, 1985), p. 1. Mr. Chishty is the Secretary, Ministry of Establishment, Government of Bangladesh. In this capacity, he is one of the highest ranking civil servants in the public service. Chishty was a key figure in the important privatization of jute and textile mills in 1982-83 as the government's chief negotiator.

6. Nyrop, op. cit., p. 12.

7. Sobhan, Rehman and Ahmad, Muzaffer: *Public Enterprise in an Intermediate Regime: A Study in the Political Economy of Bangladesh* (Dhaka, Bangladesh Institute of Development Studies, 1980), pp. 28-29; Yusuf, Fazlul Hassan: *Nationalization of Industries in Bangladesh* (Dhaka, National Institute of Local Government, Oct. 1985), pp. 35-36. Of course, the Fourth Five-Year Plan was never implemented because of war with and independence from Pakistan.

8. Nyrop, op. cit., p. 44.

9. Yusuf, op. cit., p. 53f.

10. Sobhan and Ahmad, op. cit., p.33.

11. ibid, p. 57. See also Chafkin, Sol. H., et al: *An Approach to Accelerating Industrial Growth in East Pakistan* (Washington, D.C., American Assistance Corporation, 1970)—A Report to USAID/Dhaka, pp. 19-21; Nyrop, op. cit., p. 32.

12. Chishty, op. cit., p. 1. For further information regarding PIDC/EPIDC and the Pakistan period, see also Sobhan and Ahmad, op. cit., pp. 36ff; Ahmad, Qazi Kholliquzzaman: "The Manufacturing Sector of Bangladesh—An Overview," *The Bangladesh Development Studies*, Vol. VI, No. 4, Autumn 1978, pp. 389-91.

13. Chishty, op. cit., p. 2.

14. ibid, p.1; Sobhan and Ahmad, op. cit., p. 21, 36.

15. Nyrop, op. cit., p. 266.

16. Chafkin, op. cit., p. 23. No figures are available for the percentage in the hands of non-Bengalis.

17. Sobhan and Ahmad, op. cit., pp. 64-65.

18. Chafkin, op. cit., p. 24.

19. For a fairly complete listing of PIDC/EPIDC ventures from 1952-70, including public and private shares, see Sobhan and Ahmad, op. cit., pp. 49-51; and regarding divestiture, see ibid, pp. 37-38.

20. ibid, p. 38.

21. ibid, p. 195. Bangladesh's share of total jute exports from both Bangladesh and India jumped from 8% in 1955-56 to almost 50% in 1969-70. The Export Bonus Scheme was evidently the key in giving Bangladesh the edge. Bangladesh undersold India by 7-23% during the sixties. Surprisingly, India took no particular countermeasures. Ahmad, Q.K., op. cit., pp. 394-95.

22. Chafkin, op. cit., p. 22.

23. Ahmad, Q.K., op. cit., p. 390.

24. Sobhan and Ahmad, op. cit., pp. 65-66.

25. ibid, p. 68.

26. Ahmad, Q.K., op. cit., p. 386, 393.

27. Sobhan and Ahmad, op. cit., p. 192.

28. ibid, p. 193.

29. Leaders of the Awami League had declared independence for Bangladesh from Pakistan on March 26, but full liberation was not achieved until the commanding general of the Pakistan army surrendered on December 16. The Industrial Enterprises Nationalization Order (Presidential Order No. 27) was symbolically announced on March 26, 1972, the anniversary of the first "Liberation Proclamation."

30. The full title was *The Bangladesh Abandoned Property (Control, Management and Disposal) Order, 1972* (President's Order No. 16 of 1972). The edition used for the present study was P.O. No. 16, "as modified up to 31st May 1983."

31. Sobhan and Ahmad, op. cit., p. 117; see also Chishty, op. cit., p. 4; Conversation—M. I. Rabbani, Secretary, Ministry of Industries, 10/28/86.

32. Yusuf, op. cit., p. 277; Sobhan and Ahmad, op. cit., p. 122 and passim. While there was opposition to nationalization from a number of quarters, the

consensus among observers is that the policy did have the support of the general public.

33. Statistics vary widely in connection with the number and type of entities that were abandoned, vested or otherwise taken over and later divested in one way or another. For example, estimates of the number of abandoned industrial enterprises listed in the sources analyzed for the present study varied from 620 to 786, commercial enterprises from 2,000 to 8,000, the number of state-owned enterprises (SOEs) from 313 to 423, and the number of SOEs placed under the new corporations were variously listed as 224 to 350. As late as 1986, estimates of the SOEs still in the public sector varied from 150 to 281. The figures cited in this study have been drawn from the most reliable sources available. They can be regarded as reasonably accurate and useful as approximations. Principal sources used were Chishty, op. cit., p.4, 5; Sobhan and Ahmad, op. cit., p. 116, 142, 192; Yusuf, op. cit., p. 69, 103, 112; Nyrop., op. cit., p. 267; Ahmad, Q.K., op. cit., p. 407; and World Bank: *Bangladesh: Public Sector Industrial Enterprises*, an unpublished working paper of the World Bank Office in Dhaka, 393/4, 1985, p. 1, 2. This and similar papers are used in preparing the Bank's annual country reports. Further citing of this particular working paper will appear as "WB/Dhaka—Pub. Sec." See also Rahim, A.M.A.: *Current Issues of the Bangladesh Economy* (Dhaka, Bangladesh Books International, Ltd., 1978), p. 93. Chapters in the Rahim book that were especially useful were "A Review of Industrial Investment Policy, 1971-77" (pp. 88-111) and "The Performance of the Banking System, 1971-77" (pp. 1-21). Dr. Rahim has been Economic Advisor to the Bangladesh Bank.

34. Sobhan and Ahmad, op. cit., p. 400. Incidentally, agriculture represented 60.1% of GDP and trade 7.8%. Further, apart from 33 tea gardens and related facilities, there were only 20 foreign-owned industrial enterprises in Bangladesh, mostly in pharmaceuticals. They were given special treatment and exemptions in connection with the nationalization program. Foreign investments were not, however, a major factor in the economy at the time. Sobhan and Ahmad, op. cit., p. 211.

35. ibid. Information is almost completely lacking about the commercial enterprises that were abandoned, nationalized and disposed of. Estimates of the number of commercial enterprises involved vary from 2,000 to 8,000. This subject is discussed in some detail in Chapter 4.

36. Yusuf, op. cit., pp. 112-13. Note that not all of the nationalized enterprises were placed under the corporations, which partially accounts for the differences between 352 and 392. Others were placed under the corporations later, some were shifted, and some remained autonomous. The number of corporations listed in the table above is 11, but the number has varied over the years from as few as 6 to a maximum of 14. Finally, throughout the text of this study the word "Corporation" will be capitalized when referring to the umbrella entities set up by the Bangladesh government in order to distinguish them from the generic corporate entity of the private business sector.

37. WB/Dhaka—Pub. Sec., op. cit., p. 5; Chishty, op. cit., pp. 5-6; Ahmad, Q.K., op. cit., p. 405. Rehman Sobhan strongly argues that the traditional

bureaucracy scuttled the Rules of Business to keep control of the nationalized enterprises from passing to the Corporations. See Sobhan and Ahmad, op. cit., pp. 152, 173-77. His objectivity in this and related matters is somewhat suspect, in that he was one of the principal authors of the nationalization policy. He has spent most of the years since then arguing that nationalization did not fail and, if it did not accomplish all it set out to do, this was due to self-serving obstructionism of opponents in the bureaucracy and the private sector.

38. Chishty, op. cit., p. 7.

39. ibid, p. 4.

40. ibid.

41. The four were Rehman Sobhan, Nurul Islam, Anisur Rahman and Mosharaf Hossain, all long-time supporters of Mujib and the Awami League, the first three having drafted many of the provisions of the Manifesto of 1970.

42. Sobhan and Ahmad, op. cit., p. 198, 209.

43. ibid, pp. 201-202.

44. ibid, pp. 203-204.

45. ibid, p. 252. Another issue was the use (for purchasing the units) of "black money" gained from dealings on the black market, where much of the country's economic activity took place (and still takes place). At the time, it was one of the few commercial activities left to the private sector. Potential investors feared complications with the tax authorities if they used such funds to buy an enterprise being divested. In a classic example of theory versus reality, Rehman Sobhan has argued that the government should not "reward smugglers and black marketeers ... on spurious grounds of expediency and pragmatism." ibid, p. 244. The question has never been fully resolved, although since 1986 there have been some indications that the government might be willing to grant amnesty if such funds were used for investment. It must be kept in mind that the resources of a large number of very important people are involved.

46. Chishty, op. cit., p. 7; WB/Dhaka—Pub. Sec., p. 3. Of the estimated 2,700 firms in the private sector at liberation, only 27 had fixed assets exceeding Tk1 million (US$132,000), and only a handful had assets over the Tk2.5 million (US$330,000) ceiling. Ahmad, Q.K., op. cit., p. 407f. The currency conversion used is the official exchange rate of Tk7.60/US$1 in force in 1972. Throughout this study, conversions will be made on the basis of the official rate prevailing in each year, according to *International Financial Statistics*, International Monetary Fund (1979-87) and a variety of sources for earlier years, especially Nyrop, op. cit., p. 255.

47. Yusuf, op. cit., p. 178.

48. Chishty, op. cit., p. 8.

49. Chowdhury, Tawfique E.: *Privatization of State Enterprises in Bangladesh (1976-84)*, Case Study III (Seoul, Korea Development Institute, 1987), p.2; a paper presented to a Joint Seminar on Economic Change and Government Process, co-sponsored by the Korea Development Institute and the (international) Economic Development Institute in Seoul, Nov. 9-12, 1987. Tawfique Chowdhury, currently Joint Secretary for Banking, Ministry of Finance, is one of the more highly respected financial experts in the Bangladesh

government. He holds a Ph.D. from M.I.T. For similar comments, also see Ellis, William H.: "Bangladesh: Hope Nourishes a New Nation," *National Geographic*, Sept.1972, p. 329; Yusuf, op. cit., pp. 286-87; Alamgir, Muhiuddin Khan: *Development Strategy for Bangladesh* (Dhaka, Dhaka University Centre for Social Studies, 1980), p. 144.

50. Yusuf, op. cit., pp. 277-78, 287; Ahmad, Q.K., op. cit., p. 407.

51. Yusuf, op. cit., p. 25. One highly respected former civil servant told me that "Mujib used nationalization to reward his partisans and placate his Russian friends, who had helped him when the Americans didn't." Conversation—Shafiqur Rahman—9/22/86. This was one of the very few times that the USSR was ever mentioned in interviews or written materials encountered while researching this study. At first, I wondered if this was a conspiracy of silence, but ultimately came to the conclusion that the Soviets were a minor factor in both the debate and the process of nationalization (and, ultimately, privatization), even though they had been prominent supporters of Bangladesh at the beginning. Evidently, they did not inundate Bangladesh with advice on nationalization or on how to run SOEs, possibly because, as some say, the Soviets did not want to be associated with a socialist experiment that was doomed to failure.

52. Rahim, op. cit., p. 87; Yusuf, p. 296.

53. ibid, p. 93, 94, 272.

54. Baxter, Craig: *Bangladesh, A New Nation in an Old Setting* (Boulder, Colo., and London, Westview Press, 1984), p. 84.

55. Yusuf, op. cit., p. 24; Sobhan and Ahmad, op. cit., passim; Rahim, op. cit., pp. 93-94; Timberg, Thomas A.: *An Essay on Golden Bengal: Contemporary Bangladesh: Assets, Liabilities, and Challenges* (draft manuscript), p. 30. I am extremely grateful to Dr. Timberg in making available the draft of his forthcoming book. I know of no other observer of Bangladesh affairs who possesses Dr. Timberg's knowledge and, perhaps even more important, his insights into how the society functions. His assistance to me has been less in providing factual material than in suggesting approaches. For example, it was Dr. Timberg who pointed out the anomaly of a situation where the principal characteristic of Bangladesh's Martial Law Authority was not the iron hand usually associated with such regimes, but an inability to control much of anything. I shall speak of this later in the study, when discussing performance of the public sector in Chapter 7.

56. Conversation—Chishty, 9/29/86. Secretary Chishty is the author of the ADB conference paper cited above.

57. Sobhan and Ahmad, op. cit., p. 201; Yusuf, op. cit., p. 24, 282.

58. Conversation—Shafiul Azam, 10/3/86. Shafiul Azam was the Minister of Commerce and Industries under both Presidents Zia and Ershad, and is generally conceded to have been the guiding force behind the design of the privatization effort in Bangladesh. He suffered a severe heart attack in 1985. I was granted one of the first interviews Minister Azam was able to give (in the eleventh month of a twelve-month convalescence).

59. Ahmad, Q.K., op. cit., pp. 404-405; Yusuf, op. cit., p. 273, 284, 293; Rahim, op. cit., p. 93, 94; T. Chowdhury, op. cit., p.2; Conversation—Mahfuzul

Islam, Deputy Director General of Industries, Ministry of Industries, in Washington, D.C., 7/6/88, while Mr. Islam was attending a seminar on privatization jointly sponsored by the Center for Privatization and the International Management Group.

60. Conversation—A.S. Mahmud, President, Dhaka Chamber of Commerce and Industry, 10/9/86. William Ellis, in his *National Geographic* article previously cited, quotes Enayetullah Khan, the editor-owner of *Holiday* (a highly critical Dhaka daily) as saying, "The Awami League simply is not geared to the ideals of Socialism. They have nationalized some industries, yes, but they have no long-range plans of how to run them," op. cit., p. 329.

61. Rahim, op. cit., p. 10.

62. It is revealing that the government decided that the SOEs should not have to "carry the burden" of debts that had piled up during the difficult period preceding liberation. Yusuf reports that the plan for 1974-75 included a provision whereby, "All liabilities on capital account were to be converted into long-term debentures with five years' moratorium on payment of interest and capital." op. cit., p. 165. This is doubly interesting when one recalls that during later negotiations with private sector buyers of SOEs, the government required that the purchasers accept all the liabilities amassed during the period of nationalization.

63. For an excellent coverage of economic conditions during the period, see Yusuf, op. cit., pp. 257-62 and 293-94.

64. Sobhan and Ahmad, op. cit., p. 366.

65. World Bank: *Bangladesh: Industrial Sector*, an unpublished working paper of the World Bank Office in Dhaka, 1986, p. 3. This primarily deals with the industrial sector, is not be to confused with the working paper cited earlier that was more directly concerned with the public sector. The paper referenced in this footnote will hereafter be cited as "WB/Dhaka—Indus. Sec."

66. Chishty, op. cit., pp. 8-9. The exchange rate by this time was Tk7.74/US$1.

67. As cited in ibid, p. 22; see also pp. 8-9 and Rahim, op. cit., p. 87.

68. WB/Dhaka—Pub. Sec., p. 3; Chishty, op. cit., p. 9.

69. T. Chowdhury, op. cit., pp. 5-6,20; see also Sobhan and Ahmad, op. cit., pp. 247-48.

70. This estimate is based on my study of two lists of divested enterprises provided at two different times in 1987 by the Ministry of Industries. The former Indian properties confiscated by the Pakistan government were labeled as "enemy property" under P.O. No. 29 of 1965. After liberation, the tile was amended to read "vested property" because India was an ally of Bangladesh in the struggle against Pakistan. I regard the lists as accurate enough for the purpose of this study, but not perfect. See Appendix A for the combined listing of divested enterprises.

71. In Bangladesh "disinvestment" is used to designate the process whereby nationalized "abandoned" or "vested" properties are divested, whereas "denationalization" refers to divestiture of enterprises to their original Bangladeshi owners. While "disinvestment" has some meaning in the

Bangladesh context, it may be misleading. One could get the impression that the government is getting rid of something in which it had "invested." That was true in only a few cases. Actually, the government had not *invested* in most enterprises; it had merely nationalized or taken them over. I have opted not to use the terms "disinvested" or "disinvestment" in this document, unless it appears in direct quotes, usually from Bangladeshi sources.

72. This data was obtained from the same lists cited in footnote 70 above.

73. Conversation—Alihussain Akberali, 10/12/86. Mr. Akberali is a director of several of the firms in the family complex of companies, including H. Akberali & Co., Ltd.; Bangladesh Steel Re-rolling Mills, Ltd.; Meghna Engineering Works, Ltd.; Section Steel Industries, Ltd.; and National Iron and Steel Industries, Ltd. As is so often the case with family business complexes in Bangladesh (and elsewhere in the developing world), it is extremely difficult to figure out which company in the complex is being discussed in any given instance, particularly when financial matters are the subject.

74. Lorche, Klaus: *The Privatization Transaction and Its Long-term Effects: A Case Study of the Textile Industry in Bangladesh* (Cambridge, Harvard University, April 1988), p. 17. This was a paper done for the Harvard Institute for International Development, Center for Business and Government, John F. Kennedy School of Government under a contract with the United Nations Development Programme (UNDP).

4

The First Phase (1975-1981)

The Zia Government

The overthrow of Sheikh Mujib ended the doctrinaire approach to management of the Bangladesh economy. The regime of General Ziaur Rahman that followed showed a more pragmatic appreciation of economic and social reality. The early post-liberation constitution had sanctified socialism as both the goal and the vehicle of national reconstruction. In 1977 the constitution was amended and, in a politically sensitive bit of tightrope walking, the word "socialism" was qualified to mean "economic and social justice."[1]

The altering of the constitution's language represented more than semantic legerdemain. While divestiture of abandoned properties could be accomplished merely by administrative decision, divestiture of enterprises (including banks and also firms formerly owned by Bengalis) nationalized under various ordinances required a two-thirds vote of the parliament. A Martial Law Proclamation of 1977 amended Article 47 of the constitution in the manner noted above. By this subtle diluting of the language (and concept) of socialism, it was now possible to undertake denationalization within the framework of ordinary law. This change made transition to a mixed economy much easier, and paved the way for the major privatization moves of 1982, which we will analyze in considerable detail in the next two chapters.

Bangladesh launched its economic development program with an overextended public sector. The original belief had been that by "controlling the commanding heights" of the economy, the government and its socialistic program could mitigate "the evils of capitalism,"[2] and could direct the country's resources in ways that would serve the common good. Ironically, a policy that ideologically was "anti-bourgeoisie" had the effect of being "pro-bourgeoisie." Even its most ardent supporters have reluctantly admitted that.[3]

The Planning Commission ideologues had tried to force a European Fabian socialist model of the forties and fifties onto a primitive, subsistence economy that was in chaos. The inept and corrupt state control system they installed only exacerbated the basic problems, which were still not being addressed. In their fervor, the planners not only did not come up with a coherent plan that was relevant to conditions existing in Bangladesh; they showed they did not really understand their own society, with all its foibles, its peculiar traits, and the highly individualistic motivations that drove it.

President Zia decided to steer a different course. Relying heavily on the advice of his able and dedicated Minister of Industry and Commerce, Shafiul Azam,[4] he announced in December 1975 that:

> The government is ready to extend all possible support to the private sector for utilizing the full potential of the private entrepreneurs in stepping up of the productive economic activities in the country.[5]

Zia's approach to the policy reorientation was, however, cautious. He was open-minded about gradual privatization, but only after he had consolidated his own political power.[6] He did not feel strong enough to take the full plunge right away, but he had the courage and wisdom to take the first necessary steps.[7]

When I asked well-informed officials, who had been in responsible positions at the time, what was in Zia's mind when he opted for privatization of the economy, the consensus was that he basically believed that private enterprise was more efficient and dynamic. Zia assumed that the best chances for growth would come from the private sector, not the public sector. He was generally aware that the Asian countries that had emphasized private sector development had progressed faster than socialist countries, but his knowledge of such matters was not deep.[8]

Revised Investment Policy of 1975

The Revised Investment Policy of December 1975 [9] represented a watershed in reorienting the economy toward more dependence on private sector activity. As periodically amended, it remained the basic policy statement and guideline until the major shifts of 1982.

Technically, the new policy maintained the 18 reserved categories, but it opened 10 of them to joint ventures between the public corporations and private investors indigenous or foreign. The government would, in all cases, hold at least 51 percent of the equity. The limit on private investment was raised to Tk100 million (US$8.3 million).[10] The eight categories still reserved to the public sector were:

- arms, ammunition, and allied defense equipment
- atomic energy
- jute (sacking, hessian and carpet backing)
- textiles (excluding handlooms and specialized textiles)
- sugar
- air transport
- telephone, telephone cables, telegraph, and wireless apparatus
- generation and distribution of electricity

In other words, the fields that were now open, at least partially, to the private sector included paper, iron and steel, shipping and ship building, heavy engineering, minerals, oil and gas, cement, forest extraction, and chemicals. In actuality, the doors had been opened only a crack. The government was giving ground slowly. As Shafiul Azam told me, "Once anything is in the clutches of the government, it is difficult to dislodge."[11]

The Revised Investment Policy of 1975 stated that, "In view of the misgiving that has been created in the minds of investors by the reference in the New Investment Policy (of July 1974) to the moratorium on nationalization for a period of fifteen years, this provision has been deleted."[12]

Tax holidays and other incentives were increased. It should be kept in mind that tax breaks are only useful as incentives if the tax collection system operates efficiently, which it does not in Bangladesh. If taxes are inconsistently and inequitably collected in the first place, there is no added advantage to a tax break.

A special provision was included in the act to state that the official Bangladesh Shilpa Bank (BSB) had been "directed to provide equity support in deserving cases to small industries, particularly agro-based, agro-supporting and export-oriented industries." This was intended as a response to complaints that government banks (a) gave preferential treatment to state enterprises and (b) tended to favor assistance to large, urban-based industries.

An Investment Corporation of Bangladesh (ICB) was authorized (actually established in 1976); and the Dhaka Stock Exchange, which had been shut down during the nationalization fever of 1972, was reactivated. It reopened to little fanfare and less interest in July 1976 with two listings on the board.

The final substantive paragraph of the act put the government on record for the first time as having an official privatization program. It read:

> With a view to allowing the sector corporations to improve the efficiency of management, some industrial units under their control which were declared abandoned and handed over to them for management will be disinvested to Bangalee (sic) entrepreneurs on cash payment. Persons receiving compensation under President's Order No. 27 will be allowed to adjust their compensation money against the sale price of such disinvested units.[13]

While what the Zia Government put forward was definitely better than what the Mujib regime had offered, it turned out that most of the enterprises initially identified for divestiture were small units that were losing money under Corporation management and which were outside the 18 categories on the reserved list. Quite a few were located in remote areas of the country.

One source[14] has reported that by late 1977, 21 units under the jurisdiction of the Corporations had already been divested and possession turned over to the new owners. Another 15 were divested but not handed over. A total of 33 were in process, and 17 more were under consideration for divestiture. Altogether, these 86 would represent almost 40 percent of the 224 originally confided to the Corporations. A total of 110 of these enterprises were privatized during the Zia period; so this sequence appears on schedule and reasonably accurate.

That same source was on less firm ground when reporting that of the 462 enterprises placed under Boards of Management, 159 had been released in favor of owners, 144 sold and possession transferred to the owners, and 56 sold but not yet handed over. According to this source, the remainder were under consideration for eventual divestiture. This second group of figures is undoubtedly high, and must include some commercial enterprises in addition to industrial companies.

A Disinvestment Board was established to facilitate the process set in motion by the policy announcement of December 1975. A decision was made to return several specialized textile units and jute twine mills to their former owners. This was significant because jute and textiles belonged to the core of major industry taken over. The specialized textile and jute twine units were evidently selected because they were operationally better suited to small-scale management.[15]

For some time, there had been a strong lobby of shareholders of private firms that had been nationalized without compensation. The government set in motion a compensation plan that involved repayment of 20 percent in 1975-76, 30 percent in 1976-77, and the remaining 50 percent in 1977-78. The schedule was more or less adhered to. Over 15,000 claims were received through 1977, amounting to about Tk320 million (US$21 million).[16]

"Privatization" of the Commercial Sector

The lobbying effort also led to a decision by the Disinvestment Board to put up for sale a large number of commercial and trading firms that had been taken over as "abandoned" Pakistani property or Indian firms taken over as "enemy property" during the 1965 Indo-Pakistan War (and renamed "vested property" after the War of Liberation, in which India was an ally).

Twenty-three of the "vested" industrial enterprises had been returned by the Mujib regime. Another 31 were returned by the Zia Government between late 1975 and 1981.[17]

The commercial and trading entities presented a vastly different problem. There is no aspect of the study of privatization in Bangladesh more shrouded in mystery, obfuscation, and general lack of information. It has been almost impossible to find out even such basic information as how many commercial firms were nationalized and how many were privatized. Estimates of privatized commercial enterprises have varied from 2,000 to 8,000. Comprehensive official figures are nonexistent, or at least not available. Even in scholarly studies, the question of what happened to the commercial enterprises is only vaguely alluded to, often in a footnote.[18]

It is as if people either don't know much about this matter or, more probably, don't want to talk about it (particularly with a foreign researcher).[19] The situation related to the commercial enterprises is an embarrassment.

The reason for this apparent reticence is not difficult to deduce. From what information one can piece together, it becomes obvious that a great deal of corruption, malfeasance, and outright pillage was involved. Some of this started even before the war with Pakistan ended. Many Pakistanis, realizing that the West was losing, fled in the Fall of 1971. They pulled out what funds and belongings they could, but had to leave behind most of their business holdings. Scavengers descended on the thousands of enterprises thus left unguarded. Looting was widespread, and participation was not confined to the abject poor. Friends, neighbors, competitors, former employees, and stray passersby all expropriated furniture, equipment, inventory (sometimes in substantial amounts), family possessions, etc., or simply took over the premises. The situation did not improve markedly after the government nationalized these entities. The pillage merely became institutionalized. Officials systematically stripped the firms of what was left, or used their stewardship role to operate the businesses for their own personal gain. A company's name and reputation or its customer lists were often the most valuable assets of commercial/trading firms.

In the chaotic socioeconomic situation that existed in Bangladesh, such firms disappeared in the maze. With several changes of name, they became untraceable. Many ceased to exist once they had been completely drained of resources. Others became the basis upon which substantial, respectable businesses were built. More than a few fortunes in both official and business circles were launched from such beginnings. Abandoned houses were parcelled out to political cronies and supporters, including quite a few former Freedom Fighters.

It is no wonder, then, that useful information, much less hard data, is difficult to come by. The Ministry of Commerce was not at all cooperative in supplying data for this study. Higher officials were willing to discuss the general subject, often quite frankly. But everything bogged down in the middle bureaucracy when statistical information was requested.

The Ministry of Commerce finally came up with a hastily concocted, handwritten note stating that 745 commercial units had been nationalized.[20] This figure was patently ridiculous. When pressed on the point that thousands had been taken over, the Ministry haltingly responded that the 745 represented the "larger" abandoned companies that had been nationalized. No clarification was given as to how the dividing line between large and small was determined. The note stated that up to late 1986, 417 units had been sold, 214 were "awaiting sale," 66 were under litigation, and 48 had been returned to "Bangladeshi owners" (of whatever dubious documentation). No names of firms, sale prices, or dates of transactions were provided. The impression given was that only this number had been nationalized, and that all of them had already been privatized or were in process.

The Ministry of Industries has admitted that monitoring of divested industrial enterprises has been intermittent and selective at best. In the case of commercial firms it has been nonexistent. To be fair, keeping track of divested firms in the labyrinth of commercial trading houses in the bazaars of Dhaka, Chittagong, Khulna, and other Bangladesh towns would be a most difficult task.

One reason for this lack of information is that many of the so-called divestiture transactions probably never took place, because the enterprises had for all practical purposes ceased to exist as functioning businesses. They remained on the registers only as legal entities. It is probable that they were finally written off by a simple entry as "disinvested."

When one considers that commerce and trading have traditionally constituted the major participation of the Bengali business community, this is a sorry tale that is, however, unfortunately symbolic of economic activity in Bangladesh.

One should keep this in perspective, however. Despite these murky intrigues, the percentage of the private part of the commercial/trading sector increased from only 30 percent in the heyday of state control to 65 percent by 1977,[21] due to heightened confidence and improved access to credit.

The Industrial Sector and the Public/Private Mix

Industrial output finally reached 1969 levels by 1977,[22] although the mainstays, jute and textiles, were still only at 85 percent of pre-liberation output.[23]

The improved investment climate resulted in increased and broader activity by the private sector, especially in 1976-77. Approved investment projects included ventures in deep sea fishing, synthetic and specialized textiles, garment manufacturing, footwear, weaving, canning, pharmaceuticals, plastics and rubber, ship repair, building of river barges, engineering works, etc. It should be noted that all of these were areas in which the public sector was not active, or had recently reduced its presence through divestiture.[24]

The government also sold 10 of 29 tea "gardens" (estates) in 1977 at a time when the industry was booming.[25] Predictably, this prompted some criticism from entrenched circles who seemed incapable of realizing that the economy as a whole profits (not just a few grasping capitalists) if the government unloads "going concerns," and not just the losers that no one wants.

It was also about this time that a notable trend started in earnest. Bengali businessmen in commerce and trade began to show more interest in longer-term industrial investments. Their dependence on public support and patronage was still strong (perhaps even stronger than in EPIDC days because of less favorable economic conditions in the mid-seventies),[26] but they were beginning to venture into larger, more sophisticated, longer-term activities. This has been a common pattern in many LDC economies. In Bangladesh, there were quite a few people with a lot of money in their hands who hadn't quite decided what to do with it.

Although the diversification of economic activity was encouraging, the public sector still dominated the modern industrial sector. As Q.K. Ahmad wrote in 1978, "The most fundamental implication of the nationalization of industries for private capitalism in Bangladesh is its virtual elimination from large-scale industrial ownership."[27]

The major industrial concerns were housed in the sectoral Corporations. In 1976, the scope and size of the holdings was as represented in the following table:[28]

Corporation	No. of Enterprises	Fixed Assets*	Annual Sales*	No. of Employees
Bangladesh Jute Mills Corporation (BJMC)	78	1,700	2,938	199,600
Bangladesh Textile Mills Corporation (BTMC)	75	611	1,813	65,500
Bangladesh Sugar and Food Industries Corporation (BSFIC)	58	407	1,401	31,600
Bangladesh Chemical Industries Corporation (BCIC)	65	2,017	1,849	25,300
Bangladesh Steel & Engineering Corporation (BSEC)	54	804	1,424	14,500
Petrobangla	4	177	220	2,800
Bangladesh Petroleum Corporation	7	148	560	2,800
Bangladesh Minerals Exploration Development Corporation (BMEDC)	10	—	211	1,100
Bangladesh Forest Industries Development Corporation (BFIDC)	20	338	78	4,000
Totals	371	6,202	10,494 (US $404 million)**	347,200 (US $684 million)**

*In Tk million.
**The official exchange rate in 1976 was Tk15.35 to US$1.

When the new privatization policy went into effect, the enterprises under the Corporations still accounted for almost 90 percent of the fixed assets in major industrial areas and 78 percent of government revenues.[29] Raw jute and jute manufacturers amounted to 75 percent of the foreign exchange earned through exports.[30]

Meanwhile, the Corporations and the ministries continued their tug-of-war over control of the SOEs. In the later stages of the Mujib regime, a move was made by the government to give the Corporations the status of Divisions within their respective ministries, which would have increased both their power and operational freedom. Four were in fact given such status and their chairmen awarded Secretary status.[31] The process, however, was halted when the Zia Government came to power. Power reverted to the regular ministerial Secretaries.

Consequently, while policy was being liberalized under Zia, operation of the SOE system was not. An insecure government was tightening the reins. Renewed ministry control insured that SOEs would be run on bureaucratic rather than commercial principles. Ministerial interference increased and managerial autonomy at the enterprise level decreased, with a parallel loss in both initiative and accountability[32] (to say nothing of profitability).

This situation continued until May 1976, when the government felt secure enough to issue the Rules of Business that had been such a bone of contention for years. Under the new Rules, the functions of the ministry were to be confined to policymaking, appointment of Corporation chairmen, budget approval, review of audits, and evaluation of SOE performance. An accompanying intention was to increase both the autonomy and the accountability of the individual enterprises under the general supervision of the Corporations.

Despite such well-meaning phrases as "the Ministry/Division shall scrupulously refrain from interfering in day-to-day management . . . and shall scrupulously respect the operational freedom of the Corporations/autonomous/semi-autonomous bodies," the Rules, in practice, did not much improve the situation.[33] Like many other public pronouncements in Bangladesh, rhetoric was not matched by performance.

Industrial finance has always been a critical factor in the development of the modern sector of Bangladesh's economy. One of the major objectives of the nationalization of financial institutions was to improve credit allocation among different sectors.

Imbalances existed throughout the economy. For example, the rural agricultural sector produced 80 percent of the GDP in the mid-seventies, but had only about 10 percent of bank deposits.[34] Bank nationalization had not adjusted that imbalance. It had only increased the tendency of financial institutions to first meet the needs of the public sector on a priority basis, thereby reducing the amount available to the rest of the economy.[35]

Banks gave little scrutiny to loan requests from BJMC and BTMC. Bad repayment experiences with these and other public institutions induced greater caution in bankers; but most of their reticence was directed, ironically, at private sector applicants. As Rahim points out, the lending strategy of commercial banks was not based on development, much less commercial, considerations. Politics had historically dominated in both the official development finance institutions (DFIs) and the nationalized commercial banks (NCBs).[36]

During the seventies, 43 percent of the financial resources provided by the commercial banks went to the manufacturing sector; and the bulk of these went to SOEs.[37] The situation, extreme during the Mujib period, did change under Zia. For example, the Bangladesh Shilpa Bank (BSB), the leading DFI, directed 20 percent of its loan assistance to the private sector in 1973-74, 17 percent in 1975-76, but 90 percent by 1976-77.[38]

In dealing with the private sector, however, commercial banks have tended to go for quick returns in the trading sphere rather than longer-range returns in industrial development.[39] Most of Bangladesh's entrepreneurs had the same predilection.

This, when coupled with lack of equity capital and excruciatingly long delays encountered during the DFI approval process, helped to create an investment climate in which private industrial sector investment was slow to pick up steam. Obstacles like this (and there were others) had more influence on private investment than pious policy statements. Initial investor reaction to the reactivation of the Dhaka Stock Exchange was almost nil.[40]

Despite limitations, the performance of the private sector, though still behind the unrealistic goals of the Mujib government's First Five-Year Plan (1973-78), was superior to that of the public sector, mainly because of the somewhat less constricting investment climate.[41] By the end of the decade, the disparity in performance was becoming obvious. Between 1973-74 and 1980-81, industrial production went up 45 percent. The private sector grew 64 percent, but the public sector grew only 39 percent.[42] Of course, the private sector had begun from a smaller base. The private sector's greatest gains were in chemicals and electrical equipment manufacturing.[43]

The following table shows the comparative performance of both sectors in terms of investment and output during this period:[44]

Year	Investment (in Tk millions) Private Sector	Public Sector	Industrial Output (with 1973-74 as base) Private Sector	Public Sector
1973-74	N/A	N/A	100.0	100.0
1974-75	5,091	5,102	89.5	100.0
1975-76	6,102	5,056	103.4	105.4
1976-77	5,664	4,935	112.5	114.0
1977-78	7,454	9,049	122.5	125.2
1978-79	9,004	9,808	145.2	128.6
1979-80	11,424	17,786	151.1	126.9
1980-81	13,941	19,784	164.3	136.9
1981-82	15,215	14,959	166.3	135.7

Note: Investment figures are economy-wide; output figures do not include micro and cottage industries.

It is revealing that after a slow start in the mid-seventies, a number of public policies and entrepreneurial initiatives began to pay off in the form of more rapid private sector growth by the late seventies and early eighties. Production in the public sector increased, but more slowly. Public sector losses also increased, averaging about US$250 million annually in the early eighties. These recurrent public sector deficits, with consequent drain on the strained budget in an impoverished economy were among the prime motivations behind the government's decision to turn up the privatization throttle another notch in 1982.[45]

One side effect of increased private sector activity is that the public sector began to feel the bite of competition. One economist critical of private sector objectives and methods was forced to admit that private jute traders were "devastatingly effective" in under-bidding the BJMC on jute carpet backing in 1976-77 and 1977-78 through price flexibility.[46] Elliot Berg, in his worldwide survey of divestiture for the World Bank, postulated that the introduction of competition from the private sector was having a beneficial effect on the way SOEs were being run. He said that, at a minimum, the government now had a measuring stick for their performance.[47]

Summary of the Zia Period (1975-1981)

During the six years of the Zia regime, a total of 255 SOEs were divested or privatized in one way or another.[48] Thirty of these were

the last of the "enemy" cum "vested" properties originally confiscated from Indians during the Pakistan period. Another 115 were
small firms divested through the Office of the Director General of Industries (DGI), similar to the small units unloaded during the Mujib
period.

The remaining 110 were somewhat larger entities housed in the
Corporations, the first such enterprises let loose. Of these, 84 had
been classified as "fully abandoned" and 26 as "partially abandoned,"
meaning that there had been other original owners as well as Pakistanis. Most of these had been Bengali minority shareholders, although there were also a few Indians and Europeans.

It is difficult to describe with precision the size and makeup of
these divested entities. I have previously commented on the perils of
trying to gauge their value (especially the smaller units dispensed by
the DGI). Nevertheless, the best available data suggests that among
the 30 enemy/vested properties were 18 rice mills, 5 vegetable oil
companies, 4 chemical/pharmaceutical firms, an ice company, a printing operation, and a trading company.

Of the smaller firms divested through the DGI, the list includes:

metalworking	8
rubber products	11
paper and printing	7
vegetable oils	16
rice and/or flour mills	21
textiles and hosiery	10
soap and chemicals	4
films	3
jute rope	2
ice and cold storage	3
hotels	2
trading	3
engineering	5
wood products	4
glass and optical	3
salt	2
miscellaneous	11
Total	115

Finally, in the 110 divested from the corporations were:

tanneries, hides, and bones	25
metal works	17
textiles	11
jute products	7
tobacco	6
rubber products	5
food products	5
wood products	5
vegetable oils	5
matches	4
ice and cold storage	4
engineering	3
chemicals and pharmaceuticals	3
miscellaneous	10
Total	110

Although generally larger than the entities released by the DGI, few of these enterprises were among the largest or most important corporation holdings.

In sum, privatization and private sector development were advanced significantly during the period of President Zia (1975-81). The policies were basically liberal, but carried out with more caution than conviction.[49] Policy was emphasized more than implementation and, as with the predecessor government, no well-thought-out plan with coherent objectives was ever developed.[50]

Only a few, like Shafiul Azam and Shafiqur Rahman, had a well-developed idea of where they were going or should go in the future. The concept of a mixed economy and what that entailed in defining roles for a public-private partnership was not widely understood, much less accepted and implemented.

Nevertheless, the ground was well-prepared for the next logical step in the evolution of a privatization policy,[51] even though the turmoil and insecurity engendered by the assassination of President Zia in May 1981 made the future uncertain for a time. This was not new to Bangladesh.

Notes

1. The significance of this alteration, often overlooked by foreign observers, is discussed thoroughly in T. Chowdhury, op. cit., pp. 3,9-11; see also Rahim, op. cit., p. 86.
2. ibid, p. 93.
3. Sobhan and Ahmad, op. cit., p. 563.
4. Shafiul Azam can quite properly be called the design architect of Bangladesh's move toward privatization and private sector development. He convinced President Zia in 1975 and President Ershad in 1982 to institute the two major privatization initiatives. He was, reportedly, the sole cabinet officer who voted against nationalization in 1972. He left the Mujib government a few months later, returning to office when Zia took over in mid-1975.
5. *The Bangladesh Observer*, 8/4/76, as cited in Yusuf, op. cit., p. 97; see also T. Chowdhury, op. cit., p. 7. Chowdhury says that Zia wanted to redirect the economy from socialism to a mixed economy, with a substantially larger role for the private sector.
6. Conversation—Azam, 10/3/86; Conversation—Chishty, 9/29/86.
7. Conversation—Azam, 10/3/86.
8. ibid; Conversation—S.Rahman, 3/3/87; Conversation—Chishty, 9/29/86; Conversation—Dr. Shahadat Ullah, Commissioner, Planning Commission, 10/7/87; Conversation—M.R. Siddiqi (President), Habibullah Khan (Vice President), and C.K. Hyder (Secretary), Metropolitan Chamber of Commerce and Industry, 9/23/86.
9. *Revised Investment Policy*, Ministry of Industry and Commerce, Industries Division, Government of Bangladesh, Dec. 7, 1975. However, applications above Tk10 million still required approval of the Investment Board.
10. The limit was completely abolished in 1978. The exchange rate in 1975 was Tk12.02/US$1.
11. Conversation—Azam, 10/3/86.
12. *Revised Investment Policy*, op. cit., p. 2. A nervous investor could interpret that two ways. The government assured investors that it should be taken to mean that the government had discarded any idea of nationalization. Conversely, the Revised Investment Policy of 1975 went on to say,"However, it is reiterated that if any industry is ever nationalized, compensation will be paid on [a] fair and equitable basis."
13. ibid. p.3.
14. Rahim, op. cit., p. 91, 95; see also Yusuf, op. cit., pp. 104-105; Conversation—S. Rahman, 9/22/86; Conversation—Rabbani, 10/28/86. Rahim has also pointed out that in 1976 and 1977, a total of 684 investment applications were sanctioned, a significant jump from the immediate post-liberation era. The average size of investment was also up substantially. Rahim, op. cit., p. 92.
15. Chishty, op. cit., p. 10; Yusuf, op. cit., p.97.
16. ibid, pp. 97-98, 166-67.
17. These figures were compiled from a list of 482 divested industrial enterprises provided by the Ministry of Industries. It should be noted that

industry and commerce have been combined under one ministry or split into two at various times over the years. From this point on in this study, they will be referred to as separate ministries, which has been the pattern for most of the last decade.

18. For example, Yusuf in his otherwise meticulous study, says only that the Disinvestment Board decided (in 1976?) to sell 2,187 commercial and trading firms that had been nationalized. Yusuf, op. cit., p. 101. He obtained his data from the government sources he normally quoted. Also, he gave no indication whatsoever of what was actually done after the decision to divest was made. In the case of divestiture of industrial enterprises, he usually followed the process through as carefully as statistical information permits in Bangladesh.

19. Conversations—S.Rahman, 9/22/86 & 12/2/86; Conversation—Chishty—9/29/86. These two and other senior officials were very cooperative in discussing this situation in general terms, but specific information was difficult to obtain. At lower levels, there was reluctance to talk even in general terms.

20. Conversation—Abu Sayeed Chowdhury, Joint Secretary, Ministry of Commerce, 11/24/86. Mr. B.R. Khan, Deputy Secretary, was also in the meeting.

21. Rahim, op. cit., p. 94.

22. Ahmad, Q.K., op. cit., p. 399; Nyrop, op. cit., p. 244, 268.

23. Ahmad, Q.K., op, cit., p. 401.

24. Yusuf, op. cit., p. 101; Nyrop, op. cit., p. 268.

25. Yusuf, op. cit., p. 101.

26. Ahmad, Q.K., op. cit., p. 409.

27. ibid, 408. As mentioned in an earlier section, the public sector represented only a small number of larger firms (between 375 and 400 in 1977), whereas private sector enterprises numbered approximately 7,850 (340,000 if one includes rural micro-enterprises and cottage industries). Sobhan and Ahmad, op. cit., p. 193.

28. Yusuf, op. cit., p. 116. The names of the Corporations have been changed regularly, as have been the rosters of enterprises within the various Corporations. A 1986 listing appears in Appendix B.

29. Yusuf, op. cit., p. 117.

30. ibid, p. 116.

31. Chishty, op. cit., p. 6. A Secretary is the highest ranking career civil servant in a ministry and carries enormous prestige and power.

32. WB/Dhaka—Pub. Sec., op. cit., p. 6.

33. ibid, p. 7; Chishty, op. cit., p. 7.

34. Rahim, op. cit., p. 6. Only 8% of private investment was in agricultural activity. Alamgir, op. cit., p. 190.

35. Rahim, op. cit., p. 3.

36. ibid, p. 11, 15. A useful discussion (with supporting data) of the shift in government strategy concerning assistance to the private sector during this period can be found in *Bangladesh: Promoting Higher Growth and Human Development*, a World Bank Country Study (Washington, D.C., World Bank, 1987),

pp. 77-79. To differentiate among this and other World Bank reports, we will hereinafter refer to this document as WB-'87.

37. Yusuf, op. cit., p. 118. This preference of the banks to provide loans to SOEs was mentioned in almost all sources.

38. ibid., p. 98.

39. Conversation—Azizul Haque, 2/29/87; Conversation—Serajul Islam Chowdhury and Zafrul Islam Chowdhury, 10/11/86. Several other sources, including the banks themselves, made similar comments. Serajul Islam Chowdhury is one of the old guard of Bangladesh industrialists. He owns jute mills, a steel mill, and has one of the country's largest shipbreaking operations. His troubled personal empire is run along very conservative, patriarchal lines.

40. Rahim, op. cit., p. 97.

41. Alamgir, op. cit., p. 189. Dr. Alamgir, who is the Managing Director of Bangladesh Shilpa Bank (BSB), obtained his Ph.D. in the United States.

42. Baxter, op. cit., p. 85.

43. ibid.

44. Chowdhury, Nuimuddin: "Economic Management in Bangladesh, 1975-82," New Series No. 32 of *Research Report Series* (Dhaka, Bangladesh Institute of Development Studies, undated, but circa 1983-84), p. 51. See also T. Chowdhury, op. cit., 7, 8.

45. Rahman, Md. Ataur: "Bangladesh in 1982: Beginnings of the Second Phase," *Asian Survey*, Feb. 1983, p. 154.

46. N. Chowdhury, op. cit., p. 45f. Dr. Chowdhury ended up decrying "price cutting," but admitted that the government's rigid price setting was unrealistic and self-defeating. Many academics in Bangladesh have trouble with competitive business practices, particularly when the government is at a disadvantage. While recognizing that the government's approach is too rigid, they cannot help expressing a feeling that the more flexible practices of the private sector are in a way unfair, almost unethical. In some cases, they are, but the accusation by some academics is a reflex reaction.

47. Berg, Elliot: *Divestiture of State-Owned Enterprises in LDCs*. A Consultant's Report prepared at the request of the World Bank (draft), Alexandria, Virginia, Nov. 1985, p. 97. An edited version of this paper was circulated by the Public Sector Management Unit, Projects Policy Department, World Bank, under the title of *Divestiture in Developing Countries*, July 1986 and published under the same title in an even more edited form as #11 in the series of World Bank Discussion Papers. Mary Shirley was listed as co-author of the 1987 edition.

48. These figures and the numerical and functional breakdowns that follow were compiled using previously cited lists and information provided by the Ministry of Industries. The figures and descriptions are as reliable as available information allows, i.e., basically sound, but not perfect. Tawfique Chowdhury has put the figure at 326. T. Chowdhury, op. cit., 10. He noted that most of that number were small, older firms that were losing money, and which represented a small percentage of total industrial output.

49. "I did not go to break up the party," *The Tide*, A Special Issue, Feb.-Mar. 1987. Stated by Moudud Ahmed, then Deputy Prime Minister and Minister of Industries, in an interview with the Dhaka publication. Similar comments were made in a number of conversations the author had with officials, particularly, Shafiqur Rahman, Azizul Haque and Shafiul Azam.

50. Conversation—S. Rahman, 10/16/86; Conversation—Muhuddin Azad, Joint Secretary, Ministry of Finance, 10/7/86; Conversation—Azam, 10/3/86; Conversation—M. Islam, 7/6/88; Yusuf, op. cit., p. 273; Rahim, op. cit., pp. 93-97. See also Islam, Syed Serajul: "The State in Bangladesh Under Zia (1975-81)," *Asian Survey*, May 1984, p. 561. It is noted in this article that management of the Corporations and enterprises was, by and large, in the hands of the political elites when the Mujib regime ran the country; but under Zia there were more military and police officers and civil servants in these positions.

51. T. Chowdhury, op. cit., p. 12. Chowdhury believes the groundwork was prepared in three ways: (a) increasing the role of the private sector, (b) divesting smaller abandoned enterprises, and (c) removing legal difficulties for eventual denationalization of larger entities formerly owned by Bengalis. We shall return to this last point in the following chapters.

5

The Second Phase (1982-1988)

Despite uncertainty and instability brought about by the assassination of President Zia, 1981 was a relatively good year economically for Bangladesh.

Some of the earlier policies and programs began to pay off, albeit modestly. GDP increased 7 percent, which was significantly more than earlier years. Industrial production increased 8 percent; and improved domestic food production lowered prices somewhat, helping to bring the inflation rate down to 10 percent.

However, in 1982 a drought dimmed prospects for continued agricultural growth. It was again made clear that agriculture's marginal capacity for growth was insufficient for the economic expansion the country desperately needed. Because of the drought, food grain production dropped and food imports increased. Consequent budgetary strain meant cutting back on public sector expenditures at a time when state enterprises were performing poorly. This in turn resulted in shortfalls in profits and high debt service payments on many large public enterprise loans.[1]

Given the limitations on employment creation in the agricultural sector and persistent balance of payments problems, the country's planners believed that greater emphasis should be placed on industrial growth and export earnings.

A review of public sector enterprises convinced government leaders that SOEs were not capable of leading a rapid industrial expansion. SOEs were viewed as too bureaucratic and inefficient, lacking accountability, ambivalent about social and commercial goals, and most were consistently losing money—hardly a formula for dynamic leadership of a troubled economy.

The government decided to make a major break with the past and embark on an economic development effort in which the private sector would play a much more prominent role. This would necessitate a change in the relative roles of the private and public sectors, along with an improvement in the investment and regulatory environments that would permit the private sector to operate effectively.

After several years of inconsistent planning and cautious opening of the economy to the private sector, the Bangladesh government, now led by General H. M. Ershad, took a bold step to dramatically force the issue.[2]

Shafiul Azam was again at the helm of the Ministry of Industry and Commerce.[3] His presence undoubtedly provided the impetus for the decision to take action. Azam had long held that "the role of the public sector is to supplement the private sector, not supplant it." He viewed conditions in 1982 as ideal for more aggressive pursuit of his economic philosophy. He said, "I got my life's chance!"[4]

Azam says he told Ershad in the Spring of 1982 that the government "must denationalize in a big way," further stating that, "Your name will be written in gold letters; it will be electrifying!"[5] Azam recounted further, perhaps diplomatically, that it had been a "true meeting of the minds—the President was already thinking along the same lines."

Ershad was more familiar than Zia with private sector successes in Korea, Taiwan, Japan, and Hong Kong, but he used no models as such and little ideology. According to Azam, Ershad's approach was "pure pragmatism."[6]

After the presidential go-ahead, Azam gave two trusted deputies, Shamsul Haque Chishty and Shafiqur Rahman, until November 1982 to get the privatization program started. In his methodical way Azam set deadlines, required progress reports and background studies, and periodically checked up on the progress of the project.[7]

The core group promoting privatization knew that their best hope for pushing through significant changes would be to act quickly, "while the iron was hot," as they said. They felt action must be taken quickly before the opposition solidified and, especially, before the military (up to then uncommitted and even unconcerned), took a firm position.[8]

Also, the government held a series of discussions with representatives of various chambers of commerce, trade associations, and industrial enterprises. Not only was it unusual for the government to consult with the private sector *before* a major action was taken, it was doubly surprising that those discussions had considerable influence in the formulation of the policy that followed.[9]

New Industrial Policy of 1982

The result was the New Industrial Policy (NIP) announced on June 1, 1982. Its stated general purpose was "to provide a new dimension and greater thrust to industrialization of the country."[10]

The NIP, like most Bangladeshi policy statements, contained a long list of objectives covering all conceivable bases, but the most important were:

- to expand the manufacturing sector with increased participation of the private sector
- to limit the role of the public sector to the establishment of basic heavy and strategic industries
- to improve the efficiency and profitability of public sector enterprises
- to protect and promote local industries by reasonable tariff measures and/or by banning imports where there was adequate domestic capacity
- to promote export-oriented industries
- to encourage efficient and economic import substitutions, and
- to create additional productive employment opportunities in the rural areas through promotion of rural and cottage industries

The list of industries reserved for the public sector was trimmed to six: arms and ammunition, atomic energy, air transport, telecommunications, electricity generation and distribution, and mechanized forest extraction.

The other 12 industries formerly on the Reserved List were placed in a new category called the Concurrent List, which permitted both public and private investment, and even encouraged public-private joint ventures. The door had been opened a bit for this in the Revised Investment Policy of December 1975. What was implicit in 1975 was made explicit in 1982. The concurrent list included:

- jute industry (sacking, hessian, and carpet backing)
- cotton textiles (excluding handlooms, power looms, and specialized textiles)
- sugar
- paper and newsprint
- iron and steel (excluding re-rolling mills)

- shipbuilding and heavy engineering
- heavy electrical industry
- minerals, oil, and gas
- cement
- petrochemicals
- heavy and basic chemicals and basic pharmaceuticals
- shipping
- appliances and equipment for telecommunications service [11]

In other words, all but six industries were opened to the private sector, and joint venturing with foreign investors was permitted with few restrictions.

The NIP even suggested that, in some "deserving cases" where there was public-private collaboration, management could be awarded to the private investors even though the major shares were still held by the public sector Corporation.

Corporations were to divest "abandoned" enterprises or units established by the Corporation when such enterprises continually lost money or could not compete effectively with the private sector. The NIP took another bold step by stating:

> In order to stimulate the share market and raise additional funds, shares up to 49% of some enterprises managed by the sector Corporations will be unloaded for public subscriptions or operation by the Investment Corporation of Bangladesh.[12]

This provision caused a furor that prompted the government to slow its pace in this area for a while. The government put the stock selling idea on the back burner. It was returned to the front burner again in late 1986, as we will see later.

The blockbuster in the NIP was the decision to return the jute and textile mills nationalized a decade earlier to their original Bangladeshi owners. The jute and textile lobby had been pushing hard for this for several years. There is no doubt that this issue had been the central point of political, as well as economic, discussions between the government and business leaders prior to promulgation of the NIP. The move to privatize these two major industries was made, "in order to create a favorable investment climate and confidence in the minds of prospective entrepreneurs."[13]

The move represented the first privatization on a major scale of large industrial enterprises in strategically important areas of the economy. The denationalization of 27 textile mills and 33 jute mills was accomplished within a year.

The government turned over to the private sector 38 percent of the jute capacity, and 45 percent of the spinning and 57 percent of the weaving capacity in the textile industry. The government subsequently sold another 4 textile mills through sealed tender.[14] Later sections of this report will deal with privatization of the jute and textile industries in more detail.

Other NIP provisions warrant at least passing attention. Bangladeshi policy statements seem to have an inherent predilection for "covering the waterfront," and the NIP was no exception. Like its predecessors and successors, the NIP's provisions were so voluminous that the improbability of their being implemented increased in direct proportion to the number of propositions. Inclusion of these propositions, however, at least indicated awareness of the manifold problems facing the modern sector of Bangladesh's industrial economy. The basic thrust of the document was the government's position that the greatest potential for economic growth and progress rested with private enterprise, not the public sector.

The NIP stressed rehabilitation and reform of existing industrial establishments and use of local resources, whenever possible, in order to better balance development and distribution of industry around the country. A recommendation to increase subcontracting by large enterprises to small companies was prominently mentioned. The NIP also expressed a desire, considered by most observers as premature, for Bangladesh to move away from assembly-type operations to actual manufacturing.[15]

Various incentives for investment, both domestic and foreign, were included in the NIP. An encyclopedic total of 84 industries were identified where technology was desired, mostly from foreign investors. The system of Investment Schedules was supposed to be streamlined. These Schedules had compiled a remarkably consistent record of earmarking the wrong industries for investment and expansion.

The list of "free sectors," where no formal governmental permission was required prior to investing private funds, was greatly expanded. These were mainly in industrial areas where the public sector was not active, and also where relatively small private units were doing quite well. In those cases where governmental sanctions were still necessary, the NIP made a gesture at streamlining and shortening the process. Deadlines for approval were set, but rarely met.

A Foreign Investment Cell and a "One Stop" Service were set up to facilitate investment applications from foreign companies. The ineffectual performance of the latter unit prompted frustrated applicants and local wags to suggest its name be changed from "One Stop" to "Dead Stop."

The performance and profitability of SOEs were to be improved by installing and monitoring a management information system (MIS), permitting more flexibility in pricing, encouraging greater efficiency and more autonomy in operations.

Reaction to the New Industrial Policy was mixed. Everyone acknowledged that something dramatic, even drastic, had to be done to turn around the faltering economy. All but the diehards realized that such hopes could not possibly rest with the lumbering, graft-ridden state enterprise system.

But privatization, as such, had few passionate advocates. The leftist-leaning academics and intellectuals were almost universally opposed, as is so often the case in former colonial societies. Like their counterparts elsewhere, the Bangladesh academics decried the influence of foreign ways, but loathed even more the traits and backwardness of their own traditional society. In some ways, they have been more foreign than the foreigners. They speak in grand humanitarian terms, while building elaborate state control systems within which they can play olympian guru roles.

There are competent and dedicated scholars in Bangladesh, but generally the scholarship is slanted and polemic. This is particularly so on the subjects of privatization and private enterprise. Few have business experience, except in hawking their scholarly wares.

The Awami League, now the opposition party, was a dedicated foe of privatization of the mills, holding to the tenets of its socialistic manifesto. There was a certain irony in this, in that quite a few of the mill owners, who had originally been set up in the business by the EPIDC, were early and important supporters of the Awami League. They had obviously split from the party on this issue.

The workers were loosely aligned with the Awami League, although their opposition to privatization was based on practical issues, not ideology. They feared that divestiture of the vastly overstaffed public enterprises would result in loss of jobs in the name of efficiency and profitability. Unemployment in a subsistence economy of an overpopulated country like Bangladesh is a very serious matter. The labor force has the traditional fear of the powerless at times of dramatic change. As bad as their current lot is, the turmoil and doubts associated with the unknown is worse.

Unemployment in Bangladesh has consistently hovered around 37-38 percent, and underemployment is even higher. The workers had been given false hopes by the nationalization of 1972. In 1975, they had been worried, but went along with the government's tentative moves toward privatization in the hope of better times. Their attitudes had hardened by 1978-79. By 1982, they viewed privatization as a threat, particularly since the principal denationalization was to take place in jute and textiles, the two industries employing the most people.[16]

Cynical after centuries of exploitation, the workers saw a dynamic private enterprise economy as a way for the rich to get richer, rather than as a way to create more jobs or generate increased income. Self-serving leaders of the violent labor union movement, fearful of losing power, made certain that those fears and forebodings were constantly reinforced.

Meanwhile, the rural and agricultural population, which comprised more than 80 percent of Bangladesh's people, played their usual passive role, unconsulted and apparently unconcerned about privatization of the "modern" industrial sector. The farmers, the country's most influential private sector, felt little kinship with urban businessmen. Whatever contact they had experienced had been characterized by exploitation.

Many in the bureaucracy viewed privatization as a threat to their jobs, their power, and their access to graft. More than a few, particularly at higher, policy levels, did realize the weaknesses of the current system, and had come to the conclusion that the government was a poor businessman anyway. They would be relieved to unload the burden of the stumbling state enterprise system.

The biggest support of privatization came, of course, from the business community and the traditional elite who had influence with the political leadership. But even in the business community, there were some who looked upon privatization with unease. A few shared the view of the academics and bureaucrats that Bangladesh's private sector was not sophisticated or public spirited enough to take the primary leadership role.

A few of the business elite saw the rise of the private sector, the broadening of its base, and increased competition as a potential threat to their own business empires; and they quietly colluded with sympathetic circles in the bureaucracy to keep privatization policies and programs within palatable limits that served, not endangered, their interests.

One cannot help but wonder what prompted the political leadership to undertake such a bold step in the face of almost universal antagonism in a society so factionalized and riddled with self-interest.

The primary reason for pushing privatization in 1982 was the same as in 1975. The previous experiment—nationalization and public sector domination—had failed miserably. The situation had deterio-rated even further by 1982. One senior official in the Ministry of Finance said, "We had wasted 35 years [1947-1982]. We had to do something different and definite!"[17]

As noted earlier, most governments don't opt for privatization for positive reasons, but usually because something else has failed. That is why the first moves toward privatization in Bangladesh and, in-deed, in most LDCs, were cautious and lacking in confidence. Such a move is inherently unfamiliar to governments, who only vaguely sense that privatization is the way to go.

As Shafiul Azam said, "Few saw the only hope as private sector growth." [18] Ershad and Azam struck quickly and decisively before the antagonistic but scattered factions could coalesce into a more for-midable opposition.

Many of the Bangladesh government's actions over the years have been ad hoc, poorly planned, and even more poorly carried out. Some, however, have been handled thoughtfully and planned meticu-lously. As always, the personalities involved have been the decisive factor.

In key instances, for example, the government was fortunate in having the services of Shamsul Haque Chishty and Shafiqur Rahman, the two senior aides of Shafiul Azam mentioned earlier. Azam gave them the following guidance regarding the disposition of state enter-prises, "Dispose of each file (1) objectively, (2) quickly, and (3) apply-ing high standards of quality. Then follow it up - keep at it. Also, build a good library for reference."[19]

One of the problems of Bangladeshi bureaucracy is that careful, step-by-step planning by such people as Chishty and Rahman is not followed up by consistent implementation. All too often, the ten-dency has been to turn out a meticulously crafted policy statement and then proclaim, "Well, that's done, " as if that was all there was to it.

Chishty was in charge of important phases of the negotiations for the sale of abandoned mills and the return of other mills to former owners. He was well informed on the subject and knew all the principals, having been Chairman of the Board of BJMC a few years earlier. Because he handled return of the jute mills so efficiently, he was subsequently appointed to oversee the process for the textile mills as well.[20]

Four basic forums handled the claims:

1. Tender Committee—to open and examine the validity of tenders

2. Scrutiny Committee—to verify the title and nationality of the former shareholders/owners (a terribly complicated process, given the great variety of tangled relationships that existed)

3. Working Group—to evaluate the assets and shares of the enterprises and principles, and to make recommendations for disposition, and

4. Disinvestment Board—to make the final decisions.

A floor price (the National Reserve Price or NRP) was marked out and used as a basis for negotiating with former owners over their bids. The final selling price was the NRP or the winning bidder's (there were several bidders in some cases), whichever was highest, other things remaining the same.

The successful bidder was to make a down payment of 25 percent before the final transfer if the mill was located in a developed area (such as Dhaka, Khulna, Chittagong, and the like), or 20 percent if it was in a less-developed area. The balance was to be paid off in 3 equal annual installments for mills in developed areas or 4 installments in less-developed areas. The payment was to begin 24 months after execution of the Deed of Agreement for sale. The major details of the complex agreements are included as an appendix[21] at the end of the study.

One of the immediate problems facing Chishty and his colleagues was to sort out which mills were fully "abandoned" property and which ones had been fully or partly owned by Bangladeshis. Even the determination of citizenship was not uncomplicated. There were cases in which Bengalis had owned the majority of the stock, and others in which they owned less than 50 percent, but could be considered in the majority when their shares were combined with the holdings of financial institutions.

There were other cases in which Bangladeshis owned less than 50 percent but were to buy enough shares to reach majority status. There were still other instances in which they had been in minority status, but had managed the mills. They were allowed to buy enough shares to take control, provided their original holdings were not less than 30 percent (this requirement was apparently relaxed in some cases). As one can easily see, this situation could be very complicated, but also very important.

Eventually, previously owned shares could be bought at par or face value or at the compensation price determined in 1972. Due to appreciation, this was to the advantage of the former owners. If they had owned less than 51 percent, they had to pay a revalued price for the shares to bring them up to 51 percent. In some instances, they were required to purchase such additional shares if they were to recover even their original investment.

All shares above 51 percent not previously owned were to be purchased at market value, which was much higher than par. Most purchasers opted not to buy at inflated prices. Therefore, the government retained considerable portions of stock (and control) in the "privatized" firms, a fact not generally realized outside of Bangladesh. As a matter of fact, only one or two mills are 100 percent private. The degree of government participation or interference in the operation of individual privatized businesses varies markedly from case to case. There does not appear to be any set pattern.

Another principal bone of contention was the liabilities of the SOEs being divested. The first position of most buyers was that they should not have to accept any liabilities, even the ones existing at the time of nationalization. Their argument was that if they had kept their firms (i.e., no nationalization), they could have liquidated those liabilities.

Since it was obvious that the government would not agree to that, the buyers fell back to another position: while they would accept the liabilities existing in 1972, they should not be held responsible for the liabilities built up during 1972-82, when the firms were operated by the government.

Ultimately, after prolonged and frequently bitter debate, the buyers had to accept all liabilities. Several sources (both public and private) told me that the President personally intervened and, in essence, told the buyers, "Take it or leave it!" Mill owners said, "We had no real choice. We had to accept or we'd never get our businesses back."[22]

Thus, the buyers had to accept a price that they felt was unreasonably high. Inflation worked two ways. Valuation of fixed assets, based on earlier market values, favored the buyers because of appreciation (although most equipment and facilities were old and in bad shape). On the other hand, inflation had made debt service intolerable.

The result was that the buyers came to the conclusion that they could not or should not pay back the loans out of the proceeds of the business. They accepted the government's deal with no intention of paying back the loans. Some mill owners state that after the President laid down his ultimatum, officials in the Ministries of Finance and Industries told them to accept, intimating that the government would compromise later.

Nonpayment of these loans remains a major unresolved problem to the present. It must be faced and concessions from both sides must be made. The two principal government development finance institutions, BSB and BSRS,[23] have repayment rates of approximately 10-12 percent. The loans related to the divestiture of the jute and textile mills are certainly not the only ones past due—nonrepayment is general throughout the society—but the loans in jute and textiles are large and prominent enough to draw attention.

Another key stipulation, which highlighted yet another recurring issue, concerned personnel. The buyers were obligated to take over all officers, staff, and workers, as well as their public service benefits. They also had to agree to take on board a negotiated number of BJMC officers and staff made superfluous by the transfer of the mills out of the Corporations. No terminations were to be made for one year. As it turned out, termination of workers even after that time was politically difficult, in fact, near impossible.

Negotiations over the privatization of the jute and textile mills lasted six months and involved innumerable lengthy sessions.[24] It is worth noting that the government accepted the Bangladesh Jute Mills Association as the spokesman and broker for the private jute owners, a break in precedent. Shafiqur Rahman reported that between June 1982 and June 1984, he supervised the divestiture of 87 public enterprises, in addition to the 33 jute mills and 31 textile mills.[25]

He also reported that another 92 small and medium enterprises were in the process of being divested. In most of these cases, the formalities were completed and agreements signed; down payments had even been made; all that was left was to turn over the enterprises to the buyers. The government was legally bound to the transactions.

At this point, Shafiqur Rahman gave the President a full report, including the matter of legal obligations. The President gave him the go ahead.[26]

Everything was, however, put on hold after President Ershad made a speech in August 1984 to the Bangladesh Steel and Engineering Corporation Employees and Workers Forum, in which he announced that no more public enterprises would be "disinvested or returned to private entrepreneurs." A news story at the time reported[27] that this announcement was greeted with "applause and welcome slogans." The President implied that the government's New Industrial Policy had really been designed to protect local industries, a policy which he promised to continue.

One cannot be certain whether the President's speech signalled a major policy shift or was merely another instance of an insecure politician catering to the strong feelings of a major pressure group. Subsequent events and pronouncements have not shown a consistent pattern, either for or against privatization. That very lack of consistency, however, has indicated a lack of firm commitment to privatization, or at least to its implementation.

The fact remains that no significant divestitures have taken place since mid-1984. Shafiqur Rahman has stated that 70 to 75 of the 92 small enterprises in process were eventually handed over quietly, but it has been difficult to obtain any kind of satisfactory verification. The same is true of reports of another 20 "disinvestments" in 1985-86.

What probably took more out of the drive for a privatized economy than the President's speech was the departure of Shafiul Azam from his position as Minister of Industries. Informed sources have said that "95 percent of the accomplishments of the privatization movement were made while Azam was in office." After he left in mid-1984, "the opposition in the bureaucracy got the upper hand."[28]

Reorganization and Revitalization of the Public Enterprise System

One of the more heralded thrusts of the NIP was reorganization and revitalization of the public sector. An NIP-generated special task force, called the Committee for Reorganization of Public Statutory Corporations (CRPSC), submitted its report in 1983. Among other things, the CRPSC recommended that 13 SOEs should be abolished, 30 others amalgamated into 12 units, and 21 restructured. The remaining SOEs were to remain in the government stable, but under continuing scrutiny.[29]

Other recommendations included the perennial ones of increasing the operational autonomy of individual enterprises, giving them greater flexibility in pricing, and running them along more commercial lines, particularly in such areas as marketing and sales. Better monitoring was recommended both by CRPSC and an excellent study carried out under United Nations Development Program (UNDP) auspices.

The government has also experimented with management contracts. For example, Fabrique National of Belgium was contracted in 1984-85 to run the ailing Bangladesh Machine Tool Factory. Similar arrangements were discussed in regard to GEM Co., Ltd.; Chittagong Dry Dock; Pragoti Industries; and North Bengal Paper Mills.[30] Outside management contracts may marginally increase the efficiency of some SOEs, but the practice does not solve basic issues and, above all, fails to face the issue of commercial survival.

As the World Bank has noted:

> The recommendations of CRPSC, while accepted by the Government of Bangladesh, have only been partially implemented . . . and those dealing with the respective roles of Government, Corporation and enterprise; as well as issues of autonomy and accountability have not been implemented.[31]

The major CRPSC recommendation that was carried out was converting enormous SOE debt to equity. By early 1984, 24 SOEs had been financially restructured by converting Tk6.1 billion (US$244 million) from debt to equity, plus extending another Tk900 million (US$36 million) in equity. Grants of Tk1.3 billion (US$52 million) were given, and the remaining debt service repayments were scheduled.[32] This made the books look good and eased some pressure on the budget, but did not solve the basic problems.

Debt-equity swapping has, however, become popular in financial circles. It is being tried in a number of countries, most notably in Latin America. The keys are the use of local currency and the presence of an active secondary market. The swap is made at perhaps 70 percent of value. Supporters of the concept say it is good for all parties, particularly in transactions involving sale of SOE debt to foreign investors. Foreign banks like it because it makes the books look better. LDCs like it because it serves to reduce international debt and gets corporations involved in improving industrial SOEs. Of course, the middle man gets a cut.

USAID has shown some interest in the concept, but is proceeding cautiously because of the built-in possibility that speculators can get wind of the sale, buy in advance, and quite possibly destabilize the market. Debt-equity conversion is an extremely complex process, the full potential and pitfalls of which are yet only dimly understood in most LDCs.

Something had to be done in Bangladesh, however, when the debt-equity ratio had reached 90:10 on the average. According to the World Bank, public enterprises have survived only because of cash subsidies from the government and loans from the nationalized commercial banks.[33]

In 1971, it had been hoped that the SOEs would generate profits, but they actually became a serious drain on the budget. It is difficult to determine just how much public enterprises lose or make money, mainly because of the way they structure their accounting. Subsidies are often disguised, as are interest liabilities or huge loans. Profits are usually shown *before* interest, which gives a warped picture. For example, in FY 1984-85, the net profit of the public enterprise system was 5.1 percent (of sales) before interest, but -4.2 percent after interest.[34] The net profit of the five main Corporations progressed from a profit of Tk900 million (US$36 million) or 4.9 percent of sales in FY 1982-83 to -Tk2.2 billion (-US$70 million) or -9.2 percent of sales in FY 1985-86.[35]

In most years, the losses in the industrial enterprises more than offset profits made by public financial institutions, with BTMC and especially BJMC the big losers. The World Bank states that the current financial position of many SOEs "would be untenable under normally applicable commercial criteria."[36]

Even though the number of SOEs has decreased over the last decade, their influence on the modern sector of the economy is still profound, especially in large-scale industry producing intermediate and capital goods with high forward linkages. This being the case, the efficiency of SOEs also affects all downstream users.

The following table shows the number of enterprises in all six major public Corporations, the ministries under which they operate, and a rough estimate of the share they have of certain industries: From even this sketchy picture, one can easily see that the public sector is still a dominant factor in Bangladesh's industrial economy.[37]

Corporation	Ministry	No. of Units	Share of Selected Markets
BJMC	Jute	35	jute products—63%
BTMC	Textiles	48	textile—25%
BFIDC	Agriculture	14	mechanized forestry—100%
BCIC	Industries	23	cement—100%* fertilizer—100% pharmaceuticals—8% rubber footwear—20%
BSEC	Industries	25	basic steel (not including rerolling)—100%* water vehicles—36% bicycles—47% pumps—50% radios and TVs—20%
BSFIC	Industries	18	refined sugar—100%
	Total units	163	

*These are probably high estimates. See footnote 36.

Just how much have the divestitures of state enterprises carried out by the various Bangladeshi governments contributed to the private sector component of the industries listed in the table to the economy as a whole? Also, how much of this contribution is due to general private sector activity and growth, accomplished with or without government encouragement or support? The answer to these questions is only clear in the case of jute and textiles, where the linkage is direct and unambiguous.

Privatization and Private Sector Development Since NIP-'82

There is no question that the NIP-'82 contributed significantly to improving the environment for private sector activity. Investors' confidence increased. A new breed of industrial entrepreneur began to emerge from the commercial trader ranks.

Economic activity became more varied. Industrial growth reached 9 percent in 1984 and 1985, after having been almost nil in FY 1982 and 3.7 percent in 1983[38] as the result of political instability. Growth came from labor-intensive private sector industries such as ready-made garments, food processing (especially shrimp), light engineering, and pharmaceuticals, areas where the public sector was not directly involved.

The public sector grew less rapidly and stressed investment in capital-intensive industries. Patterns began to shift. The combination of jute, cotton, textiles, paper, and tobacco, which had represented 60 percent of production in FY 1974 shrunk to 40 percent by FY 1985.[39]

But this was still a troubled economy. Unemployment and underemployment were still high, and productivity remained abysmally low. Private sector performance, while mildly encouraging, was spotty; and public sector performance was sluggish. Foreign exchange earnings were tied to a declining industry (jute), and the country was using 80 percent of the scarce foreign exchange for purchase of petroleum.[40] And always lurking in the background was the disturbing fact that the "unofficial economy" (i.e., black market and smuggling) was almost as large as the official economy and, as a consequence, influenced the application of resources.[41]

By 1986, two-thirds of domestic savings were in the private sector. Allocation of credit between the public and private sectors, which in 1982 had slightly favored the SOEs, had by 1986 shifted to the private sector by a factor of 2 to 1. Unfortunately, the repayment problem continued, and even increased. It became more profitable to borrow than to produce.[42]

The rate of inflation slowed slightly to 12 percent in FY 1985 and 11 percent in FY 1986. Manufacturing was still only 12 percent of GDP and 8 percent of total employment. The large-scale modern sector employed 18 percent of the manufacturing labor force, but generated

58 percent of value added. Small and cottage industries employed 82 percent of the work force, but only 42 percent of value added.[43] The industrial sector grew to 14 percent of GDP in FY 1987. Growth was greatest in labor-intensive export and import-substitution activities. Manufacturing declined slightly in the first six months of FY 1988 (after a rise of 6.4 percent in FY 1987), mainly because of drops in jute, textiles, tobacco, and basic metals industries. Food and chemicals showed modest increases. Leading indicators projected only a 1.8 percent increase in GDP in FY 1988.

Private investment slacked off due to political instability, the threat of strikes in late 1987, and uneasiness over government treatment of major loan defaulters. As the World Bank noted,"The uneven performance of the manufacturing sector in recent years—high growth rates followed by virtual stagnation—points to the need for continued and coordinated political reforms, as well as the need for further diversification of the sector."[44]

Given the inelasticity of the agricultural sector, it was recognized that rapid economic development in general, and job creation in particular, would have to depend heavily on promotion of industry. Further, it was also recognized that the potential for the growth the nation so desperately needed did not rest with the ponderous public sector, but with private enterprise.

The Third Five-Year Plan (1985-1990) was surprisingly frank about the problems of the economy and the persistent gap between the rhetoric of policy and the actuality of implementation.[45] The Plan traced the increased role of the private sector in the development process. Allocation for the private sector was 11 percent under the First Five-Year Plan (1973-78), 16 percent under the Two-Year Plan (1978-80), 35.5 percent under the Second Five-Year Plan (1980-85), and 35.2 percent under the Third Five-Year Plan (1985-90).[46]

The Plan also spoke of the NIP as a "momentous step compared with any earlier measures," noting that denationalization of the jute and textile mills had "significantly improved capacity utilization."[47]

The importance of increased private investment was stressed. The Plan posited that the improvement in the performance of the private sector and, hence, its contribution to national development would depend on improvement of the environment within which it must operate. While noting the need of the private sector to "earn the confidence of the society," the Plan saw the government playing more of a "catalytic role," reducing "direct interference with the economy to a minimum" as the country moved "towards the market economy." It continued,

The Third Plan will strengthen the process by increasing the private sector, on one hand, and increasing substitution of direct control by indirect control through macro-economic policies reforms on the other. The Plan thus emphasizes a greater reliance on policy planning than before to ensure a harmony between social and private goals.[48]

These eloquent words authored by the Planning Commission for the Third Five-Year Plan in December 1985 are worlds apart from the socialistic ideology espoused by the Planning Commission in 1972 when it launched the nationalization program. Yet they share a common trait—detachment from reality—although it is manifested in vastly different ways. While the 1972 pronouncement forcefully led the government along a certain path (nationalization), it was, as we have seen, divorced from the realities of the socio-economic conditions of the time. The 1985 statement, while reflecting economic reality, was not in sync with the direction, or lack of direction, the government was demonstrating.

In the last several years, Bangladesh has pursued an on-again, off-again, affair with privatization. The government has plunged boldly forth at times, veered or backed off at others, and generally vacillated. It is fascinating, if depressing, to observe the tortuous, ambivalent pursuit of major national policy—policy by whim, if you will. To demonstrate this, a sampling of headlines and clips from newspaper articles during the period follows, starting with President Ershad's speech of August 25, 1984.

"No more disinvestments"
The New Nation, 8/26/1984

"Industries Minister Defends Privatization Policy"
"NIP a progressive measure"
The Tide, Fall 1984

"Some disinvested units may be taken back"
Bangladesh Observer, 10/18/1984

"A fast diminishing public pressure in Bangladesh"
"government may sell up to 49% equity stakes to private investors in government-owned banks, shipping lines, the national airline, and the telephone industry via the stock exchange"
Far Eastern Economic Review, 7/25/1985

"536 industrial units divested so far"
"Minister of Industries says process of disinvestment will continue to encourage the private sector"
The New Nation, 8/5/1985

"Another dose of privatization: Ershad announces disinvestment of existing NCBs" (nationalized commercial banks)
Holiday, 10/11/1985

"DISINVESTMENT"
"Recognizing the importance and impact of PRIVATIZATION, the Government will continue to pursue the following policies:

(i) abandoned, vested and taken-over industrial enterprises and shares and other proprietary interests will continue to be disinvested;
(ii) industries established with Corporation's own resources or ADP (ed: national budget) may also be disinvested;
(iii) Corporations may develop industries . . . and then disinvest them or unload their shares;
iv) shares (of state enterprises) will be unloaded mainly through public subscription or through the Investment Corporation of Bangladesh"
Industrial Policy—1986
Ministry of Industries, July 1986[49]

"More enterprises likely to be disinvested"
Holiday, 9/19/86

"New Industrial Policy realistic says Moudud" (Deputy Prime Minister and Minister of Industries)
Bangladesh Observer, 10/9/86

"No more special protection for public sector says Moudud"
The New Nation, 10/26/86

"Public sector units to be turned into companies"
"must survive in open market competition"
Bangladesh Observer, 12/26/86

"Disinvestment of NCB soon likely" (Rupali Bank)
Bangladesh Observer, 12/20/86

"Shares ready for public offer"
Holiday, 1/9/87

"No more subsidy to public sector"
Bangladesh Observer, 1/14/87

"Rupali Bank to remain in public sector"
The New Nation, 1/22/87

"Jute mills disinvested for corruption: Zafar (Minister of Jute)
Bangladesh Observer, 2/4/87

"Private sector to be made dynamic: Ershad"
"government-owned industries and banks will remain in public sector"
Daily News, 2/6/87

"Private, public sectors must co-exist: Ershad at CONOPE*"
Bangladesh Times, 2/6/87
* Consulting Committee of Public Enterprises

"Ershad rules out bank disinvestment—public sector units won't be privatized"
Bangladesh Observer, 2/6/87

"132 disinvested units failed to pay"
"Moudud said that there were provisions to scrap the agreements with the lawyers and take over the disinvested units by the government again"
Bangladesh Times, 2/24/87

Ershad: "I believe in a mixed economy in a country like ours"
"Certain industries—we have reserved—no private enterprise coming in—but, by and large, small and medium industries must go for privatization."
"the stock exchange is activated—so this is also in a way privatization."
The Tide, Special Issue, Feb-March 1987

Industry: "After privatization . . . poor performance . . . led to national consensus to visualize the whole thing once again"
"Recognizing the importance and impact of privatization, the government will continue to pursue disinvestment."
The Tide, Feb-March 1987

Moudud: "The process of privatization accelerated and it achieved the desired goal."
"This is now a policy of consolidation of the privatization of our industries."
"There will be balanced growth between public and private sectors."
"We would like to make the public sector competent and profit-making."
The Tide, Feb-March 1987

Finance: "The introduction of the 1982 industrial policy with a new look toward withdrawal of government discretion from public sector and encouraging private sector is now experiencing a transitional hazard regarding efficient management, procedural discrepancies and political commitment."
The Tide, Feb-March 1987

"Abandoned industries to be made public limited companies"
"51% to be retained by corporations."
"15% reserved for workers"
"34% subscribed by public through stock exchange"
The New Nation, 4/27/87

"Call for strike at industries tomorrow"
"protest against the disinvestment policy of the Government"
The New Nation, 4/27/87

While all this flip-flopping and platitudinous posturing was going on, senior officials of the government were saying privately to me in late 1986 and early 1987 that privatization policy would and should continue. For example, on October 23, 1986, Moudud Ahmed (then Deputy Prime Minister, later Prime Minister, and now Vice President) responded to my query about future divestiture of state enterprises by saying, "In my personal view, we should give up all of them." Other senior people in key ministries said such things as:[50]

"The government should get out of manufacturing and do what government should do."

"Sick or not sick—sell the public enterprises."

"We should start selling the viable ones."

"Bangladesh should denationalize in a big way."

By early 1987, however, it was becoming clear that despite confidential endorsement, privatization would not be aggressively pursued as public policy. In backing off, the emphasis shifted to promoting a "mixed" economy[51] and to making still another try at improving the performance and profitability of the public enterprises, while still declaring a continued strong commitment to developing the private sector.

Over the years, opposition to privatization, if vocal and persistent, has been effective. The Awami League has been the most strident in its criticism of the government's privatization policy, even recommending renationalization in some industries.[52]

However, the noisiest and most effective public opposition has come from organized labor. Strikes are almost automatically called whenever a public enterprise is even rumored as a potential candidate of privatization. Several union-sponsored Disinvestment Resistance Committees sprang up over the proposed privatization of the Rupali Bank in early 1987. Small demonstrations are almost a daily occurrence in the central commercial district of Dhaka.[53] Citywide and countywide strikes are in vogue. Not infrequently, striking workers actually kidnap factory managers and their principals, holding them hostage until labor demands are met.

Mobs in South Asia are volatile and unpredictable. Deaths are not uncommon during these demonstrations. Such demonstrations have become even more prevalent and dangerous since organized labor has found out that violence pays off when dealing with an indecisive, insecure government.

One of the more striking revelations for a person studying Bangladesh affairs is that the Martial Law Authority (MLA) has not lived up to the usual image of such regimes, one of exercising no-nonsense, iron-fisted control. Instead, the Bangladesh version of MLA government has been characterized by impotence. (It should be noted that martial law was officially cancelled in 1988, although most of the trappings are still in evidence just beneath the surface.)

While loss of jobs and making the rich richer are the principal charges leveled against privatization, the accusation of pressure from foreign donor agencies is another frequent and effective criticism. Accusations of excessive foreign pressure is an effective political device in a former colony; but in this case, it seems to have been exaggerated. The role of donor agencies will be discussed in some detail in a later chapter, but for the present, I will only say that I found that outside pressure has been exerted in Bangladesh less than expected.

There is no doubt that the World Bank and the U.S. Agency for International Development (USAID) both favor emphasizing the private sector approach to economic development. They have both expressed such beliefs frankly to various Bangladesh regimes. But I found little evidence of undue pressure or ultimatums of "privatization or else."

There has been donor pressure for instituting various reforms, particularly in financial management; but the relationship to privatization appears to have been more indirect than direct. Until very recently, what pressure there was was apparently neither forcefully exerted nor terribly effective.

The World Bank has generally advocated private sector development; but has shown more interest in backing reform and revitalizing of SOEs than in privatizing them. Structural adjustment and financial discipline, with particular regard to repayment of privatization loans, have been hallmarks of World Bank/International Monetary Fund (IMF) policy.

USAID in Bangladesh has generally encouraged private sector development over the years; but the effort has, by AID's own admission, been scattered and intermittent. Although it sponsored this study, USAID/Dhaka has only carried out one major project directly related to privatization; however, that one project was a most substantial and significant one.

For eight years, USAID has been the prime mover in privatizing the distribution and sale of fertilizer, an extremely important commodity in an agriculture-based economy such as Bangladesh's. Interestingly, in this case privatization did not result from the divestiture of a government entity, as was usual in Bangladesh. Rather, USAID helped in the establishment and development of a private sector sales network that gradually replaced the government distribution system.

In effect, the government apparatus was marginalized or frozen; and the private alternative network was gradually built up, first at the retail level, then at the wholesale level, and most recently at storage points. Liberalization of regulations governing the importing of fertilizer and related materials by private entrepreneurs is under discussion. However, direct importation and, especially, actual manufacture of fertilizer will probably remain in government hands for the foreseeable future.

This experiment in fertilizer distribution is a form of the "quiet liquidation" that other LDCs, such as Taiwan, have used so effectively; but it is, to date, unique in Bangladesh. The project has not been without its problems or critics, and is still politically sensitive. Nonetheless, it involves an approach to "privatization of the economy" that warrants close scrutiny for application in other fields in Bangladesh and elsewhere.[54]

Industrial Policy of 1986 and the "51-49 Plan"

In the midst of the headlines and media clips listed earlier, one official government policy document was also quoted. That was the important "Chapter VI—Disinvestment" statement of the government's Industrial Policy—1986 (IP-'86).[55]

The IP-'86 is basically a refinement of the NIP of 1982. Like its predecessor, the IP-'86 includes an encyclopedic list of objectives and strategies (15 of each). Most are similar to the 1982 proposals, though in 1986 some additional attention was paid to incentives for both foreign and domestic investment and to promotion of small and medium agro-based industries.[56] Generally, IP-'86 broadens the scope of NIP-'82 in regard to private sector development. Bangladeshi officials are prone to say it has now "opened the window fully" for the private sector.[57]

The industrial categories reserved for the public sector were raised from 6 to 7 to include security printing (currency notes) and mining. The "Concurrent List" was dropped, replaced by a statement that, "All industries not reserved for the public sector will be meant for the private sector."[58] The very successful "free zone" concept (initiated in 1980) that allowed investment without prior approval in many fields was continued.

A new feature was the appearance of lists of "priority" and "discouraged" industries. There were 6 categories of "priority" industries: (a) agro-based industries (with 5 sub-fields); (b) Textiles (with 6); (c) tannery, leather, and rubber products (with 5); (d) chemicals, pharmaceuticals, and allied products (with 12); (e) engineering (with 11); and (f) electric industries (with 5). Certain industries were listed as "discouraged" because of over-capacity or under-utilization of capacity. They included automatic rice mills, cigarettes, cold storage, deep sea trawling, distilleries, edible oils, sugar mills, specialized jute products, wooden tea chests, tanneries (for wet blue), and safety matches.[59]

The 1986 policy mentioned more prominently than before the possibility of joint public-private ventures in industrial fields where the private sector lacked sufficient funds; the government would gradually bow out of these ventures once they were functioning.[60] Also, another attempt was made to streamline sanctioning and licensing procedures.[61]

Here, however, we are interested in only two aspects of IP-'86: (1) the restatement and elaboration of a program introduced (but never implemented) in NIP-'82 —of converting the public Corporations into "public limited holding companies" and the consequent offering of shares to the private sector of up to 49 percent of enterprises under the sector Corporations; and (2) the emphatic endorsement of privatization and continued "disinvestment" at a time when the government's resolve was wavering.

At this point in this study, it is only necessary to mention the highlights of the stock selling plan, describing (with some commentary) what has taken place to date. More thorough analysis and alternate scenarios will be reserved for concluding sections. (See especially Chapter 7.)

In the summer and fall of 1986, considerable fanfare was given to the government's intention to sell shares of public enterprises through the reactivated Dhaka Stock Exchange or the Investment Corporation of Bangladesh. Statements varied as to whether the government would offer shares of all or only some enterprises.

It was obvious to most observers that many of the enterprises would not be attractive investments. Who would want to buy shares of an enterprise that had been consistently losing money for years? Further, the potential for reform or revitalization might be limited because of the government's published intention of retaining 51 percent of the shares and, hence, control of the enterprise's fortunes.

Privately, officials have stated frankly that the government would be willing, eventually, to sell 100 percent of the shares of most public enterprises, but it would be politically impossible to admit this just before elections. Given the undeveloped state of capital markets in Bangladesh, the government only expected to be able to sell about 20 percent of the stock of most enterprises initially.

The stated purposes of the program were to increase opportunities for private sector participation in the larger and more important phases of the economy, to broaden the base of the public-private partnership, and to add badly needed cash to the exchequer.

Critics in the private sector said the plan was a way for the government to save its floundering industrial empire with private capital, but without giving up control, which would severely limit chances for reform and improvement. In response, the government has intimated that it would be willing to consider making concessions to substantial buyers in regard to management of the enterprises.

For example, if a buyer or consortium of buyers were purchasing, say, 33 percent of the shares of a given enterprise, they would normally expect to get 3 of the 9 positions on the board of directors. Instead, the government intimated that it would be willing to offer such a purchaser 4 slots, which is only one less than a majority and, additionally, to turn over management of the enterprise to the private sector.

The buying of minority shares in a company is not a well developed concept in Bangladesh's business world. Investors traditionally want complete control. Also, the private sector lacks confidence in the government's willingness to actually surrender control. They fear continued bureaucratic interference.

In a public relations sense, the program is vulnerable to the criticism that the shares will be bought by the already wealthy, dealt out to cronies, or both. The government seems to feel, however, that the 51-49 Plan is more palatable to the general public, and especially, to the labor force than outright divestiture.

One stratagem the government has offered to allay fears is to show interest in offering 10-15 percent of the shares to employees, individually or to their retirement trusts. Shares would be priced at 100 to 200 taka to enable poor workers to participate.

This is a new idea for the government, and one that deserves priority attention. The Employee Stock Option Program (ESOP) has been a successful ploy in other LDCs. In Bangladesh, it could be an effective method of lessening labor unrest and disruptive activities. It is amazing how attitudes change once a worker becomes an owner.

Perhaps it is for this reason that union leaders, feeling possible loss of their own power, are showing less enthusiasm for the plan than one might expect. Incidentally, several government officials expressed strong feelings against permitting unions to buy shares. They tend to believe that would be like letting the fox into the chicken coop.

The stock-selling plan has obvious weaknesses and has not been carried out effectively; but in an economy like Bangladesh's, the 51-49 Plan should not be dismissed out of hand. It can be a way to gradually build up a capital market. Extreme care must be taken, however, to avoid over-concentration of shares, money, and power. Restraint along these lines has not been one of the cardinal virtues of Bangladeshi political leadership to date.

More thoughtful planning will also be required than the government has shown so far. For example, the initial entities proposed for the share-selling scheme were four enterprises under Bangladesh Chemical Industries Corporation (BCIC), the two large development finance institutions (BSB and BSRS), and one of the nationalized commercial banks (NCBs). It is not at all clear what criteria were used to select BCIC as the trial case, although it is at least encouraging that the four medium-sized enterprises selected are all profit-making.[62] The assumption is that the choice of BCIC was an ad hoc decision. It may turn out to be a fortuitous decision, but one would not normally select the chemical industry for such a program because of costs, required level of technology, and dependence on expensive imports (and consequent onerous red tape).

It is difficult to figure out what prompted the government to believe that investors would seriously be interested in buying shares of BSB and BSRS. The sums involved are vast, and the two are virtually insolvent. It would take a real plunger to speculate on these stocks.

Rupali Bank was proposed as the NCB to be put on the block. Since Rupali is the most profitable of the four NCBs, it is again encouraging that the government is aware of the need to offer attractive enterprises at first. But the government handled the situation so badly that it has endangered the entire deal.

The Managing Director of the Rupali Bank walked into the bank one morning to find three senior government officials in his waiting room. When he ushered them into his office, they promptly informed him that his bank was to be privatized in two weeks. This lack of thorough preparation, consultation, and consideration of all relevant factors is typical of the compulsive way the Bangladesh government handles its affairs. It frequently operates from *en haut* or as if it were in a vacuum.

The result in this case was that when the bombshell was unloaded on the staff, they walked off *en masse*. Rupali was pulled off the market, then later put on again. It has been offered three times, but interest has been minimal. This is doubly unfortunate because, on purely economic grounds, this is an attractive offering.

A similar situation transpired in regard to the Dhaka Stock Exchange, the private instrumentality that would be required to handle a large percentage of the stock sale and transfer transactions. Even though there had been countless public pronouncements and newspaper reports about the 51-49 Plan for several months, no one from the government discussed the situation with the Dhaka Stock Exchange (DSE) as late as October 8, 1986, when I called on them to determine what preparations were being made to handle the tremendous increase in their business that would inevitably result from the proposed stock sale program.

As a matter of fact, no one from the government came to the DSE until February 23, 1987, when the Deputy Prime Minister appeared to give what amounted to a "pep talk," but not to engage in substantive, technical discussions.

The Stock Exchange in Dhaka has gradually increased in activity and sophistication since its reactivation in 1976. Nevertheless, it is still a relatively primitive institution, manifestly incapable of responding effectively to the demands of the enormous program the government is launching.

Finally, the government has not adequately researched the complex legal and constitutional issues involved in converting the Corporations into public limited holding companies and sorting out questions of transferring shares and control of assets. The government may be in conflict with its own laws. These matters must be handled before anything else can proceed.

Nevertheless, in a conversation on October 23, 1986, the Deputy Prime Minister stated that he expected the program to get rolling soon, noting that he was counting on 30-40 crore taka in revenue from the program in the current budget. He also mentioned that while he personally favors a broad base of investors, the Ministry of Finance would prefer to restrict the number of shareholders.

The government has not resolved the delicate financial-political question of how you allow the certain amount of concentration of wealth necessary to build a viable capital market without creating over-concentration as has happened in many countries. The government should be very conscious of the adverse political and financial ramifications of the domination of the Pakistan economy by the famous (or infamous) "22 families." Fortunately, the fledgling capitalist class in Bangladesh does not appear to have the potential for that degree of over-concentration of wealth and power.

Despite the ambitious language of the IP-'86, no major divestitures followed. Few observers felt that anything significant would happen prior to the elections in November 1986. There was speculation that the government might feel secure enough after the elections to move forward again on major economic problems. For one thing, many felt that the government would clamp down on rampant labor movement violence. This had not happened by mid-1988.

Second, it was thought that the administration might move again toward divestiture of selected public enterprises. That, also, has not transpired. In fact, the government seems to be moving further away from that option. The sale of shares is the substitute privatization measure.

Third, it was hoped that the government would move aggressively against loan defaulters or act in some other manner to solve the serious nonrepayment dilemma. Action was not taken here either. Previously, the government had not staunchly backed the DFIs, but did in December. BSB had set a December collection target of Tk175 million (US$5.8 million).[63] By virtue of aggressiveness they actually pulled in Tk250 million (US$8.2 million). The total collected for July-December was Tk3.6 billion (US$119 million), which for the first time in history exceeded its target, which was Tk4 billion (US$112 million).[64]

All of the excess came from the private sector. Because the December target for collection from the public sector was not met, Tk20 million (US$667,000) was collected against a target of Tk34 million (US$1.1 million).

BSB had targeted 16 of the larger defaulters (all jute mills) and got 12 of them to bring payments more up to date. When the other 4 found out that they could not get credit anywhere else, 2 of them settled.

A list of 132 firms in default was published in local newspapers. Four debtors were summarily thrown in prison, which caused a furor in the business community. The lesson was not lost on other defaulters. Repayment picked up. But investment rates dropped. Some observers, both in and out of government, felt that the "legal system is being completely upset and distorted" by the jailing of the 4, in that criminal law was being applied in a civil law situation.[65]

There is no question that something had to be done about the desperate default problem; and it is hoped by the World Bank and others that the pressure will be kept on. The government certainly made its point, but its impetuousness may have spawned a whole set of new problems. One partially redeeming feature is that stricter collection activity may help in some measure to improve the ghastly financial situation of the DFIs, but probably not enough to make their shares more attractive on the stock market.

Outright opposition to privatization has lessened by mid-1988. Highly ballyhooed national strikes in the fall of 1987 were not as disruptive as feared. There were a number of reasons for this, but there is no doubt that the offer of 15 percent of the stock of any SOEs to the employees had a quieting effect on labor.

Also, by mid-1988 opposition parties are badly splintered. They are somewhat discredited because they have not been able to come up with any coherent alternative to the government's basically pro-private sector program. The Awami League has talked a great deal about renationalizing industry; but few have believed the rhetoric. In the final analysis, people have come to believe that drastic reversal of the privatization program is neither possible nor desirable. Only a handful of the most ardent Awami Leaguers still believe that the SOEs can be turned into profit-making entities.

SOE performance has remained unsatisfactory. The Public Enterprise (Management and Coordination) Ordinance of 1986 granted substantial autonomy for SOEs and established measures for monitoring and accountability, but they have been inconsistently implemented. Of the 16 SOEs listed for selling of shares, only three were marketed successfully in FY 1987.[66]

Economic performance in 1987 was a mixed bag. Heavy monsoon rains in July-September caused the most serious flooding in 30 years. Agriculture and agricultural investment were adversely affected. Private industrial investment and production, both of which had dropped off sharply in FY 1986, picked up somewhat in FY 1987. Manufacturing was up 6.4 percent in FY 1987, mainly due to increased production of jute products for export and greater domestic demand as stronger measures curbed smuggling. Manufacturing showed a slight decline in the first six months of FY 1988, mainly because jute, textiles, and basic metals fell off again.[67]

Conversely, what economic progress there was during the period continued to come almost entirely from the private industrial sector, especially from the 125 "free sectors." Regulatory liberalization also began paying off. In short, while privatization of state enterprises was not touted publicly, privatization of the overall economy proceeded quietly but steadily. [68]

Privatization in Bangladesh—A Recap

This brings the Bangladesh privatization story up to the present (mid-1988). Before we proceed to in-depth analysis and evaluation of various aspects of the subject, it might be useful to recap what has transpired.

Successive governments in Bangladesh have divested or denationalized 609 industrial enterprises, 2 banks and an estimated 465 commercial businesses, for a grand total of 1,076.

One can add in another 3,000-4,000 if one wishes to cover the small commercial trading firms that sank out of sight, as described earlier. For the record, of the 609 industrial firms, 12 were hangovers from EPIDC, 120 were unloaded quietly during the Mujib period (1971-75), 255 under the official privatization policy of the Zia Government (1975-81), and 222 (including most of the larger ones) under the NIP-'82 and IP-'86 of the Ershad regime.

The numbers are impressive. As we noted in the introductory chapter, even a recognized authority such as Elliot Berg was prompted by such figures to call Bangladesh "a champion performer in the world of privatization or divestiture."[69] The preceding pages should convince any thoughtful reader that while Bangladesh's experience with privatization has indeed been remarkable, the performance has not been of championship caliber. The numbers are impressive, but they are also misleading.

Bangladesh's privatization effort has been carried out without a coherent and consistent plan. After one gets past the sloganeering, it is difficult to determine just what specific objectives the various Bangladeshi governments had in mind when they issued privatization policy statements. There has also been an enormous gap between policy statements and implementation. It is as if once the policy is issued, that is the end of it, that's all that needs to be done. The Bengalis' renowned love of words that has carried them to the heights of South Asian poetry and literature may have betrayed them in the tangled world of politics and economics.

The several Bangladesh governments have not sufficiently understood that the formula for success in privatization involves more than the unloading of large numbers of unprofitable state enterprises. Real, lasting success also requires a well integrated set of concrete programs that ensure that the private sector can flourish. What is involved is not just divestiture, but privatization of the economy. To accomplish this, the roles of the public and private sectors must be clearly defined and consistently acted out.

Given these shortcomings, it is remarkable that privatization in Bangladesh has proceeded as far as it has, and accomplished as much as it has. In the following chapters, we shall investigate some of those weaknesses and strengths and, in the process, come up with some conclusions and recommendations for future policy and courses of action.

Notes

1. World Bank: *Bangladesh: Recent Economic Developments and Selected Development Issues—Summary and Conclusions* (Washington, D.C., South Asia Programs Department, March 18, 1982), Report No. 3768-BD, pp. 1-4.

2. U.S. Embassy/Dhaka, cable #0 148658Z Jan. 1987; Chishty, op.cit., p. 10; WB/Dhaka—Indus. Sec., p. 1.

3. Technically, Azam's position was Advisor in Charge of the Ministry of Industry and Commerce, a title occasionally assumed by senior officials before they actually take on the mantle of a cabinet minister (which he did a short time later).

4. Conversation—Azam, 10/3/86.

5. ibid. For the reader's information, the term "golden" has a special significance in Bangladesh, which used to be called "Golden Bengal." Jute, the leading crop, is known as the "Golden Fiber."

6. ibid.

7. Conversation—S. Rahman, 12/2/86. As already mentioned, Chishty is Secretary of the Ministry of Establishment, in which capacity he passes on all of the senior appointments to the public service. Shafiqur Rahman retired in August 1986 as Joint Secretary of the Ministry of Industries and Chief of the

Disinvestment Wing. Rahman assisted Chishty with the latter's outstanding paper on privatization. Rahman is generally recognized as Bangladesh's leading expert on privatization. I had a two-hour meeting with Chishty and eight long sessions with Rahman. With regard to the Nov. 1982 deadline, Rahman reports that Azam jocularly admonished him and Chishty, saying that he would fire them if they didn't meet the deadline. ibid.

    8. Conversation—S. Rahman, 11/20/86; Conversation—Azam, 10/3/86. While I have highlighted the role of Shafiul Azam, Shamsul Haque Chishty, and Shafiqur Rahman in formulating and pushing through privatization policy measures, Ershad has also drawn upon the advice of other trusted confidants. Among them is Anwar "Monju" Hossein, editor/publisher of *Ittefaq* and other liberal journals oriented toward business, and later Minister of Energy and Minister of Commerce. Another has been A.M. Muhith, Secretary, Ministry of Finance and External Resources, who was responsible, in large measure, for implementing the IMF's stabilization program. He is now at the UNDP in New York, working on postwar Afghan affairs. Another is Moinul Islam Chowdhury, a retired Lt. Colonel who reportedly has had a strong ideological influence on Ershad. Then there is Shadi Isphani, one of the country's wealthiest industrialists, and the highly respected Murshed, who was head of the Jute Board and then Secretary of the Ministry of Industries during the early years of the Ershad regime. More recently, he has been Ambassador to Indonesia. This list is selective and illustrative, not in any sense complete. Additionally, the limits on this study make it impossible to document the actual influence of these people on Ershad.

    9. "Private sector given greater participation," *The Bangladesh Observer*, June 2, 1982.

    10. *New Industrial Policy*, Ministry of Industry and Commerce, Government of Bangladesh, June 1, 1982, p. 1. Hereafter, this document and program will be referred to as "NIP-'82."

    11. ibid, pp. 2-3. There was some juggling and reshaping of industrial categories. Forest extraction, for example, was put back on the reserved list because of rampant deforestation.

    12. ibid, p. 3.

    13. ibid. I wish to note here the tendency in Bangladesh to use the term "entrepreneur" very loosely. Among the Bangladeshis, it has become almost interchangeable with "manager" or "businessman" or "industrialist" and, in the process, has lost much of its special significance. Entrepreneurship has come to mean only risk taking. Because of the commercial trading background of most businessmen in Bangladesh, the emphasis on risk taking and being a "plunger" has perpetuated this narrow image of the entrepreneur. Consequently, it has become too easy to overlook the deeper and broader needs of industrial entrepreneurship. That same narrow stereotype persists to a surprising degree in developed countries as well.

    14. Chishty, op. cit., pp. 13-14.

    15. This overly ambitious attitude has continued to surface periodically. It was used as one reason for turning down a Singer Co., investment application for an electronic assembly plant in early 1987. Bangladesh seems to forget

that places like Taiwan, Korea, Singapore, Malaysia and Thailand eagerly sought assembly operations for a number of years before launching into their own manufacturing operations. Bangladesh is far from being sophisticated enough to make that jump at the present stage of its industrial and technological development.

As one Swedish electronics businessman pointed out to me in early 1987, even if a foreign investor gets over the initial hurdle of training a very unskilled labor force to work on the assembly line, he runs into the biggest obstacle in trying to locate good foremen and supervisors. They simply do not exist in Bangladesh at the present time. Bangladesh cannot jump into manufacturing until sufficient numbers of such professional and technical specialists are readily available. See also Lorche, op. cit., p. 40, for similar comments about deficiencies at supervisory levels in the textile mills.

16. Conversation—S. Rahman, 9/22/86. There were a reported 1,700 labor unions in the mid-seventies, Nyrop, op. cit., p. 268. One reason unions went along with the reforms of 1975 was President Zia's obvious desire to "take care of the workers." Conversation—Chishty, 9/ 29/86. Worker support faded when concrete results were not forthcoming. Several official sources estimate that the industrial labor force is 90% unionized. Conversation—S. Rahman, 9/22/86.

17. Conversation—Muhiuddin Azad, Joint Secretary, Ministry of Finance, 10/7/86.

18. Conversation—Azam, 10/3/86.

19. Conversation—S. Rahman, 12/2/86.

20. Most of the material in this section dealing with the government's divestiture negotiations and processes has been taken from Chishty's paper, op. cit., passim, and my long conversation with him.

21. Appendix D, as cited in Chishty, op. cit., pp. 25-28.

22. Conversation—officials of the Bangladesh Jute Mills Association, 9/ 29/86; Conversation—officers of the Metropolitan Chamber of Commerce and Industry, 9/23/86 and 11/9/86; Conversation—officials of the Bangladesh Textile Mills Association, 10/2/86. See also, T. Chowdhury, op. cit., pp. 27, 35-37. Chowdhury's comments provide support for the argument that Ershad adopted a "take it or leave it," stance.

23. Bangladesh Shilpa Bank (BSB) and Bangladesh Shilpa Rin Sangstha (BSRS).

24. Conversation—Chishty, 9/29/86.

25. Conversation—S.Rahman, 3/3/87.

26. ibid.

27. *The New Nation*, 8/26/84; Conversation—S.Rahman, 3/3/87.

28. Conversation—S. Rahman, 3/3/87.

29. World Bank: *Bangladesh: Economic and Social Development Prospects,* in four volumes (Washington, D.C., World Bank, South Asia Programs Department, Report No. 5409, April 2, 1985), Vol. II: "Recent Developments and Medium Term Prospects," pp. 86-87. This publication will be referred to frequently throughout this study. Therefore, for reasons of convenience, it will be cited hereafter as "WB-Bangladesh '85-2." Also see World Bank:

Bangladesh: Recent Economic Developments and Medium Term Prospects, in two volumes (Washington, D.C., World Bank, South Asia Program Department, Report No. 6049, March 17, 1986), Vol. I: "Executive Summary and Main Report," p. 35. This document will also be used frequently and will be cited hereafter as "WB-Bangladesh '86-1." The World Bank listed 155 "organizations under public statutory corporations" when the CRPSC started its work and 160 in the 1986 report. This is not the correct number of SOEs. Dr. Muhiuddin Khan Alamgir, Managing Director of BSB lists a total of 281 SOEs in his *Public Enterprises & the Financial System in Bangladesh*, unpublished paper, Sept. 1986, pp. 29-40. Even this list, while more complete than the World Bank's total, leaves out several. An otherwise excellent overview of SOE monitoring by Mallon erroneously states that there were only 185 SOEs in July 1985. See Mallon, Richard D., et al: *Overview on Policies to Improve Performance Monitoring of Public Enterprises in Bangladesh* (Dhaka, Trade and Industrial Policy Reform Program, Management Unit, TIP-MU-1, Government of Bangladesh, May 1986), p. 1. From these brief notes, one can begin to see the difficulties inherent in gathering data in Bangladesh.

30. *The Bangladesh Observer*, 6/2/82. See also WB-Bangladesh '86-1, p. 131; WB-Bangladesh '85-2, p. 89; and NIP-'82, p. 3.

31. WB/Dhaka—Pub. Sec., p. 12.

32. WB-Bangladesh '85-2, p. 87. The figures were converted (for illustrative purposes only), using an average rate of Tk25/US$1 between a rate of 24.62/1 in 1983 and 25.37/1 in 1984.

33. WB/Dhaka—Indus. Sec., p. 16.

34. WB-Bangladesh '86-1, p. 129. The World Bank also states that "data on public sector enterprise profitability is scattered and conflicting." WB/Dhaka—Pub. Sec., p. 14.

35. WB/Dhaka—Indus. Sec., p. 16. The five main Corporations are BJMC, BTMC, BSEC, BSFIC and BCIC. For some unknown reason, BFIDC was not included.

36. ibid.

37. WB-Bangladesh '86-1, p. 127; Alamgir, op. cit., pp. 29-40. See also U.S. Embassy/Dhaka cable #0 140658Z, Jan. 87. The data from this cable was drawn from the sources just cited and combined in such a way as to be most useful.

38. WB-Bangladesh '86-1, p. 33, 101.

39. WB/Dhaka—Indus. Sec., p. 8.

40. Rahman, Md. Ataur: "Bangladesh in 1982: Beginnings of the Second Decade," *Asian Survey*, Feb. 1983, p. 154.

41. When the "unofficial" economy is combined with the "informal" economy of a myriad of unregistered micro-enterprises, cottage industries and the ubiquitous street vendors, the total jumps to more than 60% of the Bangladesh economy. For an interesting coverage of the informal economy, see WB-Bangladesh '86-1, pp. 153ff.

42. Frequently businessmen borrow the money from the government at relatively low interest and immediately reinvest in a quick turnover, high-return deal, just like they have been accustomed to doing in the world of

commerce and trade. There are an infinite number of variations on this scenario.

43. WB-Bangladesh '86-1, p. iii, 102.

44. *Bangladesh Adjustment in the Eighties and Short-Term Prospects* in two volumes (Washington, D.C. World Bank, 3/10/88), Vol. I, p. 8; see also p. ii, 3, 13, 30. This publication will hereinafter be referred to as "WB-'88-1."

45. Third Five-Year Plan, p. 115.

46. ibid, p. 127, 132.

47. ibid, p. 128.

48. ibid, p. 132.

49. NIP-'82, Chapter VI, p. 6.

50. I have decided that it would be best not to give attribution for these remarks. They can, however, be verified from notes of conversations.

51. This common economic term has only recently come into use in Bangladesh. Beleaguered politicians have grasped upon it as a useful equivocation.

52. *The Bangladesh Times*, 1/4/87; *The Bangladesh Observer*, 2/2/87.

53. A few days after I arrived in Bangladesh in September 1986, I was asked to come to the window of the 4th floor offices of USAID in downtown Dhaka. A steady stream of people was exiting rather animatedly from a building across the street. My companion, Nizam Ahmed of USAID's Programs Office (the indispensable collaborator to whom this study is dedicated) said without any frills, "There's an example of the initial results of privatization." It seems that the employees of the nationalized commercial bank, Janata Bank, had just been informed that the bank was to be turned back to the private sector again. So they walked out. They struck on the spot. As of mid-1988, Janata Bank is still not privatized, although some of its shares have been sold on the open market under the 51-49 Plan. The bank has not done too well in recent years and there have been press reports of malfeasance and corruption. See "Misappropriation in Janata Bank branch: 15 held," *The Bangladesh Observer*, 11/25/86, "Nationalized banks lose Tk. 26 crore in 10 yrs," *The Bangladesh Observer*, 3/3/87.

54. Further discussion of the important fertilizer distribution project will be given in later chapters.

55. *Industrial Policy—1986*, Ministry of Industries, Government of Bangladesh, July 1986, p. 6. Hereafter, this document will be referred to as "IP-'86."

56. ibid, pp. 1-2, 12-13, 16-17, 19.

57. Conversation—Moudud Ahmed, Deputy Prime Minister and Minister of Industries, 10/23/86. Expecting a routine audience with the DPM, I was pleasantly surprised when the interview lasted for more than an hour-and-a-half. Moudud, like many Bangladeshi officials, is a former general. He has twice been imprisoned by former regimes, ostensibly for corruption, though many say it was politically motivated. He is an articulate and energetic spokesman for the present government's economic development programs. He has been the point man for the Ershad government's privatization effort the last couple of years and, as a consequence, has been the source of many of the conflicting quotes listed above. He is well acquainted with privatization

issues, having been the attorney for a number of British firms affected by nationalization. In 1988, Moudud was elevated to the position of Prime Minister. In 1989, he was elected as Ershad's Vice President.

58. IP-'86, p.3.

59. ibid, in that publication's Appendix A (Priority Industries), pp. 22-23;
ibid, in that publication's Appendix B (Discouraged Industries), p. 24.

60. ibid, p. 3, 4. This provision appears frequently in government policy
statements, but is almost never acted upon. This was, however, a pattern
favored by the EPIDC in Pakistan days. It might be appropriate here to state
that IP-'86 is primarily the work of Shafiqur Rahman, whom we have mentioned on numerous occasions. In fact, the IP-'86 was the last major policy
document he prepared before his retirement in August 1986. Perhaps because
of this, Shafiqur Rahman is deeply committed to the provisions and objectives
of IP-'86, although he recognizes that the chances for implementation of some
of its pro-private sector provisions are not bright in view of prevailing political conditions and administrative shortcomings.

61. ibid, pp. 7-10, Appendix C (Sanctioning Powers), p. 25.

62. The four are Ghorasal Fertilizer, Lira (a producer of PVC pipes),
Kohinoor I (soap, detergents and cosmetics) and Kohinoor II (dry batteries).
Subsequently, there have been moves to privatize Dhaka Vegetable Oil Co.
(under BSFIC), a motorcycle assembly plant (under BSEC), and the country's
only sheet glass plant (under BCIC). See Conversation—M. Islam, Deputy
DGI, 7/6/88. Islam also told me that the government was considering con-
structing a paper mill and cooperating in the construction of a public/private
cement factory.

63. Using a 1986 exchange rate of Tk30.3/US$164.

64. All of these figures came from the World Bank Economic Section in
Dhaka during a meeting on 2/12/87 with the Bank's extremely knowledge-
able Chief Economist, Surrinder Malik.

65. Conversation—Shahadat Ullah, Planning Commission, 3/3/87; Conversation—Shafiqur Rahman, 3/3/87.

66. WB-'87, p. xvii, 10; WB-'88-1, pp. i-ii, 3-4, 30, 54-56.

67. WB-'87, p. xxvii, WB-'88-1, pp. vii, 56-57. Information on the general
economic situation was also obtained from *Foreign Economic Trends and Their
Implications for the United States—Bangladesh* (Washington, D.C., U.S. Department of Commerce, April 1987), passim.

68. Conversation—M. Islam, 7/6/88; WB-'88-1, pp. 54-55.

69. In a speech presented at AID's Conference on Privatization in Washington, D.C., in February 1986. Actually, he referred to Bangladesh as one of
two champions, the other being Chile. Chile's divestiture program, however,
was unsuccessful at first. As in Bangladesh, most of the privatization was
actually denationalization of formerly private firms that had been taken over
by the previous (Allende) government. Chile's effort was tainted by cronyism
and was ineffective until the government broadened its approach to privatization and put together a more integrated program for private sector development.

6

The Private Sector's Performance

The first question asked when privatization in a country is being evaluated is almost always, "How have the privatized enterprises performed?" This question is invariably fired in unison with the even more pointed query, "Have they made money or lost money since being privatized?"

These are legitimate questions. In most countries, they would be appropriate questions. In Bangladesh, however, they are not the right questions.

Attention should focus on the economy, on the policy and regulatory environment within which the enterprise must function, and not on the enterprise itself. This is not an attempt to avoid taking a hard, close look at the weaknesses or failures (or successes) of individual privatized industrial enterprises. Rather, it is an approach that recognizes that in Bangladesh's struggling, backward economy, there are powerful adverse forces and factors that have more influence on determining an enterprise's fate than its own "performance."

As previously stated, privatization cannot, in and of itself, solve Bangladesh's enormous economic problems. In turn, the success of privatization depends on creating and sustaining an overall economic environment that fosters dynamic growth through increased private sector activity.

The possibility of a denationalized industrial enterprise prospering is governed more by a variety of external factors, such as conditions prevailing in the enterprise's particular industry, government policies and procedures, general economic forces, and the like, than by the internalized criteria usually applied that focus on managerial skills, marketing acumen, technical know-how, or profit and loss (P&L). The latter group unfortunately, have often been the "measuring sticks" used and manipulated by critics to "substantiate" predetermined opinions.

The above is true of any private enterprise, but divested firms often possess special inherited burdens that threaten viability. These might include bloated and unmotivated staff; inefficient production and marketing systems; old, poorly-maintained equipment; and substantial debts.[1] Some, but certainly not all, divested enterprises start out with two strikes against them. In fact, these additional burdens make focusing primarily on the individual privatized enterprise even more misdirected and unproductive.

The suggested broader approach is consistent with our position that what is important to consider about privatization is not just the unloading of state enterprises, but the *privatization of the economy.*

There is a school of thought that proposes that the most efficient way to evaluate privatization is to "go to the books" of the individual divested enterprises. That approach is rejected as a primary approach in this study. Of course, it would be folly to disregard the accounting and financial records of privatized firms; they can provide the thoughtful investigator with useful information. But analyzing the books is only one of many tools and, in Bangladesh, not one of the most productive.

A principal drawback is that accounting information is extremely difficult to obtain and is likely to be unreliable. Sharing of confidential financial information is not a local tradition. The Chinese practice of keeping three sets of books (one for the government, one for your partner, and one for yourself) has its highly-developed Bangladeshi counterpart. Lack of trust of outsiders and fear of the tax man is endemic.

Also, in interpreting accounting data there is often a tendency to apply western criteria to Bangladeshi practices and procedures. Further, the accounting systems of most Bangladeshi firms are simply not sophisticated enough to develop the information and insights one is able to glean from company accounts in more sophisticated business communities. In order to evaluate the performance of a denationalized enterprise or understand what has contributed to the success or failure of privatization in Bangladesh, one needs much more than accounting analysis.

In pursuing this research project, a conscientious attempt was made through interviewing and a carefully constructed questionnaire[2] to gather accounting data, financial information, production and sales figures, and the like. While considerable data was collected, its value and limitations had to be regarded realistically. We were constantly reminded of the local joke, genially offered in business circles, that a Bangladeshi entrepreneur will tell you that, "Our production is up, production costs are down, sales are up—but, by the way, we're losing money."

Therefore, other information was considered more important in the preparation of this study. This other material included such items as prevailing conditions in the particular industry, labor problems, future plans for expansion, government policies and practices that help or hinder the firm's business activity, and the like.

The present report was guided by the dual premise that privatization in Bangladesh is a policy-oriented study and that privatization is only one aspect of a loosely integrated economic mosaic.

The problem in pursuing this subject is to keep everything focused on privatization without neglecting the broader issues that significantly affect it. This is particularly difficult when addressing the matter of "performance" by the privatized sector.

Notes on the Bangladesh Business Community

The nature and make-up of Bangladesh's business community has changed dramatically in recent years. Much of this has been due to privatization and other government policies that have increased incentives for private investment and liberalized regulations affecting the business community. There has also been a gradual maturing process as more budding industrialists took advantage of opportunities opened up for private enterprise after denationalization started around 1975.

East Bengal cum East Pakistan was dominated by non-Bangladeshis, i.e., British, Bawanis from Burma, Pakistanis, or Marwaris, Biharis, and West Bengali Hindus from India. The presence of prominent non-Bengali elements in Bangladesh's economy is still strong today, and becomes stronger the deeper one digs under the surface. Nevertheless, Bengali Muslims are increasing their presence and influence in all facets of their country's business life, not just the commercial trading paths they traditionally followed.

Nationalization put a crimp in that development for a while, perpetuating the small shopkeeper stereotype. Just prior to liberation, it was estimated that 47 percent of fixed assets were in the hands of non-Bengalis. One of the justifications for nationalization was that there weren't enough Bengali managers to run the abandoned Pakistani enterprises. I have never been completely satisfied by that argument;

and there is also a substantial body of local opinion that there were more locals around at the time with managerial experience, though perhaps few at the top decision-making levels. For example, in the two principal industries, jute and textiles, there was considerable experience, even ownership, as the NIP showed in 1982 when so many mills were returned to former owners and managers.

The fact remains that in 1972 someone had to run the abandoned businesses. One cannot but note that the public service, which took over, had to search frantically outside its own ranks to find managers. Many of these were found in the private sector. The fact that many were unfortunate choices speaks as much to the politics of the affair as anything else. The nationalization program, in the final analysis, did provide a managerial training ground of sorts, although a lot of time was lost and some inappropriate methods practiced.

The concept of corporate management, important in the modern industrial sector, is still not well understood in Bangladesh business circles. Many Bangladeshi enterprises, even most of the larger ones, are still run along family business lines. Sons, rather than professional managers, are trained or at least destined to take over from aging patriarchs to preserve the family holdings.

There are progressive industrialists, however, who see the limiting aspects of the traditional system. For example, Affsaruddin Ahmed, a Chittagong industrialist with a wide range of holdings in construction, shipbreaking (dismantling), engineering, textiles, and rubber products, is dedicated to the proposition of hiring, training, and developing professional management. In 1986, he purchased Bengal Belting, a venerable rubber products company that had been denationalized in 1983, but had failed under the first buyer.

Ahmed bought it and promptly recruited a professional management team. While Ahmed is active in policy decisions, he deliberately leaves the day-to-day running of the company to his managers. He is proud that he "hires the best" and that "it is not a one-man show." Bengal Belting is recovering nicely. Production is up, production costs are down, sales are up, and they're no longer losing money.[3]

Unfortunately, there are still not enough enlightened industrialists like this man in Bangladesh; but, then, there weren't many in Taiwan or Korea 25 years ago either. Management training of a practical and professional (in contrast to academic) sort is badly needed in Bangladesh.

The most interesting group to emerge recently is the new breed of owner/managers who are now entering the industrial scene. They come from a variety of backgrounds, but most are from the commercial/trading world. Others have made their money in the manpower business, connected with service in the Middle East. Many have profited in real estate. Some come from rural or small town agribusiness or farming, and more than a few have graduated from the ranks of small industrial shops. The majority are not well educated, and few have experience in industrial management.

Their motives are as varied as their backgrounds. A common thread among these former commercial trading types is their desire to put their money into longer-range industrial investment rather than risking all on large-scale, one-shot commercial deals every so often. The appearance of stability and permanence is attractive even if the pitfalls are only vaguely understood.

The same is true of the general attitude about quick profits. Most will say they are willing to bank on longer-term profitability, but don't seem to comprehend what that implies in an industrial setting. To them, long term is understood as two-to-three months, not three-to-five years.

Parallel to this is the conception of profit. A long-time professional colleague of mine recounted the following story. When he explained the operations and profitability of a certain American company cited in an article, his Bengali discussants were particularly interested in the 20 percent net profit of the firm. My friend, thinking they were impressed by that high return, was surprised that their reaction was exactly the opposite. They said they would not undertake such a venture unless they were able to anticipate a net profit of 200 percent, which was what they were used to in trading.[4] Such attitudes and perceptions change slowly. The main thing to keep in mind, however, is that there are quite a few people in Bangladesh who have a lot of money and don't know quite what to do with it.

Industry is more prestigious than commerce, a factor that attracts many in a society where the ordinary businessman is not held in high regard. Many of the transition types speak of thinking of their children's future.

Several who spoke to me expressed a patriotic motivation, saying that industrial development would be more important to Bangladesh's future than commerce and trading. This was usually stated almost shyly or hesitantly, as if they felt they wouldn't be believed. Yet they appeared quite sincere.

The widely-held image of business people in Bangladesh is that they are aggressive slickers out to make a fast buck in any way possible, usually at the expense of others. They are regarded as exploiters rather than builders. There is certainly a rich tradition in South Asian society to support such an impression. One does not have to look far in Dhaka or Chittagong to identify types that roughly fit that description in one way or another.

However, I was mildly surprised at the high quality of owner/managers I met. Most did not fit that unsavory popular image. There were people who were sincerely proud of turning out a quality product, treating their employees relatively well, being fair with their customers, and fulfilling their obligations. They gave the impression of being aggressive and accustomed to sharp dealing, but not utterly ruthless. They were, for the most part, representative of their society and culture. Most would be considered quality people in almost any setting.

It may be interesting to note for the reader that these "model" businessmen came from such disparate fields as steel, vegetable oil, tanning and leather products, private banking, rubber products, food processing, investments, advertising, shrimp raising, jute, textiles, shipbreaking, and road construction. Snippets of their stories and frustrations will be interspersed (though largely unattributed) throughout this and later sections of the study.

Purchase of a divested enterprise can be a good deal, despite the acknowledged burdens stated above. For an entrepreneur making an initial entry into an industrial field or for an established industrialist diversifying or adding to his holdings, there is a definite advantage to obtaining an existing physical plant and equipment, developed land and utilities, a relatively experienced staff, and an established customer list. For the neophyte, especially, this situation is better than starting from scratch, despite problems one might inherit.

This holds true only if the business has not been run completely into the ground under state management, or if the price has not been set so high that the firm is probably not viable. As a matter of fact, several former owners, who were originally interested in getting their property back, were so disenchanted by the inflated price that they decided against it. The case of a major bicycle manufacturer who made such a decision was mentioned by the Deputy Prime Minister and a respected foreign observer. Regular buyers seeking new business ventures have become similarly discouraged.

Inflated pricing is a common occurrence in LDCs where government auditors, fearful of being accused of "giving away the country's patrimony" to the wealthy, overvalue the assets and set the sale price too high. In Bangladesh, the business community frequently states that the bureaucracy has set the selling prices high to discourage divestiture or to financially burden the buyers to such an extent that they will default or fail, or both.

These and other practices have led to a number of bad effects from some divestiture transactions. High selling prices and inflation have meant that some buyers purchased state enterprises with no intention of paying off the loans. Essentially, they obtained the enterprise for the 20-25 percent down payment and profited by reinvesting the loan money.

In certain instances the money has changed hands so often or the enterprise been resold so many times that it is virtually impossible to trace the funds and obligations. It is easy to launder the money, since the government makes no more than a token effort to monitor firms after divestiture, other than for direct collection on the original loan.

Some speculators bought enterprises because of the value of the land. Others stripped the companies of their assets. This has been particularly true in the jute industry. While it is an ailing industry, there is still a lot of money to be made in jute. Huge sums of cash flow in and out. Some owners pocketed the cash while letting the business itself descend into ruin. Seven jute mills have failed for this and other reasons, and several others are on the verge of collapse. Because jute is, for better or worse, the country's leading earner of foreign exchange and employer of the largest number of workers, the government will bail out ailing firms up to a point, and may be forced to take some back eventually.

Usually, the blame for such practices is attributed to unscrupulous private profiteers; but the government is also culpable in several ways, particularly in managing the divestiture system in such a way that it made such practices and results inevitable. Collusion between public servants and buyers in such cases is widely known, and will be touched upon in the next chapter, which deals with the performance of the public sector.

Nonrepayment of debts is a national malaise that threatens economic progress. The World Bank places it as the number one obstacle to industrial development. It undermines more than just the jute mill purchases. It undermines confidence in the financial sector and adversely affects possibilities for further investment.

Generally speaking, the several major chambers of commerce and trade associations have not done the job they should have in setting and policing ethical and professional standards for their members. Such organizations have mainly been concerned with playing an advocacy role for business in its relations with the government, and have tended to represent powerful business interests who are already well connected with the political elite.

There is no chamber of commerce that actively represents the interests of the small and medium-sized enterprises that represent the greatest number of firms and the greatest potential for growth. Such a void needs to be filled, though the idea for such a federation of small and medium enterprises will not be well received by government or established business elites.

The main thrust of these remarks about the business community is to point out the new blood and new vitality that has come into the industrial sector in recent years. There is much more varied economic activity now, and almost all of it is emanating from the private sector. There is no question that much of this vigor and diversity is due to the privatization policy of the government. This is true in two major respects.

First, over 1,000 privatized firms, 600 of them in the industrial sector, have reappeared in the private sector. In an economy like Bangladesh's, this is a significant percentage of the modern sector .

Second, the divestitures and related incentives to the private sector incorporated in NIP-'82 and IP-'86 have stimulated private investment. The first contributed to the confidence that engendered positive results from the second. They are inseparably linked, and represent "privatization of the economy" in the most meaningful sense of the term.

One final and general point should be made about the business community before passing on to more specific topics. Because of the preoccupation in this study with the industrial/manufacturing sector, it may not have been made clear that outside of industry, which makes up approximately 12 percent of GDP and 8 percent of the labor force, large segments of the Bangladesh economy are almost completely dominated by the private sector. These areas include agriculture (90 percent of the labor force of 14 million), construction (100 percent of 600,000 to 800,000 workers), transportation (25 percent of 500,000 employees, but 85 percent in road and water transport), trade (almost 100 percent of one million workers), finance (75 percent of 400,000 people), and professional services (virtually 100 percent of 1.5 to 2 million people).[5] From these figures, one should not, however, get the impression that the industrial sector is insignificant, because it is not. The industrial sector possesses the greatest potential for economic growth, employment creation, and income generation; but it should be recognized that that capacity has definite limitations under the existing conditions in Bangladesh.

Included in the sectors of the economy to which we cannot give more than passing notice is the so-called "unofficial economy," the "black market" that some observers believe involves more than 50 percent of the economic life of Bangladesh. The largest portion of this market is involved with smuggling across the Indian border. Although it operates outside the normal official economic channels, it affects them mightily. It is, in a sense, the ultimate privatization sphere. The government has virtually no control over it as an institution, although individual bureaucrats are intimately involved in its affairs.

It is difficult to see how the Bangladesh economy can achieve rational progress until the government adjusts its policies and practices in ways that will make the official economy more attractive than the unofficial one. It is obvious that the black market will remain a powerful force in the Bangladesh economy for the foreseeable future. Enormous activity and resources are involved that are not being channelled into the more inflexible "official" economy. It is widely rumored that the government is ready to grant amnesty for "black money" that is used for investment in priority industrial areas of the regular economy.

Interaction With the Government and the Public Enterprises

Much has already been said in this study about the interaction between the public and private sectors. More will be covered in the next chapter, which is concerned with the performance of the public sector. At this time we will concern ourselves with only a few major aspects of the relationship.

The private sector is generally pleased with the basic thrust of government economic policy in recent years. What had been an anti-private-sector stance during the Mujib period has gradually evolved into a policy framework that, on paper at least, encourages private sector development. Most of the discriminatory policies have been rescinded or revised. Incentives for private sector investment have increased, and barriers to participation in all but a few fields have been removed. There has even been a start at liberalization of the regulatory environment, although there are still impediments that frustrate businessmen, particularly in the area of import restrictions and regulations.

The private sector's concerns and problems have shifted from policy to implementation. What looks great on paper has a way of turning out to be substantially less than that in practice. The gap between policy and implementation, between rhetoric and action, is enormous.

The degree of bureaucratic lethargy, ineptness, obstructionism, red tape, and downright venality that exists in Bangladesh must be seen to be believed. I, personally, have not seen its equal in thirty years of dealings in Asian affairs. Bangladeshi businessmen must deal with it on a daily basis. Indeed, they are part of it.

Some of the public service obstructionism stems from distrust of or disdain for the private sector. Other bureaucrats resent loss of power and opportunities for illicit money making as the public sector has shrunk and private sector activity increased.

Some very large and lucrative bureaucratic empires were broken up by divestiture and related liberalization programs. For example, numerous businessmen have commented on how difficult it is to deal on even minor items with the Office of the Director General of Industries since that bureau lost its powerful sanctioning power and control over more than 400 small state enterprises. When a visiting Oversease Private Investment Corporation (OPIC) delegation from the United States asked in early 1987 about possible fields for foreign investment, the DGI suggested only industries in which the government was directly involved, not the more active (and profitable) private sector industries. Other reports, however, indicate that the DGI has adapted reasonably well to its reduced role and power.

There is a general feeling among foreign and local businessmen that the situation in regard to official corruption and required bribes is getting worse, not better.[6] A story current in Dhaka relates that a businessman wanted to start a small venture in a field that no longer required a sanction or license. Just to be on the safe side, however, he checked with the office with which he had always dealt. They agreed that a license was technically no longer required. But unsure of his position in the more liberalized atmosphere, the businessman filled out the old form anyway, and paid the usual "expediting fee."

Nevertheless, while increased private sector activity may lead to more bribes for obtaining licenses, this corruption is petty in comparison to the enormous graft that takes place when the government runs an enterprise and the bureaucracy is, as they used to say, "controlling the commanding heights."

What follows is a series of vignettes drawn from the case studies of privatized companies gathered for this study. For lack of a better term, they are labeled "incidents." The particular incidents selected here demonstrate the types of problems divested firms encounter in their necessary dealings with the government. They are typical, not exceptional. In some cases, they are directly related to the special circumstances of divested units. Most incidents, however, could have happened to any private enterprise operating in the Bangladesh environment.

Incident #1. In many instances, the problem faced by businesses is not deliberate obstructionism or venality, but ignorance. For example, a Chittagong garment company imported some materials related to the manufacture of shirts. Since the company was in the Export Processing Zone and under the Bonded Warehouse Scheme, the materials were eligible for importation without duty. The local customs officer, apparently unaware of these regulations, seized the shipment and held it for payment of duty. He did not accept the arguments of the manufacturer. At first, the supposition was that the customs official was really jockeying for a payoff; but it became apparent that he sincerely believed that duty was due. He simply wasn't current on the regulations. Finally, after *four months* of fruitless argument, the manufacturer got the Minister of Industries to personally intervene with the customs officer's superiors. Import duty was waived, as it should have been in the first instance. In the meantime, the manufacturer had literally lost his shirt. But he wasn't through yet. When he finally received his approval, he also received a bill for four months' demurrage.

Incident #2. The manager of a privatized steel rerolling mill informed the marketing manager of the enormous government-owned Chittagong Steel Mill that he had happened to run onto a potential buyer for a large inventory of metal ingots that had been sitting unsold in the government mill's yard for a very long time. The private mill owner proposed to the marketing manager a joint sales contract wherein he (the mill owner) would take only a reasonable commission for moving the merchandise. Although the government mill could have moved unsold inventory and come out ahead in the transaction, the marketing manager turned down the offer with only the explanation that, "I can't do business with you because you are private." Not only does this demonstrate why SOEs lose money, it was done at a time when IP-'86 was specifically recommending public-private sector joint activity. As in incident #1, the left hand did not know what the right hand was doing. Additionally, the public mill reflected the commonly held feeling that the private sector is a competitor.

Incident #3. The Minister of Industries, who was concurrently Deputy Prime Minister, recounted an incident he had encountered recently in which the import duties on raw materials for the manufacture of small motors were greater than the cost of importing the finished product. As a result, the proposed venture to start a company to manufacture the motors was scrapped. The machines were imported from India, mainly through the black market. Local industry was the loser, and so was the government (because it didn't even collect duty). The Minister said that this was not an isolated case wherein import regulations were directly in conflict with national development goals.

Incident #4. After purchasing a nationalized soap manufacturing company, the new owner discovered that the government, just before the final transfer took place, dumped the firm's huge unsold inventory of soap at fire-sale prices at auction. This made it virtually impossible for the new owner to sell his product for six months because of the precipitous flooding of the market by the auction sale. Second, some of the chemicals he was supposed to receive as part of the sale transaction were transferred at the last minute to another state-owned soap factory. Other promised materials and technical manuals disappeared.

The government tendency to favor state-owned enterprises is fairly common. The practice is devastating to recently privatized firms which have not had the opportunity to arrange alternate sources of supply or service, something which long-time private firms had learned by bitter experience that they must develop. Incidentally, in the case of this particular entrepreneur, he never really recovered from the cash-flow crisis created by government unfair practices and irregularities at the critical point of launching the privatized venture. His business is expected to go under.

Incident #5. During negotiations between USAID and the Ministry of Labor and Manpower over a multi-million dollar management training program, the Ministry noted that 60 percent of the funds for training were destined for the public sector and 40 percent for the private sector. The Ministry said they could not be responsible for the portion provided to the private sector, despite having been shown precedents. The issue was eventually resolved, but the fact remains that the government bureau responsible for the nation's manpower development failed to understand the role of government in promoting development through the private sector. The government refused to see the partnership aspect. They were only interested in their own bailiwick, the public sector.

Incident #6. The government sold one of the chemical plants under BCIC, telling the buyer he would have virtual monopoly in that particular area of the chemical business. The supposition was that unprofitability and inefficiency could be turned around under more dynamic private management. Almost immediately after the transfer, the government began construction on a similar plant with new, up-to-date equipment. Evidently, the government wanted to get rid of a failure. Also, considerable side money could be made out of the construction and purchase contracts on the new plant, which was not expected to be profitable anyway. Because of this overcrowding of a limited market, neither enterprise has any reasonable potential for profit.

Incident #7. An entrepreneur bought a cold storage plant from the government, but didn't get title right away. In the meantime, the government allowed unlimited investment in the cold storage field. Plants mushroomed everywhere (the so-called herd instinct in action).[7] As a consequence, when the original purchaser finally got title, the field was overcrowded, few were making money, and cold storage was put on the "discouraged" list of industries.

Incident #8. This is actually a composite of several incidents. A universal complaint is that it takes an inordinate amount of time to get any kind of approval out of the government. This is particularly true of time consumed by the loan approval process. The new owner of a privatized food processing company related a horror story of how he waited two years to get a crucial plant improvement loan only to be told by BSRS that even though the loan was approved, the bank had no money, and he must wait an estimated two more years before he could expect funding. Businesses and business opportunities cannot wait four years. The owner went to a foreign commercial bank and received the loan within three weeks, based on his excellent credit record (however, he did have to pay a higher rate of interest).

A trade association reports that its members wait 2-3 years for approvals, while faltering SOEs with abysmal repayment records get quick loan service. A study conducted by scholars favorable to the state enterprise system still had to concede that less than 50 percent of the sanctioned projects were funded within three years.[8] The World Bank estimates that 50 months elapse between application and production, including 12 months for the banking decision, 23 months for imported equipment to arrive, and 15 months for other start-up procedures.[9]

Incident #9. Almost without exception, privatized firms inherit old equipment that has been poorly maintained, requiring major rehabilitation or replacement. In few instances did the government purchase new equipment during the period of nationalized operation. In cases in which equipment was updated, the government had a far greater tendency to keep the plants.

In one case, a privatized rubber products company found in going through records that just before being nationalized in 1971, the original owners had purchased an expensive mixing machine. It was still in the dock warehouse 15 years later! It had rested there during the entire nationalized period. Amazingly, it was put into operating order with minimal problems (beyond taking possession).

Incident #10. Vegetable oil processing and distribution is a major industry in Bangladesh. Most SOEs of this type have been privatized. One of the most respected private owners commented on government importing in the vegetable oil business that has directly affected his privatized (formerly "abandoned") firm. The table below was written out to demonstrate his point that the government policy was "not very intelligent":

Bangladesh's total requirement for
edible oil is	250,000	metric tons
Locally available	− 15,000	
Leaving	235,000	

Produced out of rapeseed, sunflowers
and mustard from Canada	− 125,000	
Leaving	110,000	

Crude degummed from PL480	− 80,000	
Leaving	30,000	metric tons

This 30,000 metric tons is the amount that should have been imported to meet requirements. Instead, the government imported indiscriminately a total of 180,000 tons of palm oil in 1985. The flooding of the market forced several mills to close down. This also came at a time when the price of palm oil (actually best for industry, but used as edible oil after purification) plummeted from $550 per metric tons in 1985 to $315 in September 1986. Informed sources verified the accuracy of these figures and this analysis, only adding that some bureaucrats had made personal gains by this importation policy.

Incident #11. A similar instance in which government import policy directly affected the private sector in an adverse way is in the textile industry. For political reasons, the government imports low quality raw materials from the People's Republic of China under the terms of a barter treaty. In 1984 a particular shipment was of such poor quality that it was unsuitable for spinning. While BTMC was forced to take most of the large shipment, great pressure was put on the private mills to accept 10-15 percent of it. Evidently, most of it is still in stock, unused and unsold.

Incident #12. Shortly after divestiture in 1982, a number of privatized mills received past-due electrical bills amounting to millions of taka. The unpaid charges related to the period when the mills had been government operated. The public utilities company said presentation of the bills was delayed because of "faulty meter reading." Similar bills were subsequently presented to mills still publicly run. After prolonged negotiations, the utilities board agreed to substantial reductions. Inconsistent and generally inadequate power supply is still a major problem, however.[10]

Stories similar to the 12 cited above are endless. These represent a sampling of cases discovered through the normal interview process and were not specifically sought out as "worst case" examples.

In brief, the business community is ambivalent about the government. On the one hand, it distrusts government and is constantly frustrated by bureaucracy. On the other hand, the private sector constantly looks to the public sector for guidance and support.

For generations, businessmen in South Asian society (and for that matter in most other parts of the Third World) have depended on royal or governmental patronage. Even today, the Bangladesh business community is strangely uneasy and unsure of itself under the more liberal regulatory environment. The weaning process can be painful and prolonged. Bangladesh's business community is not unique in this respect. Sustained growth and success will increase confidence, particularly if political stability and consistent policies continue.

Some say that the mendicant attitude is due to a propensity of the private sector to use government funds for financing expansion, while risking as little as possible of their own capital. Some say also that there is a tendency on the part of the business community to view "profits as theirs and losses as the banks' or the government's."[11]

There is more than a little truth in that sentiment. Experience elsewhere has demonstrated that such an ambivalent attitude can be ameliorated once both parties consistently act in ways that foster greater mutual trust and cooperation.

The Volatile Labor Question—
The Dilemma of Unemployment in a Poor Country

Organized labor in Bangladesh has declared war on privatization. Every time privatization raises its head above the trench, labor starts sniping and, if the threat of privatization persists, calls out the troops for a direct frontal attack. For example, a general strike was called for April 28, 1987, in protest against the government's privatization policy.[12]

The issue is, of course, fear of loss of jobs if a divested enterprise believes that to increase efficiency and profitability it must reduce personnel. That specter is constantly raised by unions to their public service members at the first hint of privatization of a particular state enterprise. Partly, this is recognition of the fact that SOEs are overstaffed, with an inordinately high percentage of unproductive employees.

Any worker will fight when he thinks his job is threatened. In a country like Bangladesh, the resistance is understandably stronger, because unemployment can mean abject poverty, even starvation for a family. Unemployment also means loss of union members and loss of power for the leaders of the rough and tumble labor movement. Privatization is a perfect target.

Reliable statistics are difficult to come by in Bangladesh. In the field of labor, they are impossible to come by. Reports are fragmentary, frequently conflicting, and usually self-serving. For example, the most widely used figure on unemployment is 37.5 percent. The Bangladesh Bureau of Statistics (BBS), however, says that the unemployment rate is only 2.76 percent. BBS also disputes the extremely high figure quoted for underemployment. Part of the difference lies in definition of terms. But even if one accepts the equation that enables the BBS to cite a figure of 2.76 percent, one has to ask what that realistically means. If a worker is putting in enough hours to qualify as employed, even fully employed, but cannot earn enough to feed his family, then the employment figure doesn't really mean very much.

Despite the uproar over the supposed relationship of privatization and termination of employees, there is very little published material on actually how many people have been either laid off or employed as the direct result of privatization. One early discussion (published in mid-1984) by Rehman Sobhan is somewhat useful, but flawed by bias and questionable data.[13]

An example of the confusion appeared in two press reports appearing in Dhaka papers on February 18, 1987. The accounts both quoted the Minister of Jute as saying that employment in the jute industry has declined from 176,972 to 143,349, or a loss of 33,623 jobs; but they differed in major respects. The *Bangladesh Times* said those figures reflected employment reduction in privatized mills from "before denationalization" (1981) to the present. The *Bangladesh Observer*, however, used the same figures to reflect employment reduction in the "nationalized" jute mills from after liberation (1972) to the present. Both papers quoted the Minister as saying that the jute industry had lost Tk621.44 crore (U.S.$205 million) from 1971 to 1987, which is very low. One can guess that the employment figures were for the overall industry, reflecting reductions in both public and private sectors.

In a late 1986 conversation, the Minister of Industries stated that 27,000 jobs had been lost across the board because of privatization; but he did not elaborate on either the source or breakdown of that figure. This seems very high for the modern industrial sector, which only totals around 500,000 in employment[14] out of approximately 980,000 in the entire industrial labor force.

The fact is, no one really knows (or is willing to report) the actual situation. It would not serve the interests of the various interest groups to report factually what has actually taken place.

There is no doubt that there have been some staff reductions in privatized jute and textile mills. Responsible officials with whom the author discussed the situation estimated total reductions as around 10 percent or slightly higher, but they could not or would not document that.

The private sector argues that reductions in the mills have been less than 10 percent and that increases in industrial growth have more than offset them. This is doubtful. The private sector is on firmer ground when they point out that the greatest growth in recent years has been in labor-intensive industries such as garment manufacture, where 140,000 jobs have been created in the last three years.[15] Nevertheless, creation of jobs in another industry or another company means little to the man laid off in Bangladesh's labor surplus economy.

Mill owners support their argument that reductions have been modest by pointing out that the government still sets the rules of hiring, firing and pay scales. Divestiture agreements, for example, contained a provision that there would be no terminations for one year, and that subsequent reductions must adhere to certain restrictions (which vary considerably). Some employers forced the issue by paying one year's severance pay. Owners are emphatic in stating that it has been practically impossible to terminate more than a few even after the passage of the year because of extreme political and union pressure, and threats of strikes and violence. It should also be noted that there was constant labor trouble in the years preceding denationalization.[16]

Mill owners further state that most of the reductions that have taken place have been at the officer and staff levels, replacing unnecessary or incompetent bureaucrats. The previously cited survey by the Canadian International Development Agency (CIDA) indicated a reduction of only 1.4 percent among workers.

Private mills were forced to follow when the government gave two 30 percent pay hikes in recent years in the ailing jute industry. They even had to pay workers when the mills were idle, although they did not offer the 75 percent of normal wages awarded by SOEs. Nor did they pursue the commercially disastrous course followed by the public mills of producing at capacity to keep workers on the payroll, even though inventories were building up to extreme levels because of lessening demand.

A 10 percent total reduction would seem reasonable in view of the fact that several jute and textile mills have gone broke and closed down. In some of those instances, however, the government hired some of the employees. Some of those enterprises were on the verge of bankruptcy anyway.

Further, there has evidently been some shifting of regular employees to casual labor status in private mills. The extent of this practice is not known precisely. It is an important matter, because casual laborers do not receive as many benefits. Private sector companies do not offer employees the fringe benefits accorded by state enterprise.

This aspect is one of the most intensely debated in connection with the 51-49 Plan. The parties have not worked out how the status and benefits of employees will be handled. The employees may, however, be permitted to purchase up to 15 percent of the stock and to fill one of nine board members seats.

The Employee Stock Option Program (ESOP) is being resisted in some quarters (in the Ministry of Finance and among business leaders), but it is politically attractive. The parallel hope is that workers will begin to think more about the welfare of the company once they have a stake in it, however small.

Because most workers are too poor to buy regular shares, their pension funds, mutual funds, or similar instruments may buy them. The workers can then purchase in increments of Tk100 or 200 (US$3 to $6). The stock buying option is not the ultimate solution, but it is a sound and progressive step forward. ESOP does seem to have had a soothing effect on public employee opposition to privatization.

Incidentally, there is almost universal agreement among government and business leaders that unions should not be allowed to buy shares. Political realities dictate that ultimately unions will participate in the stock-buying scheme. Unions in Bangladesh are hard to classify. While in principal they protect workers, who certainly need someone to look out after their interests, many union leaders make small fortunes through payoffs. Rumors are prevalent about ties to the underworld.

To return to the question of employment, the enterprises involved in case studies gathered for this study generally indicate increases in employment after privatization. For the record, a sincere attempt was made to balance the admittedly small sample between successful and unsuccessful enterprises.

In three textile mills studied, employment has held even in one, and increased 20 percent in the other two. In the former, the owners say this actually represents an increase. When they took over, the new owners discovered the presence on the books of a large number of bogus or "ghost" employees, that is, names of people who never existed. The senior civil service managers pocketed such salaries. In addition, the auditors found listed as enterprise employees two cooks, two bearers, and a gardener, all working at the Managing Director's residence.

Employment increased 14 percent in one jute mill investigated and decreased 5 percent in another. The reduction in the latter was almost all at the officer and staff level.

A food processing company had 150 employees at the time of nationalization, grew to 192 under government operation (while share of the market plummeted), and in three years of private ownership grew to 257 because of increased business. (Also, use of outside part-time vendor/salesmen increased threefold). Total employment was expected to double by mid-1987, with the opening of a second manufacturing plant in a provincial capital.

A leading vegetable oil business found that the number of employees doubled during nationalization. Because of rejuvenated business, the returning management kept almost all of the workers (though there was some shifting of duties);[17] but higher level staff was reduced markedly. The owner/manager said that relations with union leadership were strained, but manageable. The union had fought privatization.

Two metal products firms were analyzed for this study. One showed 108 employees when taken over. This increased to 154 under government management, and was back to 140 in late 1986. The staff was expected to increase significantly in 1987 as electricity becomes more dependable, enabling the company to install new equipment to handle increased demand and productive capacity.

The other firm, which operates in a more traditional, "one-man show" fashion, has experienced consistent labor problems and lessening of profits. During three days of intense labor negotiations in mid-1986, labor leaders kidnapped two company officers from the government labor office, took them to the factory and held them (and reportedly beat them) for two days until they got what they wanted. No legal action was initiated against the union by either the government or the company.

Other case studies demonstrated a similar pattern of reducing management and staff, but few workers. At one chemical company, the government terminated the entire staff just before transfer to the new owner. The owner hired 80 percent of them back because of their experience, although the government tried to divert them to another government enterprise in the same field.

Low productivity is a pressing problem. The work force is largely unskilled. Cheap labor is what the government tries to sell to foreign investors, but that is a two-edged sword. A contract team of Chinese from a Southeast Asian country, imbued with their accustomed work ethic, was appalled and frustrated that the employees of the government maintenance facility they were advising balked at working more than three hours a day. The International Labor Organization (ILO) believes that privatization will fail in Bangladesh unless productivity is increased substantially.

A Swedish electronics expert made the observation that while it was difficult but possible to train electronics assembly line workers, the real problem was locating, training, and motivating supervisory personnel. The Bangladesh system simply does not develop foremen who are technically competent and who know how to train and supervise workers.

Vocational training is limited and of low quality. The government is financing few training or retraining programs. Bangladesh will be severely hindered in any attempt to improve industrial productivity until this situation is vastly improved.

The top levels of the government reportedly turned down applications from the Singer and Phillips Corporations for electronic factories, mainly because the companies were contemplating assembly plants rather than manufacturing operations. Bangladesh is not ready for the latter on a large scale. Their unrealistic expectations should be tempered by a closer look at the experience of countries such as Taiwan, Korea, Singapore, and Thailand, all of which were quite willing to build their industrial capacities gradually, relying on labor-intensive assembly operations for a number of years to create jobs, gain experience, and increase local capabilities.

In fairness, it should be mentioned that the government paints a somewhat different picture of the Singer turndown. While acknowledging disenchantment with the assembly line aspect, spokesmen point out that Singer's lack of experience in the electronics industry was also a determining factor.

The areas where the greatest number of new jobs have been created are garment manufacture, food processing, light engineering, and pharmaceuticals. The private sector has provided the motivating force, with little or no direct participation from the public sector.

With the enormous influx of landless workers from rural areas into the urban economic maelstrom, it has also been the private sector that has absorbed by far the greatest number of people, mainly through the "informal sector" of vendors, repair shops, and miscellaneous "industrial" subcontractors and micro-enterprises. While many of these workers are still on the edge of disaster economically, half of Bangladesh's so-called "industrial work force" is working full-or part-time in endeavors at this level. This type of economic activity occurs completely within the private sector.

The Traditional Tests—Management and the Bottom Line

We are now back at the point at which we started this chapter—the question of how the privatized enterprises have "performed" in terms of the traditional measuring stick, i.e., profit or loss. As previously stated, trying to determine a company's profit or loss is a legitimate exercise, but it is not the place to start, nor does it provide the ultimate answer. This chapter has attempted to show the many factors that must be considered in order to put consideration of the P&L aspect in proper perspective. We are then better prepared to address the ultimate question: Has privatization been good or bad for Bangladesh's economic development?

The availability and reliability of profit and loss figures for the private sector parallels the situation for employment figures. The government does only a barely adequate job of reporting on its own entities and does little or nothing to monitor and provide information on private enterprise. The tax department is incapable of collecting revenue, much less reporting on private enterprise earnings. The banks are only slightly better.

Therefore, one must rely on Bangladesh's private sector itself, an interested party that has not earned a reputation for openness, or the academic community, which has not been noted for its neutrality.

The main indicator that money is being made by Bangladesh business is that the industrial sector continues to grow at 6-8% per year. Further, the growth rate in the private sector is twice that of the public sector. Also, private investment continues to show dynamism, if one looks beyond the dismal showing of the development banks and the discouraging record of entrepreneurs in repaying them.

Evidence is clear that there is plenty of money out there (both in the legal and black markets), and it is being invested in an ever-widening pattern of undertakings. Nontraditional export industries are showing the greatest growth, although the private sector's inexperience and shortsighted pursuit of quick profits continue to result in stampedes for limited markets and a cycle of boom and bust.

The profit picture is a mixed bag. Some firms profit more than others because they are better run; but for the most part, companies tend to win or lose according to the fortunes of the particular industry within which they operate. Ready-made garments, steel, shrimp-raising, hide exports, and chemicals point in one direction, while jute, textiles, and shipbreaking point in the other. Unfortunately, big industries in Bangladesh are troubled industries.

In this atmosphere, whether a company is denationalized or private from the start appears to make only marginal difference after the first few years. It is at this point that the managerial skills of individual firms begin to make a significant difference within the overall limitations of a particular industry. Bangladesh's fledgling industrial sector is only now beginning to emerge from this shake-down stage.

At this stage of Bangladesh's economic development, good management is not the norm. There is a sophisticated old guard, but it is a relatively small group. As the economy grows, the need is for a larger, more professional entrepreneurial/managerial class. This group is only beginning to emerge. It will be a decade before their voices dominate in the chambers of commerce in Dhaka, Khulna, and Chittagong. The new class of managers will be more purely Bangladeshi in their outlook and experience than those of earlier eras.

Except in jute, textiles and banking, one finds very little attention given to the performance of divested enterprises, and even there, the analysis is quite general, usually centering rather superficially on a comparison with counterpart entities in the public sector. As one of the best-informed observers of Bangladesh's economy has remarked, "There is no usable performance record on privatized firms."[18]

One early study by Rehman Sobhan and Ahmad Ahsan made an

attempt to evaluate the production, marketing, and profitability of a cross section of privatized firms. Like most of Sobhan's work on nationalization and privatization, it is commendable as a pioneering effort, but is flawed by the author's bias and selective use of data.[19]

Rehman Sobhan was one of the four principal Planning Commission framers of the nationalization policy in 1971-72, and he has been preaching the gospel sincerely ever since. Anyone who studies Bangladesh's economic development is in debt to Sobhan. It may be that he suffers the curse of the first scholar to study any complex subject. Others, probing more deeply and widely, will later detect flaws in his earlier work.

In Rehman Sobhan's case, there is something more to consider. The composite opinion of several analysts and government officials is that while a reader should be aware of Sobhan's bias and must question his data and analysis, his writings give more insight into what was going on and being said in policy circles in the seventies than any other scholar's work.

Sobhan's paper on private sector performance is less admirable than his major opus, but still useful. He tried to evaluate the process too soon after the event, telegraphed his position, accepted questionable government data without questioning, neglected the experience of other countries, and, after saying he did not have sufficient data on which to base conclusions, went right ahead and drew conclusions anyway. He had already concluded that there was nothing to support the concept that the private sector was more efficient and profitable than the public sector other than the faith of the true believers.

Sobhan's sample was made up of approximately 40-45 firms, depending on the particular question being asked. We will only touch on the highlights of his findings for illustrative purposes. His data were drawn almost completely from government sources.

With regard to production, Sobhan found 19 companies with increased production after privatization, 11 that showed a drop off, and 5 that closed down. The data also suggested that a number of firms discontinued some product lines and concentrated on a narrower range of products. Former BSFIC units seem to have fared the best, but those out of BCIC and BSEC did less well. This is interesting because other private metal and chemicals have done relatively well.

Twenty-nine firms increased their sales after privatization and 9 showed a decrease. Former BCIC units apparently did well.

The situation was more complicated with regard to P&L. The sample was smaller (24 units). Four enterprises turned losses to profits, 2 increased profits, and 2 decreased losses. According to

Sobhan's figures, however, 4 turned profits into losses, 7 raised the level of losses, and 5 went out of business. Former BCIC fared better than BSFIC and BSEC firms.

Three things should be noted about these figures. First, Sobhan accepted, apparently without question, the government's estimates of profit and loss when the units were in the public sector and afterwards. As we have seen earlier, government methods for determining and reporting "profit" are highly questionable. Second, all of the P&L estimates were drawn from units divested only 18-24 months prior to the publishing of Sobhan's paper. They were in transition, short of cash, rehabilitating worn-out equipment, and burdened with debts. Third, private sector representatives with whom Sobhan's paper was discussed in late 1986, felt that not only was the research done too soon after divestiture, but the years chosen were particularly turbulent and severe electrical shortages profoundly affected industrial production and profitability.

Bearing all this in mind, one can come away from Sobhan's paper with a far different evaluation than its author intended. Considering the circumstances, the record is not bad at all. In fact, it presents a mildly encouraging picture at that early stage. A very wise "old hand" in the country once said, "Be content with small gains in Bangladesh."[20]

Rehman Sobhan says his findings show clearly that "private ownership does not automatically lead to improved financial performance." Of course it doesn't. Few claim that it does. Privatization is untidy business with few short-term victories. Failures (such as the 5 cited in Sobhan's paper) are expected, and certainly predictable in a troubled economy like Bangladesh's. They are, in the long run, healthier than failing state enterprises kept from complete collapse by constant subsidy and bailing out by an already-strained public treasury.

A more recent and more objective study of divested enterprise performance was performed by the Canadian International Development Agency (CIDA) office in Dhaka.[21] Carried out in late 1986 and early 1987, the CIDA survey is based on information provided in questionnaires completed by 28 divested enterprises, supplemented by data from the Dhaka Stock Exchange, eleven annual reports, and data from state Corporations (particularly on pre-divestment periods).

The CIDA survey attempted to compare performance for 2-3 years before and after divestment in such areas as sales, profitability, tax payments, and employment; in addition, it provided a brief outline of problems faced by divested enterprises. CIDA encountered the usual difficulties in gathering comprehensive, reliable data, particularly from the private sector. Of the 28 questionnaires returned (57 were sent out), no more than 21 were usable for investigating any one of the points noted above.

CIDA's sample included 8 jute mills, 4 textile mills, 7 enterprises in tanning, leather, and rubber products, 4 in engineering; 1 each in chemicals, food, and ceramics; and 2 listed as miscellaneous.[22]

With regard to sales for 21 divested firms, CIDA came to the conclusion that while total sales in absolute monetary terms increased substantially in most cases after divestiture, inflation and other factors made CIDA doubt that there was much increase in real terms.[23] CIDA was prompted to make the following comment:

> We think that it will not be appropriate to draw any conclusions about the performance of the divested enterprises in general terms from the above [cited] increase or decrease in sales in absolute or percentage terms, since the sample is very small,and there is no certainty that the figures provided to our survey team are accurate.[24]

The CIDA report noted also that:

> In the case of some divested enterprises catering [to the] domestic market, the sales pattern has significantly changed after divestment. For instance, in the case of some engineering industries surveyed, we noted that during the pre-divestment periods most of their sales were to the public sector, whereas after divestment most of their sales have switched to the private sector. This is because of the procurement policy of the government which encourages the public sector enterprises if supplies are available from them in preference to making purchase from the private sector.[25]

In terms of profitability, CIDA's sample indicated a net aggregate loss in the post-divestment period in comparison with pre-divestment. They further stated that net loss increased or net profit turned into net loss "in most sectors other than cotton textile and tannery, leather, and rubber products."[26]

A few causes for this situation were suggested. The rising cost of inputs was prominently mentioned, as was the tendency of businessmen to show decreased profits or large losses for tax purposes. Oversanctioning was another factor cited in regard to certain industries.[27]

CIDA's employment survey covered 18 divested enterprises. Overall, employment dropped from 25,352 to 24,415, or 3.7 percent, from the time of divestment to the time of the survey (late 1986 or early 1987). CIDA's figures further showed that the fall at the officer level was 13.3 percent (from 737 to 639), 17.4 percent at the staff level (from

3,089 to 2,551) but only 1.4 percent at the worker level (from 21,526 to 21,225).[28] This approximates the present study's findings.

CIDA concluded its survey with a list of problems faced by divested enterprises. Principal among them was the inability of many divested firms to raise working capital because they could not pledge assets as mortgages against loans until the entire divestiture sale price was paid off. Other problems included poor management practices and inadequate, misleading accounting systems (both inherited from the time when firms were state-run); bloated payrolls and continual absenteeism; the effects of smuggling (especially in the textile industry); old, poorly-maintained equipment; the high cost of imports; government procurement policies that favor SOEs; and poor government divestiture procedures that led to unrealistic negotiated sales prices and inadequate screening of purchasers.

Using a sample smaller than either Sobhan's or CIDA's, but drawn completely from sources in the private sector, this study came up with similar results, although they differed in some significant ways. P&L figures were hard to come by and were at times estimated in percentage of increase or decrease rather than absolute figures. As previously noted, asking for information in percentages rather than monetary amounts increased chances for obtaining useful figures.

The cotton mills were divided. Production was up in all three, varying from 15 to 30 to 50 percent. Production costs increased, but averaged only 20 percent. Sales were up 10-15 percent, but in one mill they fell sharply. The mill closed down for three months. One large mill made only Tk500,000 profit; the others made a net profit of Tk5 million each. All three commented on how the black market trade in textiles severely hurts their business.

One jute mill showed an increase of 8.4 percent in production, a drop of 6.5 percent in production costs, a sales increase of 44 percent, but still reported a loss (yet this still represented an improvement over the previous year). The other mill did poorly in almost all respects as a company, but it appeared that money was being made out of the business by someone.

One food processing company saw a big increase in production in a growing industry, and a drop in production costs due to new equipment. Sales were up 12 percent. There was no major change in profit, primarily because of a substantial hike in tax payments.

The vegetable oil industry is hard to gauge because of extreme fluctuations in price. The case study showed a 10 percent increase in production and profit.

A tannery indicated increases across the board between 1983 and 1984, but a sharp drop-off in 1985. Net profit was 16 percent of sales in 1983, 16.5 percent in 1984, and 13 percent in 1984 on a much reduced volume.

A metal products company reported a 25 percent increase in production, a 40 percent increase in line production costs, a 20 percent boost in sales and a doubling of profit. A second metals firm reported losses, citing labor costs and one large loss on a shipbreaking deal. Nevertheless, it is doubtful that this complex of companies ended up losing money for the owner. This finding cannot be documented.

A chemical company continued its downward trend. It is doubtful that the principal arm of the company can survive much longer. Other companies in this field are profitable. The reason here appears to be poor management (even though the owner has an American MBA), plus a rocky start because of misunderstandings with the government. The company was never able to recover.

A rubber products firm is under new management. It is too soon to quote figures, but the outlook is quite bright for product line diversification, efficient management, and aggressive marketing.

Other firms in the sample did not provide sufficiently precise financial data on which to base profit estimates, though discussions with them were very useful in gaining insights into operating problems, relations with the government, and the like.

Profit and Loss in Jute and Textiles

The biggest controversy and largest sums of money have been connected with the privatization of the 33 jute mills and 27 textile mills, the principal act of the New Industrial Policy of June 1982. The pros and cons of that transition are still at the center of the debate over privatization. The arguments and supporting figures are partisan. This is not surprising when one considers that the stakes were the highest of any of the privatization activities. Return of the jute and textile mills had always been the top priority.

One of the leading participants in the debate, the Metropolitan Chamber of Commerce, stated in 1986,

> Denationalisation of Jute Mills has not failed. On the contrary, it yielded substantial benefit to the jute industry. Productivity per loom has increased, cost of production per ton has declined and communication with overseas buyers has improved. The average annual production of denationalised jute mills went up from 148,000 MT during the nationalisation period to 177,000 MT in the denationalisation period indicating an increase of over 19%. During the last three years (1983-86), the output per loom in operation in denationalised jute mills was

22.84 MT whereas in nationalised jute mills it was 20.32 MT. It indicates that loom productivity in denationalised mills was 12.40% higher compared to nationalised mills. During the first nine months of 1985-86, denationalised jute mills incurred a loss of Tk.3,369 per MT of production compared to Tk.5527 loss per MT of production incurred by the nationalised mills. That is, in nationalised mills the loss per MT of production was 64% higher compared to denationalised mills.[29]

The Metropolitan Chamber further advanced the pro-privatization case by pointing out certain historical and operational aspects of the question.

The record shows that 34 denationalised mills incurred a loss of Tk156 crore during nationalised period 1972-82 and government made a total cash infusion of over Tk204 crore to these mills during the period, out of which BJMC repaid to BSB and BSRS just over Tk85 crore. After denationalisation, the private mills worry about liquidity, but the public sector mills still get cash infusion from the Government; as recently as in May 26, 1986, Bangladesh Bank directed commercial banks to advance a sum of up to Tk60 crore to the public sector mills to meet all their expenses during May and June irrespective of whether the mills have drawing power, but such facilities were refused to private mills.

While appreciating the better performance of the denationalised mills it should, however, be kept in mind that operational freedom of these private sector mills was controlled, firstly by the provision of Jute Goods Trading Order 1982 and then again wage hikes were imposed ignoring the legal provisions. What is more important to note is the fact that these mills although performing better than the public mills are still making huge losses because of international market factors. Because of stiff competition from substitutes and ever rising domestic cost of production, the future of this industry also seems to be rather bleak. It is in the above perspective, that the private sector mills' escalated loan liabilities have to be seen. Unlike the public sector mills, private sector mills do not have assured financial backing of the public exchequer.[30]

The remainder of the argument centers around controversy over various aspects of the indebtedness question.

The Bangladesh Jute Mill Association claims that the 33 public sector mills lost Tk315 crore (US$10.4 million) from 1982 to March 1986, while 36 privatized mills lost only Tk135 crore (US$3.3 million), even though the SOEs enjoyed a monopoly in barter and counter trade sales and financial support from the government.[31]

Few deny that the private mills are sustaining smaller losses than the government mills, but anti-privatization, pro-government forces say that this has happened because of price cutting and other unscrupulous practices, and that the government mills have exercised greater restraint while serving the whole society. The government argument seems to be that price flexibility is unfair. It has been observed that jute mills only made "profits" in Pakistan days because of subsidies and export bonus schemes. The jute industry will always require massive subsidies to break even consistently.

Chishty, in his excellent paper on privatization, noted that the 27 denationalized mills demonstrated a 10 percent improvement in production during their first year as private companies again.[32] Those mills earned a net profit of Tk55.23 million (US$2.24 million) in 1983, whereas they had lost Tk114.185 (US$5.16 million) in 1982 under state operation, for a total turnaround of Tk169,395 (US$6.88 million). He added, that in fairness to the government, 1983 was one of the few good years for jute internationally.[33] Nevertheless, it was an encouraging performance, especially considering the transition problems mentioned above. The mills that remained in the public sector also improved. In 1984 the U.S. Embassy Commercial Section mentioned that BJMC mills were working on a 4-6 month backlog, while private mills were keeping up to date on orders.[34]

CIDA's survey of six jute mills indicated an overall absolute annual increase in sales at 13.6 percent at historical prices, but after adjustments for inflation and other factors, it came out to only 2.9 percent at constant prices.[35] The same six mills experienced an enormous increase in losses after divestiture, but no annual average was calculated by CIDA.[36]

For better or worse, jute will significantly influence Bangladesh's rate of economic growth for the foreseeable future. It is unfortunate, almost tragic, that the fate of such a poor, struggling country must rest on the fortunes of a dying industry. One is tempted to suggest that the failing jute mills should be closed down, and the country's meager resources redirected into more productive and profitable pursuits; but that is a political, social, and economic impossibility.

Instead, the government can only try to ensure that the industry—which is still the largest employer and earner of foreign exchange—is moderately well run during the painful transition period before it fades from the scene as the most important player.

The U.S. Embassy reported in 1984-85 that denationalized textile mills "seem to have performed even better than the private jute mills." Cotton textile production was up 20 percent in the privatized mills. The same mills showed a net profit of Tk400 million (US$16.25 million) in the first year of private operation, after having lost Tk130 million (US$5.9 million) in public hands the year before, an overall turnaround of US$22.15 million.[37] The Ministry of Industries announced similar figures.[38]

That pace was not sustained. The textile industry experienced difficulties over the last few years. CIDA's sample of six mills showed an annual growth in sales of 10.03 percent at historical prices, but only 0.36 percent at constant prices.[39] Profitability showed a favorable trend (though still in the red) but CIDA did not attempt to calculate annual average figures.[40]

Some textile mills have prospered, but several have gone out of business. Three heavily-indebted mills were closed down in early 1988. The owners recommended that the government take them over again, but the government declined.[41]

The private mills have tended to perform better than the public mills, even though the latter are generally larger, with more modern equipment; but the difference in performance has not been remarkable. Lorche reports that the performance of the public mills,

> got a boost from the privatization program, in 1982-83 and 1983-84. But as soon as the new sense of competition, the public attention, the Government scrutiny, and the fear of further privatization faded away, the technical and financial performance of public mills sank back to poorer levels. In 1985-86, they reported a negative 19% return on sales.[42]

Competition from black market Indian mills (goods smuggled in through the pervasive "unofficial economy") seriously threatens this industry, which imports materials and is aimed at the impoverished domestic market, in contrast to the booming ready-made garment industry, which is export-oriented. Additionally, Bangladesh's textile mills, private as well as public, have not been uniformly blessed with good management.[43]

Privatization of Fertilizer Distribution

Bangladesh's privatization effort has been overwhelmingly involved with divestiture of industrial SOEs. One of the more successful privatization programs, however, has been in retail and wholesale distribution connected with agriculture. Also, it has not involved any divestiture transactions. Rather, it has been involved in gradually building up a private sector sales and marketing network for fertilizer to replace a government operation that has been marginalized or, one could say, "quietly liquidated."[44]

Besides privatizing distribution, USAID's project has improved extension services to farmers through the new private dealer network, and has had beneficial effects on deregulating prices, decreasing subsidies, and generally creating a more vibrant and efficient competitive market milieu. The fertilizer project has been very successful and is being copied in other LDCs. Fertilizer sales increased at an annual average of 7.1 percent during the FY 1981-FY 1987 period.[45]

USAID's fertilizer distribution project represents privatization in one of its most effective forms. The project has replaced a government operation with a solidly private sector activity. This was not accomplished overnight like the denationalization of 33 jute mills and 27 textile mills. It has evolved over 8 years of careful planning and gradual step-by-step implementation. The politically sensitive aspects of the program have been met quietly but effectively.

Much has been written about this project, so there is no need to exhaustively document its progress and accomplishments here. In order to analyze performance a few of the highlights of the program follow:

- more fertilizer is being sold;
- fertilizer use by farmers has increased;
- distribution is speedier and more efficient;
- the price of fertilizer has gone up, but tolerably so, mainly because of competition;
- nationwide distribution is more even, although there are still problems in remote areas;
- extension services and technical assistance superior to that provided by the government are now available through the private dealer network;
- the government agency (BADC) is beginning to assume the role of monitoring, quality control, training and general marketing advice, besides still controlling production; and
- more people are employed in the fertilizer industry than previously.

There are, of course, many more facets to this immense and complex project. It is included here to indicate that there are many roads to privatization, and most of them do not involve divestiture.

If, as the Third Five-Year Plan (1985-90) indicates, "more emphasis will be given for promotion of agro-based rural industries and consumer industries,"[46] the approach of the fertilizer distribution project could be a useful model. It is positive in that it involves building a private sector capability, not merely unloading a public sector failure.

Few phases of the business of privatization can be labelled "win-win" situations, but this project is about as close as one can get in Bangladesh. Policy levels of the government have accepted its basic purposes, and the bureaucracy is gradually accepting the inevitable. USAID is quick to report that Phase I, which dealt with retail sales, has been more successful than Phase II, which is aimed at reforming the wholesale network. Phase II is still in process.

Summary

In sum, the performance of the divested firms has been a mixed bag. As we have seen from the several surveys cited here, attempts to use the bottom line approach are at best inconclusive and frequently misleading. The "evidence" is often contradictory.

The record, even if incomplete, does, however, permit observers to raise legitimate questions about the efficacy of divestiture as a means for promoting economic progress or even private sector growth in Bangladesh. But when this point is raised, special care should be made to maintain a clear distinction between evaluating divestiture and privatization. As was stated at the beginning of this report, the two are not synonymous. As was also noted, divestiture is one of the least attractive and, except in Chile and Bangladesh, least used vehicles for privatization.

In the case of Bangladesh, one might ask whether the SOEs to be unloaded were selected for the right reasons or, conversely, were they purchased for the right reasons. The advantages of buying an existing enterprise have been cited; but one can also wonder whether many divested enterprises started out with two strikes against them. Some observers tend to believe that the burdens more than balanced out the advantages.

Also, when one places the focus on divestiture or on performance of divested enterprises, one is evaluating special cases. Divestiture is only one of several privatization methods. In Bangladesh, it has been, for better or worse, the primary method used. Given the historical and economic circumstances, perhaps this was a logical path to pursue in Bangladesh. But there is little evidence that alternative paths were seriously considered, and not much thought seems to have been given to how best to pursue even the divestiture route. One cannot change the past, but should certainly consider very carefully different options in determining what might be the most productive way to privatize in the future.

The true test of whether privatization will benefit Bangladesh lies more in evaluating the accomplishments and potential of the private sector in general than the performance of a set of stumbling enterprises unloaded because they were losing money.

Even if a package of "performance" figures is put together, one can ask, "What have you got when you've got it?," in terms of the real economic story in Bangladesh. There are far more important and illuminating issues to investigate.

One must go further and ask whether the public sector or the private sector should be the leading actor in driving the economy. Here, the record is much more clear. What progress has been made in Bangladesh's economy in recent times has been made by the private sector. The public sector has failed as an engine of growth. The government can and should serve as stimulator, policy maker, and regulator, but not as the primary participant in the market place. So, what is required is a program capable not just of unloading, but of building. It is also a matter of sorting out proper roles and then performing them thoughtfully and consistently.

Given the overall economic morass in Bangladesh, and the way the "disinvestment" program was launched and subsequently implemented, it was probably inevitable that many of the divested enterprises would not fare very well. Critics have leapt upon this predictable lackluster performance to claim that privatization won't work in Bangladesh and that it was foisted on this impoverished country as an improved act of faith by advocates of free enterprise. That argument is flawed for several reasons.

First, the "verdict" on privatization should not be based on the inconclusive performance of the troubled enterprises that were divested. Second, concentration on the divested enterprises avoids considering the more important question of privatization of the economy in general and the establishment of a policy and regulatory environment within which the private sector in general can flourish. The debate on public-private primacy belongs here. Third, without exception the countries in Asia that have achieved the greatest degree of economic progress and prosperity for their peoples have been those that have opted for emphasizing private sector development. The government has in all those cases provided essential guidance and support, but the drive has come from the private sector and market forces. The burden of proof is on the critics of privatization in Bangladesh to prove that conditions are so unique in their country that they should not try a path that has been so successful in Japan, Korea, Taiwan, Malaysia, Singapore, Hong Kong, Thailand, and elsewhere.

Notes

1. A useful list of financial and other problems faced by divested firms can be found in Ameen, H. H. Mansurul: *A Study of Divestment of Industries in Bangladesh* (Dhaka, Canadian International Development Agency, March 1987), in two volumes, Vol. I—Main Report, pp. 143-148. This source will hereinafter be cited as "CIDA Report." Mansurul Ameen is a Canadian citizen of Bengali descent. He is a CPA/Chartered Accountant. On page 143, Ameen makes the interesting point that,"Until the entire sale price is paid, the divested enterprises cannot pledge their assets as mortgages against loans." As a consequence, they often have a difficult time arranging working capital and loan financing. Additionally, they do not get full title until the loan is completely paid off. They are caught in a "Catch 22" scenario.

2. A copy of the survey questionnaire is attached as Appendix C. A great deal of care was taken by Nizam Ahmed and me in designing the questionnaire, in consultation with businessmen and government officials. It was not designed to be encyclopedic like some we saw, which, in our estimation, would never be answered. We requested only that information which we considered essential and obtainable. Second, while we wanted actual figures, we figured that we might have a better chance of obtaining useful and reliable data if, in certain cases, we asked only for percentage increases or decreases (in production, sales, profits, etc.), rather than trying to get absolute figures. Therefore, we gave the interviewees a choice, an approach which made them more comfortable. The questions on the written questionnaire were usually asked verbally during the conversation, without much direct mention of a questionnaire. Strict confidentiality was promised. Therefore, the reader will rarely find direct attribution in the use of case study figures. See footnote 3 immediately below.

3. Conversation—S.A.M. Amanullah, General Manager, Bangladesh Chemical Complex (Pvt.) Ltd. and Bengal Belting Corporation, Ltd., 11/9/86. Also in attendance were the Purchasing Manager, Marketing Manager and Finance Manager.

4. Conversation with John A. Bannigan in Washington, D.C. 4/28/87. Mr. Bannigan, a former officer of The Asia Foundation, has been involved in South Asian affairs since the mid-fifties. He has lived and worked in Bangladesh over extended periods of time.

5. Lyell Ritchie, Demos Menegakis and K.M. Sakhawatullah: *Report on Private Sector Development in Bangladesh*, a report from Arthur D. Little, Inc. to USAID, 5/13/87, pp. 3-4. This is an excellent survey of private sector activity in Bangladesh. I met with the ADL team at their AID debriefing in Washington, D.C. on 5/13/87. Their survey was carried out under the Private Enterprise Development Study (PEDS) program of AID and will be referenced hereinafter as PEDS.

6. ibid, p. 40. A foreign businessman in Bangladesh told me that while officials used to apologize or rationalize for under the counter "expediting

fees," they now just demand it up front. I also ran into blatant examples of bribe taking. The practice is pervasive, and the effect on the speed and efficiency of government operations is deplorable.

7. See Wasow, Bernard: *Private Investment in Bangladesh—An Optimistic Appraisal*, a publication of the Trade and Industrial Policy (TIP) Reform Program, TIP-IISU-F.5, (Dhaka, Government of Bangladesh, June 1985), p. 5.

8. Sobhan, Rehman and Ahsan, Ahmad: *Implementation of Projects in the Private Sector in Bangladesh, A Study of DFI-Sponsored Projects*. A paper presented at the 7th Biennial Conference of the Bangladesh Economic Association, held at Jahangirnagar University, Dhaka, Dec. 17-20, 1985, p. 1.

9. WB-Bangladesh '86-1, p. 121; see also *Overview of Industrial Investment Incentive*, TIP series, Management Unit, TIP-MU-F (Dhaka, Government of Bangladesh, March 1986), p. 22.

10. Chishty, op. cit., p. 18.

11. PEDS, op. cit., p. 40.

12. "Call for strike at industries tomorrow," *The New Nation*, 4/27/87. Two days earlier the Deputy Prime Minister had announced the possibility of including additional abandoned enterprises still in the public sector in the proposed 51-49 Plan. That was the spark for the strike.

13. Sobhan, Rehman and Ahsan, Ahmad: *Disinvestment and Denationalization: Profile and Performance*, Research Report, New Series, No. 38 (Dhaka, Bangladesh Institute of Development Studies, July 1984).

14. WB-Bangladesh '86-1, p. 149.

15. WB/Dhaka—Indus. Sec., op. cit., p. 7. The Metropolitan Chamber of Commerce and Industry estimates total job creation as 250,000 (including 200,000 women) or 10% of the manufacturing work force. Metropolitan Chamber: *Private Sector in Bangladesh: Its Perspectives and Performance* (Dhaka, 1986), p. 7.

16. Chishty, op. cit., p. 15.

17. The Gulishan Theater, a downtown movie house, which had 20 employees before it was nationalized, reportedly found 120 on the payroll when it was privatized. The new owners faced a particularly sensitive political situation, because many of the employees added by the government were former Freedom Fighters, who had served the Bangladesh cause during the war of liberation with Pakistan. It took a long time for the new owners to solve the problem by shifting and consolidating positions, locating alternate employment, etc.

18. Conversation—Surrinder Malik, Chief Economist, World Bank/Dhaka, 3/1/87.

19. Sobhan and Ahsan: *Disinvestment and Denationalization*, op. cit., passim. Tawfique Chowdhury gives a similar evaluation of Sobhan's paper in T. Chowdhury, op. cit., pp. 39-40, pointing to "serious deficiencies in data and methodology to lead to any meaningful findings."

20. Conversation—"Pete" Peterson, Chief, Agriculture and Rural Development Division, USAID/Dhaka, 9/25/86. The *Economist* expressed a similar thought in an article in its issue for the week of July 20-26, 1985, stating,"Progress in Bangladesh means not going backwards."

21. CIDA Report, op. cit. See especially Chapter 6,"Survey of Divested Industrial Enterprises," pp.119-155. The study also provides a useful service by including lists of divestment procedures, taken from various government documents. CIDA stresses that its study was an overview of divestiture methods, not an analysis of the divestiture program. See p. viii.

22. ibid, p. 122 (table).

23. ibid, p. 125. The survey was more concerned with industries than specific enterprises, although some figures were provided for individual enterprises. See pp. 123-129.

24. ibid, p. 124.

25. ibid, pp. 128-129.

26. ibid, p. 131.

27. ibid, pp. 133-135. See also pages 137-138 regarding CIDA's inconclusive results in connection with tax liability and payment.

28. ibid, p. 139.

29. *Analysis of the Causes of Inflated Loan Liabilities of Denationalized Jute Mills* (Dhaka, Metropolitan Chamber of Commerce and Industry, 1986), p. 1.

30. ibid, p. 2, 4.

31. "Jute sector plagued by chronic loss," *Jute Review* (Dhaka, Bangladesh Jute Mills Association, July 1986). In a separate set of figures, the BJMA calculated (on 7/21/86) the comparison in the following way (numbers are expressed in crore Tk.):

Period	BJMC	BJMA
1982-83	+23.90	n/a
1983-84	−28.60	+0.79
1984-85	−146.00	−85.00
1985-86	−114.00	−47.00
Totals:	−264.70	−131.21

32. Chishty, op. cit., p. 15.

33. ibid. The exchange rate for 1982 was Tk22.12/US$1 and 24.62/1 in 1983. The reader will note discrepancies in the various sets of figures, which is typical of a researcher's problems in Bangladesh. It is curious that Rehman Sobhan did not use jute as one of the industries for comparison in his 1984 paper, because direct comparisons are available.

34. U.S. Embassy/Dhaka undated draft cable, sometime in 1984. Useful updating on the status of the jute industry was found in WB-'87, pp. 68-76, and WB-'88-1, pp. 13-14, 22. For analysis of the jute industry, I depended heavily on two related studies done by John Kelly and a Price Waterhouse team. They are *Bangladesh Jute Goods Industry: Policies and Actions for Overcoming Existing Problems* (Dhaka, Price Waterhouse Asia Pacific, 9/25/86) and *Review of the Operations of the Bangladesh Jute Mills Corporation* (Dhaka, Price Waterhouse Asia Pacific, July 1985).

35. CIDA Report, pp. 125-126. Figures on individual mills showed one averaging 30.3%, another at 22.8%, and third at 17.5%, and three others at about 8.3%.

36. ibid, p. 131.

37. U.S Embassy/Dhaka, undated draft cable (sometime in 1984). Excellent analyses of the textile industry were found in Lorche, op. cit., passim; Kelly, John: *Review of the Operations of the Bangladesh Textile Mills Corporation* (Dhaka, Price Waterhouse Asia Pacific, March 1986), Vol. I (draft), passim; Norbye, O.D.K.: *The Cotton Spinning Industry in Bangladesh* (Dhaka, Planning and Project Identification Unit, TIP, Government of Bangladesh, January 1984), Doc. TIP-PPIU, B-8, passim; and Ahmed, Nizam Uddin, "A Visit to the Bangladesh Textile Mills Association" (Dhaka, USAID, 7/18/84), a report to the USAID Mission in Dhaka. An anti-private sector analysis can be found in Chowdhury, Nuimuddin: *Towards an Understanding of Entrepreneurship in Early Development: The Case of Cotton Textiles in Bangladesh* (Dhaka, BIDS, January 1985), New Series #37, passim.

38. "176 industrial units disinvested so far" *The Bangladesh Observer*, 6/3/84. See also Chishty, op. cit., pp. 15-16. This turnaround also was not figured into Rehman Sobhan's equation.

39. CIDA Report, p. 126. Three mills had annual increases of 17.6%, one of them at 35%, and two at 1.5%.

40. ibid, p. 131.

41. Lorche, op. cit., p. 38. Lorche notes that in 1979-80 the government had taken back one textile mill (Royal Textile Mill) at the owners' request. The mill had been divested in 1976 through tenders. By early 1988, the Ministry of Textiles was planning "to dispose of it again, probably through liquidation and subsequent tender of the assets." ibid, ft. 47, pp. 53-54.

42. ibid, p. 41.

43. ibid, pp. 15-16. When the mills were denationalized,"A committee verified the legal title and, according to liberal guidelines, the nationality of the applicants. However, there was no assessment of the applicants' financial and managerial strengths." ibid, p. 15. Many were not qualified managers. Six of the mills were taken over by families who had never actually run mills, because the mills had not yet been operational when they were nationalized in 1972. ibid, p. 16. In some cases, it was the heirs or less than qualified relatives who assumed positions of authority after privatization in 1982. ibid, p. 41. Finally, Lorche points out that "... private owners tended to be transaction-oriented, rather than production-oriented, reflecting their own commercial background and the dominant role of the 'informal' aspects in the industry." ibid, p. 40.

44. Quiet liquidation of inefficient, unprofitable SOEs has been used frequently in recent years by Taiwan authorities in preference to expensive, complex, highly visible and politically sensitive divestitures. Taiwan's success is also the result of coordinating the phasing out of the SOEs' functions with sound programs that encourage and support replacement by private sector players and activities. Officials in Bangladesh are beginning to acknowledge that "quiet liquidation" might be a good technique to employ.

Conversation—Dr. Tawfique Chowdhury, Joint Secretary, Ministry of Finance, 11/14/86; Conversation—Director General of Industries, Ministry of Industries, 11/13/86.

45. WB-'88-1, p. 44. A World Bank of a year earlier stated that fertilizer use had "nearly tripled" in the past decade from 55 kg/hectare to 146 kg/ha. WB-'87, p. 58.

46. Third Five Year Plan, p. 134.

7

The Public Sector's Performance

One cannot help but approach evaluation of the Bangladesh government's privatization effort with ambivalence. On the one hand, the sheer number of privatized enterprises involved is impressive, even remarkable. No other country has divested more than a thousand state-owned enterprises. Further, it is possible that the privatization policy and related regulatory liberalization have cumulatively had a beneficial effect on industrial growth and have encouraged private investment.

At the same time, however, the thoughtful observer, once having penetrated beyond the glitter of the statistics and the clarion call of the rhetoric, is at first disappointed and ultimately dismayed. There has been more sound and fury than substance to the policy statements; they were frequently hastily, almost compulsively arrived at; and they were then foisted upon the struggling economy without sufficient planning or attention to practical implications of the development strategies they embodied.

The ultimate frustration comes with full realization of the extent of the gap between policy and implementation. Shafiul Azam and Shamsul Haque Chishty have called the privatization policy "a bold stroke"[1]—and it was. But its effectiveness has been blunted, even thwarted, by inconsistency and lack of commitment at political levels, a suffocating regulatory environment, and obstructionism, incompetence, and downright venality in the bureaucracy.

When all of these official failings, plus the machinations of a militant opposition, are added to Bangladesh's horrendous economic problems, it is amazing that privatization has continued at all. The fact that privatization has already made modest contributions to Bangladesh's economic development, and still retains the potential for even greater benefits, is testimony to the soundness of the concept in the Bangladesh context.

Considerable attention has been given throughout this study to various aspects of the government's promulgation and handling of privatization. The purpose in this chapter is to focus on government policy and operation in an integrated fashion; with a special emphasis on attitudes.

Politics and the Decision-making Process

The battle over privatization is usually fought more on political than economic grounds. That has certainly been the case in Bangladesh. Only a few diehards would recommend returning to a full-scale nationalization similar to 1971-1975. Even the professional oppositionists of the Awami League do not propose doing that, although they would renationalize some industries. It was, after all, the unfulfilled expectations of the disastrous experiment with a state-run economy that contributed to the Awami League's downfall. Rehman Sobhan continues to fly the socialist flag, but his highly ideological arguments seem to hinge more on what is good or bad for the institution of socialism, as such, rather than what is good or bad for the economy, the people, and the country.[2] For the most part, however, governmental shifts to privatization have been based on pragmatism not ideology in Bangladesh, as has been the case in other LDCs.

There were practical reasons for bringing the abandoned properties under the government umbrella in 1972, but it has been difficult for even nationalization's most ardent supporters to justify the extra step of assuming control of Bangladeshi-owned mills and businesses as well. It didn't make economic sense to take on this extra responsibility, and it was an administrative nightmare for an already overburdened bureaucracy. The step was, however, ideologically satisfying to the inner core of the Planning Commission.

In 1975 a different set of practical reasons for making the break and starting the privatization process prevailed. The main reason was that the enormous public enterprise system was floundering and losing money in large amounts.

Also, the political leadership came to believe that the best chance of reducing the growing public debt and promoting growth would be to assign a larger role in economic development to the private sector.

The leadership was generally aware that other Asian lands that had opted for the private sector approach were doing remarkably well. Moudud Ahmed provided the following "overview" of the country's industrial policy since independence. An unedited version of his 1987 statement (made when he was still Deputy Prime Minister and, concurrently, Minister of Industries) read as follows:

> . . . let us divide the period into 4 periods from 1972-75 when in the name of socialist transformation, we actually had a system by which we had nationalised 85% of our industries, banks and insurance companies, and without any planning, without having a socialist party in power, without having socialist cadres, without having a socialist bureaucracy they wanted to have a socialist transformation which was self-contradictory in its exercise. And that's why that had failed and we have seen what mismanagement, waste and corruption had taken place during that period. It was the people, not the politicians who were sincere to see that the country have a people-oriented economic system but they did not have the planning nor had they the correct conviction, nor they had the party or leadership to really implement that kind of economy. So, in the process what really happened was a shame. In the process, our economy really collapsed during those years.
>
> Then from 1976-1982 there was a period where some liberal attitude was taken. The process was the reverse but not with a total conviction—they also suffered from indecision about what to do and what not to do. But it was better; it started thinking about revitalising the economy.
>
> Then in 1982, we had the new industrial policy after the present government took over and then this policy was a bold policy in order to reverse the earlier policy which was adopted in 1972. So, a massive denationalisation took place, industrial entrepreneurship was given due recognition. Bangladeshis, who owned industries and whose industries were nationalised, were given back to them. The process of privatisation was accelerated and it had achieved the desired goal, reversing the policy.
>
> Now we have a new policy after 4 years of this phase and the whole industrial policy which has come into effect from July this year was a one-step-forward. This is now a policy of consolidation of the privatisation of our industries, of our capital, of our growth, and accelerating the industrialization of the country. . . . This policy period will be a policy of acceleration and consolidation—of the policy that was adopted in 1982. . . . Some of the main features of this policy are: there will be a balanced growth between public and private sectors; . . . we want to see a rapid growth of [the] private sector in this country. So, the people who benefitted by way of denationalisation, by way of purchasing, acquiring new industries or shares in industries in [the] last 4 1/2 years would be now expected to come forward and go for further investment.[3]

Moudud's remarks are intriguing, both for his candor regarding preceding regimes and for his lack of introspection; for much of what he has leveled against the Mujib and Zia regimes—mismanagement, corruption, no planning, lack of conviction, uncertainty—could be said of the Ershad government as well.

As evidenced by newspaper clips presented in Chapter 5, and from other material included throughout this study, consistency has not been a hallmark of the Bangladesh government's privatization policy. The Ershad government more than the others has shifted course, vacillated, plunged forward, and pulled back in the face of opposition (particularly from organized labor) on innumerable occasions.

The government's performance gives the impression that its leaders have never really figured out what they want from the policy, other than a pious wish for a "strong private sector" or a "mixed economy." It is doubtful that the government has pondered what is entailed in developing a vibrant, market-driven economy. It is also questionable that public administrators, who have presided over a failing public sector, can make sounder decisions in a free market than private entrepreneurs. Bureaucrats are usually more concerned with maintaining a spotless public image than striking out in new directions.

One sees little evidence of specific goals and targets to be met in carefully planned stages. It was as if once the policy was on paper and promulgated, the government thought that was all there was to it, especially since the enacting document had been assembled like a shopping list to include every conceivable possibility.

Little attention seems to have been devoted to planning and little thought given to the implications of the policy, the obstacles it would certainly face, the new problems it would inevitably create, and the follow-up and countermeasures that would be required. In addition, the interrelatedness of policies and problem areas does not appear to have been taken into account. As a consequence, sound ideas and good policies have been put in jeopardy more than was necessary.

For example, the major step in the entire privatization effort was the return of 33 jute mills to former owners. This was an enormously complex and sensitive venture. Prior to NIP-'82, one of the problems in the jute industry was the inflexibility of the government pricing system. Its only redeeming feature was that the industry was able to speak to the international market with a single voice through the BJMC. After privatization, foreign buyers could seek the best price from 34 sellers (the BJMC and the 33 now independent mills). What had been overly rigid became chaos. Bangladeshi was fighting Bangladeshi, and all domestic groups suffered.

If it had merely been a case of free market forces determining price, the situation would have been tolerable, even desirable. But when the mills were privatized, the settlements forced upon the buyers (if they wanted their mills back) led to all kinds of unfortunate fallout. Most buyers felt they could never get out from under the obligations imposed upon them. Some, therefore, were willing to sell jute at any price, just to generate cash, even if it meant that the mill was going down the drain. Others decided not to repay their loans. The public mills, still beholden to the price structure, could not compete in a price war and lost even more money.

What the government should have done was negotiate more reasonable terms in the first instance. Also, some kind of a public-private instrumentality should have been set up to coordinate pricing and present a unified front for selling to foreign buyers. These needs should have been foreseen. Everyone in Bangladesh would have benefited. An opportunity for public and private cooperation was missed in the country's most important industry.

The decision to turn over the mills to the private sector was not by itself erroneous; but relinquishing any semblance of monitoring or coordinating control over this vital area of the economy was disastrous. Even if all the mills had been privatized, some kind of coordinating mechanism would still have been essential. The government also neglected its responsibility to promote research and development in jute to stimulate new product ideas in this troubled but crucial industry.

Decision making in Bangladesh is too diffuse. A staggering number of councils, commissions, and committees for making economic policy exist, for example, the National Committee for Industrial Development (NCID), the Consultative Committee for Public Enterprises (CONOPE), the Executive Committee of the National Economic Council (ECNEC), the High-Powered Facilities Board (HPFB), and the Committee for Reorganization of Public Statutory Corporations (CRPSC). These are in addition to normal policy making units in the secretariat and line ministries. While these autonomous bodies are chaired by a few top people, the system is a hodge-podge. It makes one wonder whether the system was deliberately designed to avoid individual responsibility for planning and decision making. The various committees operate in their own particular vacuums, and some are even chaired by officials unfriendly to privatization and the private sector.

Meanwhile, the Planning Commission is not used as a central coordinating body for planning. It is more of a monitoring and evaluation unit, passing judgment on what has been done rather than suggesting what should be done. Its authorship of the five-year plans and participation in the budget approval process might indicate otherwise, but these are rhetorical and perfunctory services. What the government needs is a planner, overseer, and coordinator for economic policy, such as has been so successful in such countries as Taiwan, Korea, Malaysia, Thailand and Singapore. It is possible that, in consideration of the Planning Commission's enormous (and destructive) influence during the Mujib period, subsequent regimes may have decided never to allow it as much power again.

Bangladesh's dire economic circumstances have given the Ministry of Finance inordinate influence over industrial development policy, influence that should more properly reside in the Ministry of Industries. The breakup of the Ministry of Commerce and Industry into four ministries (Industries, Commerce, Jute and Textiles) contributed to this shift in influence. Certainly, the Ministry of Finance must have considerable say in both the collection and expenditure of funds; but experience elsewhere teaches that Ministry of Finance-dictated development policy will most probably not be dynamic, nation-building policy. It has not been encouraging to hear several high-ranking Bangladeshi officials say, in almost identical wording, that "finance is calling the shots" with regard to privatization.

Comparison With Taiwan's Privatization Program

Regarding policy planning and implementation, a cursory comparison will now be made between the experiences of Bangladesh and Taiwan.[4] This is presented at the specific request of a number of Bangladeshi officials and businessmen, in addition to several scholars and foreign observers. It may seem that the two situations are too dissimilar for any useful comparison, because the two countries are now at the opposite ends of the development spectrum. But contrary to expectations, informed persons in Bangladesh were most interested in the Taiwan experience, perhaps because of the great achievements made there, but also because the two countries started out with a surprising number of similarities. If that was so, logically the next question was why one has prospered, while the other is obviously struggling.[5]

This study, can present only a bare outline of some of the similarities and divergences between the two situations; but even this may illustrate some illuminating points. Both countries started out under the following circumstances at independence:

- an agriculture-based economy, featuring small holdings and a high percentage of landless tillers;
- a conservative, traditional society;
- a colonial background, wherein the economy had been geared to the needs of the colonial power (in Taiwan's case, Japan from 1895-1945);
- a backwater area dominated by nearby major commercial centers (Canton and, in Taiwan's case, Hong Kong);
- some infrastructure built by the former ruling power;
- a densely populated area, with the majority of the population in rural areas (Taiwan's concentration is greater, though the scale is smaller);
- almost no natural resources;
- a large pool of unskilled labor and widespread poverty;
- few indigenous entrepreneurs or managers with top-level experience;
- a business community oriented toward trade and commerce, not industry, and a tradition of familial rather than corporate structures;
- an economy shattered by war (Taiwan's industrial capacity was 85 percent destroyed by American bombing in World War II);
- more than 80 percent of industrial capacity residing in the public sector;
- almost no capital markets and limited domestic savings;
- encouraging prospects for considerable foreign aid; and
- an industrialized sector heavily nationalized after departure of a foreign power.

Most readers of this study will be familiar with the so-called "Miracle of Taiwan," so I will not dwell on the accomplishments that have elevated that island country to membership in the elite club of Newly Industrialized Countries. Also, such readers will know that the two countries did not start out in identical circumstances. There were differences from the start. One of the advantages was Taiwan's core of experienced administrators who came from mainland China (although the business community is dominated by local Taiwanese).

Nevertheless, there were enough common conditions, initially, to provide some valuable lessons from the analysis of differing ways the two nations subsequently performed. Although these lessons can be applied quite easily to the subjects of economic development and private sector development in general, we will deliberately restrict ourselves to those aspects which most directly bear upon the narrower subject of privatization. However, privatization and private sector development are inseparably linked. Privatization is not an isolated phenomenon.

Taiwan authorities adopted most of the tactics that make privatization work, including:

- a gradual, step-by-step, pragmatic approach to economic development;
- careful planning with clearly identified short-and long-term objectives;
- scrupulous attention to organization and details;
- demonstrated political will through consistent support of policies;
- an integrated set of practical programs promoting private sector activity;
- effective use of foreign aid;
- a privatization policy coordinated with other economic and fiscal policies;
- a planned, structured approach to transition of enterprises from the public sector to the private sector;
- privatization transactions and negotiations conducted with fairness and honesty;
- promotion of cooperation between the bureaucracy and the business community and efforts to decrease friction;
- simplified procedures, drastically reduced bureaucratic interference, and curtailment of corrupt practices; and
- rationalization of the regulatory and administrative environment for newly privatized enterprises and for the private sector in general.

Taiwan launched its program to privatize the economy with divestiture of four large SOEs, two of which were umbrella organizations containing dozens of sub-units (some of which became extremely successful spinoffs). One of the original four enterprises privatized (Taiwan Cement Corporation) became the seventh largest company in Taiwan, and one of the best run. After the original four divestitures, most subsequent moves involved (a) gradual privatization of large enterprises by periodically selling off selected sections of SOEs, (b) selling shares of SOEs, or (c) freezing an SOE budget and functions, letting it gradually fade away, while supporting replacement of it by appropriate private sector activity. By a combination of these policies, methods, and programs, the public/private ratio of 80/20 was gradually shifted to 20/80, with every indication that the trend will continue.

Taiwan's planned approach to growth has been gradual, starting with agriculture, which has driven industry. Infrastructure was built up thorough labor-intensive consumer products, with dependence on small and medium enterprises. Import substitution was followed by producing for export. Assembly operations gradually gave way to major manufacturing. (Taiwan did not have an integrated steel mill until the late seventies.) The influence of the government throughout has been pervasive, but not intrusive. Taiwan has been a textbook case on how to privatize an economy.

The Bangladesh government has not consistently followed similar precepts and programs. As a result, its bold privatization effort has not achieved its full potential for promoting economic growth and the general welfare. In the following section, material is presented that speaks to some of the more important lessons to be learned from the Taiwan model.

Implementation of Privatization Policy

Most of the influential personalities consulted in the preparation of this study agreed that "the biggest problem is implementation."[6] The government has made considerable strides in liberalizing some of the regulations dealing with various phases of economic activity. Much remains to be accomplished, however, particularly in the field of imports. Progress has been made, but that progress is threatened by the bureaucratic torpor that exists in Bangladesh. The beneficial effect of regulatory reform is blunted by administrative inefficiency and venality. Most of the interminable delays occur in the middle levels of the bureaucracy.

There are many reasons for this procrastination and obstructionism. Privatization threatens bureaucratic empires. Therefore, the bureaucracy resists change. The Minister of Industries lamented that after he had signed off on the 51-49 Plan, the paper took another 2 1/2 months to clear the ministry. He said he raised a storm over this. He saw it as an attempt of the ministry's bureaucrats to "study it to death" as a traditional delaying tactic and as a demonstration of unwillingness to surrender some of their power base in state-owned enterprises to either the private sector or the state Corporations being reconstituted as holding companies. The internal battle goes on.

Unwillingness to take responsibility is another problem. Bureaucrats shirk responsibility by hiding behind red tape or requiring numerous signatures on even routine matters. Also, in many cases, middle-level civil servants are not kept current on regulatory changes. The government must undertake a major briefing and training program for the bureaucracy. Such a program might make it possible to avoid many, if not all, of the "incidents" listed in Chapter 6.

The President of the Dhaka Chamber of Commerce and Industry (DCCI) strongly suggested that a system of deadlines be established for bureaucratic actions. Regarding the 51-49 Plan, he said that (a) there should be a deadline on implementation, (b) responsible civil servants should be accountable for meeting deadlines on this and other matters, and (c) someone should monitor their performance, enforce the deadline, and require periodic progress reports. He was not confident that his idea would be adopted. Others have broached similar ideas. Such a procedure was common practice with Shafiul Azam when he was Minister of Industries. It did not survive long after his departure.

There is a special urgency to public service reform, because a distressingly high percentage of the most capable senior civil servants will retire within the next few years. The caliber of their replacements emerging from the middle ranks is not nearly so high. This is a recognized future problem for which the nervous government does not yet have a solution. The public service is no longer attracting the best young talent. In former days, a career in public service was easily the most prestigious and most sought after type of career. Today, many of the most promising young men seek business careers. This shift has had both positive and negative consequences.

The Public/Private Mix

The President of the DCCI suggested the above idea about deadlines during a conversation in which he also lamented the deplorable state of relations between the bureaucracy and the business community. He said, "Let us forget confrontation! Let us cooperate." This is a sentiment echoed by many in the business community and at the top levels of government.

In 1987, there were some moves to facilitate dialogue through establishing liaison committees; but mistrust and animosity still rule, seriously hindering private sector development and standing in the way of general economic progress.

Privatization will be a dead letter without better cooperation between the public and private sectors. The matter goes far beyond changing rules and regulations or speeding up procedures. It goes deeply into the question of endemic corruption. Payoffs are part of even the most routine contact (one must pay "baksheesh" even to get a form to fill out).

It must be remembered that corruption was far greater when the government controlled 92 percent of the economy's resources, before a substantial percentage of the units were privatized. Some say this loss embittered the bureaucracy. Corruption is pervasive and deeply entrenched. One can attack corruption from a moral point of view, but beyond that, corruption absorbs scarce financial resources that are desperately needed for nation building. It also slows up day-to-day activities and poisons the atmosphere between business and government.

There is fault in both of these warring camps, but by far the greatest responsibility for the current state of affairs must rest with the government. The bureaucracy holds power and, therefore, the key to the situation. The Bangladesh government has never really come to terms with doing business with business. The interrelationship between government and private business sectors is not well understood, nor is there understanding of the attributes of a true market-driven economy based on open and honest competition.

There is a tendency to look at Bangladesh's economic situation in all or nothing terms. For example, a respected economics scholar, a former cabinet minister,[7] when asked about private sector development, responded, "What private sector?" His meaning was that since private enterprise borrows money from the government or obtains certain subsidies or concessions, the private sector cannot be considered truly private. He fails to see, or refuses to see, that there is no such thing as an economy that is either 100 percent private or 100 percent public. The two sectors are interdependent. The economy depends on the health and flexibility of the relationship.

A very intelligent senior official, who shall remain anonymous, declared, "I don't care if these privatized businesses make a profit or not. That's not my affair." He operates on the basis that once they are privatized, they're on their own. He should care. The future of the economy depends to a great extent on how the privatized and other private businesses fare. They, in turn, are to a great extent dependent on cooperative, businesslike cooperation and support from the financial institutions over which this particular man has considerable influence. Follow-up and continued cooperation after privatization are essential for success.

Sentiments like the two just cited, or the attitudes of managers of public steel and jute operations mentioned earlier that private companies are "the competition," must change if economic progress is to have a chance. The government must encourage, support, and cooperate with the private sector. Privatization is a key element in this evolution.

On the other side, there is much room for improvement from the private sector. There must be a more honest approach to repaying loans and meeting one's obligations. But this is a nationwide social problem, not just businessmen's lack of integrity. Farmers are also not repaying loans, and SOEs have been notorious in not paying off their loans and obligations.

Nonrepayment by recently privatized firms is a national scandal that profoundly affects the soundness of the financial community and has rightly given the business community a bad name. Public reaction has adversely affected chances for further privatization.

The government and the mill owners must come to a resolution of the repayment problem, with concessions on both sides. The government must decide if it really wants the private sector to be profitable.

The government lost money on these enterprises when they were in the public sector. It should be pleased to be spared further drain. It is often forgotten that the government coffers have benefited from the 20-25 percent down payments from privatization transactions. Also, some firms *are* paying off, although they are certainly not in the majority.

Taxes from profits of privatized firms have not been flowing in at expected rates. There are many reasons for this. One of the more important reasons is the need for drastic reform of an incredibly inept and corrupt tax collection system. Privatization and tax reform must go hand in hand.

Foreign Investment

Revenue is certainly needed by the government. One source could be foreign investment. There has been a great deal of talk about this in several highly publicized conferences, but the consensus is that Bangladesh encourages, but does not really welcome foreign investment.

Fortunately, it appears that the government hasn't set its sights unrealistically high in this area. Bangladesh has little to offer in comparison with other, more aggressive LDCs, and the regulatory environment along with the cost and bother of pervasive corruption scares off all but commodity traders. Substantial industrial firms find the atmosphere unattractive.

Cheap labor is not an incentive when it is so unskilled and unmotivated that productivity is abysmally low. Job creation can be a trap if one forgets the need for creating a viable business, as well. This is a matter of concern for domestic as well as foreign businesses. Also, the government has not squarely faced up to dealing with the more violent elements in the labor movement who have helped to create an atmosphere that concerns potential investors.

Foreign investment could be important for the country's industrial development. It is unclear just how far the government will actually permit the local private sector to joint venture with foreign firms, although recent public statements indicate that the government, in principle, favors such transactions. Many observers, however, believe that the government would prefer to keep such arrangements within the public sector. Rumors have sprung up that this has both personal and public motivations. It is obvious that foreign firms would prefer non-public partners.

The government sponsored a major conference on foreign investment in March 1987, but the results were disappointing. The meeting's agenda was too broad and the goals too grandiose. Of over 100 letters of intent, only 10 or 12 resulted in actual proposals, and the majority of even those were not very firm. The government is planning another, more modest meeting for 1989. The emphasis at that meeting and in the future will reportedly be on a few concrete, workable projects.

The 1987 decision to turn down the Singer Corporation's application is mystifying. The government says it wants to leapfrog assembly operations and go directly to manufacture. The same thing has been said about automobile production. Pride seems to have triumphed over good sense. The lessons from Taiwan and elsewhere evidently have been disregarded.

Donor Agencies and Private Sector Development

There is a natural tendency for a government to enter a new field itself rather than support private sector intervention. Bangladesh is certainly not unique in this respect. The EPIDC was commendable in its avowed intention of providing scarce capital and technical assistance to launch a venture and then gradually turn it over to the private sector. EPIDC was not overly successful (at least in this regard) for a number of reasons, one of which was the paucity of investors at the time. Domestic money and investors are more plentiful now.

The government has exhibited a knee-jerk reaction concerning direct entry into new areas. When a problem or an opportunity arises, the government opts to intervene.

Over the years, donor agencies have contributed to this syndrome, for two main reasons: (a) it is easier to provide support to a government agency; and (b) donor agencies, like the Bangladesh government, have not quite come to terms with doing business with business. Some professionals in the foreign aid field still regard direct assistance to profit-seeking private businesses as unseemly.

Attitudes are changing in the international donor community in this regard, however. In Bangladesh, the World Bank has encouraged a number of private sector initiatives. USAID has designed a strategy for general programming in privatization and private enterprise development.[8] Other bilateral programs are doing the same thing, though on a more modest scale. The United Nations has carried out a surprising number of private sector projects (some of them in cooperation with the World Bank) through the UNDP, UNIDO, FAO and ILO.[9] The Asian Development Bank (ADB) now cooperates with the private sector in a wide range of activities.

Even the private Asia Foundation is contemplating programming with the Dhaka Stock Exchange (DSE). The Asia Foundation, with support from USAID/Dhaka, will provide multi-year technical assistance to the DSE for reorganization and for upgrading its services to meet the expected expansion in its activities. The Asia Foundation also sponsored a 1985 conference on privatization by the Bangladesh Young Economists Association.[10]

None of the international donor agencies have shown much desire to program directly in privatization until very recently. They have programmed around the subject, helping private sector development in a variety of direct and indirect ways. USAID, the World Bank, and the ADB have exhorted the Bangladesh government to privatize, but this pressure has not been nearly as great as critics imply. USAID's fertilizer distribution project is the only long-term privatization program carried out by a major donor agency. At present, the World Bank energetically sponsors programs in several private sector areas, with an emphasis on financial markets. But the World Bank still tends to favor reform of SOEs over privatization, despite a continuing record of heavy SOE losses. In Bangladesh, this is both a blind alley and a bottomless pit.

Other projects are being considered by several agencies, but most will be related to private sector development, not directly to privatization as such. Privatization is still considered a political briar patch.

More private investment money is available now than previously. Nevertheless, industrial credit is still a major concern for the small and medium-sized business sectors of the economy that the government hopes to see expand.

When the idea for a special bank to meet these needs was first broached, the immediate inclination in mid-1986 was that the government should establish it.[11]   This flew in the face of what the government was saying about privatization and private sector development. There was no need for establishing a new government entity when other resources, both public and private, were available.

It is somewhat encouraging to note that the government recently revised earlier plans to sponsor a Small Industries Bank. The new bank may now be financed 70 percent from private sources and only 30 percent by the government. The government states that despite its minority equity participation, the bank will be run as a private institution, along strictly commercial lines, but with lower interest rates (10 percent) than those usually offered by private banks (14-18 percent).[12]

Concern has been expressed about the viability of the venture. There is no question that small businesses need better access to credit, but the new bank would need an extensive and expensive network to serve those needs, something potential investors would be reticent to underwrite. Some observers say existing public and private financial institutions could handle this market if given direction by central authorities.

The idea of better credit service to small business is good, but faulty planning and inadequate attention to all aspects of the situation may result in the launching of a bank with few investors and little chance to succeed. It is not clear to what extent the proposition was discussed in advance with potential investors, existing banking institutions, or business leaders. This may be another example of a policy decided in a vacuum by one of the special committees that abound in the Bangladesh government.

Improvement of the Public Enterprise System

Much of the Bangladesh government's attention these days is directed at improving the efficiency and profitability of existing SOEs. This approach appears to be the government's way to distance itself from a stronger but more politically sensitive privatization policy, while building what they now call a "mixed economy." Normally, talk of a mixed economy would be taken as a positive indication. In Bangladesh, it might be a euphemism to mask inaction and lack of political will.

Privatization may be controversial, but no serious observer of the Bangladesh economic scene can believe that the lumbering, lackluster, inefficient public sector can provide the motivating force for dynamic economic growth. The government has tried time and time again to reorganize and revitalize the SOE system, but to no avail. It is a waste of time and money, neither of which Bangladesh can afford. The public sector has required a cash infusion of Tk386 crore (US$138 million) between 1981 and 1985.[13] The World Bank reports that "There has been only one year of net financial surplus (Tk888 million—or US$28.4 million—in FY83) during the FY82-FY87 period, while losses ranged between Tk296 million (US$9.5 million) to Tk2,282 million (US$73 million).[14]

Moudud Ahmed has said that the country can no longer afford to subsidize the public sector to cover losses.[15] Nor is the prospect of replacing costly old equipment attractive. The much larger size of SOEs has not led to economies of scale or improved labor productivity.[16]

The bureaucracy does not seem willing to give the SOEs the degree of autonomy they need to operate aggressively.[17] Even if it did, the enterprises don't have the type of people needed to do the job. First of all, SOEs do not get the cream of the civil service crop, which itself is not as good as before. Second, the personnel the SOEs do have are not trained for competitive marketing and sales promotion. Third, the only type of promotion such people are interested in is moving up through the ranks of the bureaucracy (which is not accomplished by being aggressive but by avoiding mistakes). Fourth, an SOE manager would move on in a couple of years to another post. He is motivated more to "keep his nose clean" than to expand the business, especially by taking risks.

There is some evidence that increasing competition from privatized mills has had a beneficial effect on how SOEs are run,[18] but this effect has been marginal. This does not mean that all SOEs in Bangladesh are inefficient and lose money; depending on the type of operation, some SOEs operate relatively well and generate profits for the treasury. But they usually fall far short whenever any sort of consumer sales and marketplace competition are involved. Quality control is not a hallmark of most SOEs. Most implementing agencies have very little planning capacity, and the work done in their "planning cells" is perhaps better defined as programming.[19]

Many SOEs would not welcome greater autonomy and accountability. They would prefer to hide behind the system and the elaborate government accounting systems. The government is a poor businessman. A slow-moving bureaucracy can hardly be expected to move as quickly and decisively as the competitive marketplace requires.

There are many SOEs in Bangladesh that would be good prospects for privatization if the terms were right. It does not appear that in the short term the government will sell them off, except through the mechanism of the 51-49 Plan. It appears that the government would be willing to gradually sell 100 percent of the shares of many entities this way, but it is unwilling to say so publicly. That very unwillingness will decrease the effectiveness of private sector development initiatives. If the government doesn't believe in what it's doing, why should anyone else?

Selling Shares of Public Enterprises—the 51-49 Plan

For the time being, the government's principal privatization vehicle will most probably be the plan to sell up to 49 percent of the shares of its SOEs.

The general outline of the stock sale plan was described in Chapter 5. This section addresses how the government intends to conduct the program and the internal debate over its purposes and provisions.

The government has given several versions of how many SOEs will be put on the market. On occasion, the government has said that *all* of them will be; but it appears that the program will be tried out with the Rupali Bank, the two DFIs, and four units under BCIC. The choice of the Rupali Bank was a surprise in that it is the most profitable of the four NCBs. Even though the sale of Rupali stock has not gone very well due to lack of investor confidence as the result of staff discontent over the precipitous announcement of the sale, the fact that a profitable bank was put up is encouraging. Many thought the first shares offered would be from Janata Bank, which is in trouble.

Two NCBs (Uttara Bank and Pubali Bank) privatized in 1983-84 have not done very well. The two are said to suffer from shaky management and inadequate capitalization, and have engaged in some questionable lending practices. Largely in response to allegations that the new banks are not sufficiently regulated, in 1984 the government established the banking commission to analyze the banking situation.[20]

The forces within the government pushing for offering attractive investments first in order to get the program going seem to have won the day, at least temporarily. The four BCIC units, while relatively small, are all profitable. This favorable impression is clouded by the offering of BSB and BSRS, the two virtually bankrupt DFIs. In those cases, the government was evidently trying (unsuccessfully) to attract ADB and other foreign investment. A 1984 Price Waterhouse study recommended gradual liquidation of BSRS.[21]

Part of the controversy centers on to whom the government will sell the shares. There has been concern that desirable properties would go to political supporters, but there is little hard evidence of that so far. Nevertheless, caution must be exercised in entrusting an important portion of the economy's fortunes to an institution in which transactions without an element of insider trading may be the exception.

The government has received advice that it should offer only profitable SOEs to the general public. Enterprises with problems and heavy liabilities should only be offered to carefully selected buyers who would know what they're getting into. This was part of a broader debate as to whether the stock sales should generally be open to the public or directed at special, experienced buyers and groups. Because of the concern over accusations of cronyism, the government decided to emphasize open, transparent sales, while reserving the option of selective selling in special cases.

The government has expressed a willingness to be flexible about board membership and management.[22] If private shareholders purchased, say, 33 percent of the stock, they would normally get three of nine seats on the board. Instead, under certain circumstances, they might be given four seats, which is only one seat shy of a majority, plus agreement on the management being privatized. Further, if the employees were permitted to buy 15 percent, they would be given one directorship. This could mean that majority control would pass from government hands. On a five-member board, the ratio might be two government, two private, and one employee director. Several other variations were mentioned. All are theoretical at this point.

Concerning management, a government official said that the Chief Executive Officer (CEO) runs the enterprise and implements board policy. The Chairman of the Board is more of an arbitrator and monitor, who should not interfere in day-to-day affairs. Shafiqur Rahman referred to him as a "watch dog, not a bloodhound," and likened the relationship to the "parliamentary system, where the CEO is the Prime Minister and the Chairman is the Speaker." The Chairman, in all cases, would be appointed by the government until 51 percent of the shares passed into private hands.

The scenarios just described for the 51-49 Plan follow the same general pattern of board and management stipulations ironed out during negotiations on divestiture transactions in 1982 and even earlier. There has been no set pattern. Also, in some cases, the government-appointed chairmen have taken their duties quite seriously (some, in fact, over-zealously), while others have put in only token appearances, leaving the private shareholders almost free rein.

Since most workers are too poor to buy industrial shares, systems have been worked out whereby they can buy into mutual funds, 100 or 200 taka at a time, or pay 50 percent down and the rest in installments. Pension and trust funds are preferred vehicles, but not unions. One aspect that has not been worked out is the status of the employees as shares are sold. At what point do they cease to be civil servants and become private employees? This crucial question must be worked out, because government employees enjoy far better fringe benefits. The government pays great attention to employee reaction now that Disinvestment Resistance Committees are sprouting up as a result of the Rupali Bank affair.

Another interesting government strategy involved in the sale of shares is described below. What follows could apply to the sale of shares at any percentage level, but certainly for shares sold above the 49 percent level. (It was done this way in the 1982 negotiations over jute and textile mill sales.)

The government's first offer is at market value, but very few takers are expected. The second offer is half-way between par and market. If we assume, for purposes of illustration, that par is 100 and market value is 150 (a reasonable figure in Bangladesh), then the second offer is 125, with still not too many takers (they're waiting). The third offer cuts the difference in half again, i.e., to 112.5. At this point, agreement is probably reached. If it isn't, then the shares can be sold at par, but only if the sale is opened to the general public. At this point the Stock Exchange enters into the picture, which will prompt many to accept the 112.5 deal. If there are only a few buyers competing for control, the government's offer for sale at 112.5 would be stronger.

The government would prefer to manage most of the transactions directly or through the official Investment Corporation of Bangladesh. The Dhaka Stock Exchange will, however, have a major role to play. It has grown from 2 offerings in 1976 to 82 today, mostly oversubscribed. Volume of trading in the first quarter of 1987 is above 1986, and already exceeds all of 1984.[23]

Everything is governed by the Companies Act of 1913, as amended. Companies must be one of three types: (a) proprietorship, which involves a single owner (but could be a family); (b) a partnership, up to a maximum of 20; and (c) a limited company, with a minimum of 2 or maximum of 50 if it is a private limited company, or a minimum of 7 and no maximum if it is a public limited company.

Some observers believe that the government is too concerned with making a killing on each deal. The comparison is sometimes made with EPIDC, which was willing to put up seed money and then gradually turn over control. It is surprising to hear how many influential Bengalis, both public and private, hark back with some nostalgia to

Pakistan days as a period of more enlightened policies and level-headed administration.

It is not at all certain how the 51-49 Plan will work out. It will be, however, the government's chosen instrument for privatization for the immediate future.

The Future of Privatization in Bangladesh

The Bangladesh government has never really defined what role it should play in the development of the economy. It cannot restrain itself from interfering directly where it shouldn't, and won't resign itself to the role of planner, guru, coordinator, monitor, and pump primer, where it can be most productive. Also, the government has never articulated what it sees as the proper role of the private sector, other than to say it wants private enterprise to be strong. And it certainly has not spelled out how the two sectors can work in tandem.

Therefore, the government continues to give the ailing public enterprises one shot in the arm after another, while providing inconclusive encouragement to the private sector. Without coming to terms with reality or exerting the influence it should over powerful elites in the country, the government continues to drift and waver. So does the country's economy, except for some segments of the private sector that forge ahead with or without government encouragement, support, and cooperation. Those efforts will not be as productive or widespread as they would be if the government pursued a more consistent development pattern.

Hopefully, government will gradually divest additional enterprises as the politically powered pendulum swings back. It can employ the marginalization and "quiet liquidation" technique used so effectively in other countries (and that has been so successful in the local fertilizer distribution project).

Major divestitures are not the greater likelihood in the foreseeable future, given the indecisiveness of the Ershad government. But there are still 281 public enterprises of all types in all kinds of economic activity.[24] Many could be excellent candidates for privatization of one type or another; but selection of candidates must not be made on an ad hoc basis. Each Corporation and its sub-units must be carefully analyzed. This can only work in a positive fashion if the government lays out a clear road map of where it wants to go and how it plans to get there, industry by industry, in concert with the private sector.

Breaking up some of the larger SOEs is also an attractive alternative for the government to seriously consider. Some of the marketing or manufacturing arms of SOEs can be spun off to the private sector under terms that would be attractive to buyers.

The agribusiness sectoral Corporation (BADC) should be carefully analyzed for candidates. Agribusiness is an area on which Bangladesh should concentrate as a high priority. Privatization possibilities should be correlated with private sector initiatives. Government backing for these exploratory joint efforts should be made available. Privatization of all or part of a large agricultural public enterprise could be a major stimulus to expanding and diversifying the agribusiness sector. This is a trend that should be encouraged in Bangladesh's economy.

The government should keep certain arms or programs of SOEs that are important in terms of social policy. In doing so, however, the government should be aware of the tendency to blame losses on "social goals," when the cause was really poor management or general bureaucratic inefficiency.[25] Large and complex SOEs with major commitments to social programming are good candidates for contract management or franchising of particular arms by non-governmental organizations (NGOs) or private voluntary organizations (PVOs).

The idea is not so much one of getting government out of day-to-day business activity as it is to create a more varied and dynamic economy. But the government is a poor businessman. That is true in most countries, and it has certainly proved to be the case in Bangladesh.

Over the past decade, the private sector has showed more vitality. What is new and growing in the industrial sector has been the result of private sector activity, mostly without direct government participation or assistance. According to the most current figures, private sector activity has been growing at almost twice the rate of the public sector. Private investment doubled between 1981 and 1984, with almost all of the increase in the "free sectors."[26]

Even though expenditures on the public sector have decreased from 20.2 percent of GDP in 1981 to 18.7 percent in 1985,[27] the SOE network still controls 40 percent of the fixed assets in the industrial sector[28] and almost half of the production and value added.[29] Consequently, government decisions about reforming and rehabilitating the public enterprises or continuing to privatize them will be of great significance to the future economic development of the country.

The public sector carries a special importance and responsibility in a subsistence economy. In Bangladesh, while it may be necessary to keep substantial parts of basic industries in the public sector for political and social purposes, the government should be constantly alert for ways to encourage, assist, and cooperate with the private sector in new growth areas.

This effort should be given the highest possible priority, and carried out with a high degree of consistent commitment. In the planning process, special care must be given to clearly defining the complementary roles of the public and private sectors, and to identifying clear and attainable objectives for these initiatives. Special attention must be accorded to ensure forceful and coordinated implementation of privatization and private sector development programs. Such an effort will demand a capability and commitment not previously demonstrated by the Bangladesh government. Nothing less will be sufficient to meet the challenge.

Notes

1. Conversation—Azam, 10/3/86; Conversation—Chishty, 9/29/86.

2. His concern for the health of socialism as such runs throughout his book. See *Public Enterprise in an Intermediate Regime,* op. cit., pp. 197-98, 201-202, 243-44. These are far from the only examples. I cannot dismiss from my mind the thought that Rehman Sobhan's great desire in 1971-72 was to be able to say that he had socialized the country. This is distinct from accomplishing socialist goals for the nation. What we are talking about there is pride in having installed the system as such.

Rehman Sobhan is a man of talent and integrity. It is, therefore, somewhat sad that he is so preoccupied with justifying the decisions (some would say mistakes) of almost 20 years ago, when he could be applying his considerable talents to problems of the future. When he opens his mouth on many issues dealing with economics, you know what he is going to say. That is a shame, because he has much to contribute.

3. "I did not go to break up the party," *The Tide, Special Issue,* Dhaka, Feb.-Mar. 1987, an interview with (then) Deputy Prime Minister Moudud Ahmed.

4. I was resident Country Director in Taipei for The Asia Foundation from 1967-72, and was intimately concerned with Taiwan economic development planning. I have visited the country several times in recent years, including 1983, when I researched and authored *Divestiture of State Enterprises in Taiwan: A Study of an Economy in Transition,* which was AID/PRE's first in-depth study on privatization. In the fall of 1986, I condensed and updated that study for AID/PRE, stopping over in Taipei on the way to Dhaka to undertake the present study on Bangladesh.

5. The reader should be aware that Taiwan started its development program in earnest in 1952, and its privatization effort in 1953. While Bangladesh commenced its post-colonial era in 1947 and, therefore, certain phases of its economic development at that time, complete independence did not come until 1971, with the first stages of a formal privatization policy coming four years later.

6. Almost every government official and business leader contacted for this study offered this opinion.

7. Conversation—Muzaffer Ahmad, Oct. 1986. Ahmad is the co-author with Rehman Sobhan of *Public Enterprise in an Intermediate Regime.* He was Minister of Textiles at one time and, until 1986, was Director of the highly respected Institute of Business Administration at Dhaka University.

8. The present study and the PEDS project are recent examples. The aforementioned fertilizer distribution project has been going for almost a decade. There has also been support for the enterprise development activities of the Micro-enterprise Industrial Development Assistance Society (MIDAS), a fine private organization providing financial and technical assistance to small and medium enterprises of various types.

9. United Nations Development Programme, United Nations Industrial Development Office, Food and Agriculture Organization, and the International Labor Organization. Until recently, the UN has generally been reticent worldwide to promote private sector development, much less privatization, primarily because of ideological resistance within the organization from the communist bloc members. In Bangladesh, however, the UN has undertaken quite a bit of activity in private sector development, because of requests from the Bangladesh government and financial support from the World Bank.

10. See papers and proceedings of Conference and National Seminar on "Impact of Denationalization of Banks and Industries in Bangladesh," held in Dhaka, Nov. 30-Dec. 1, 1984. The papers and proceedings were published in *The Young Economist, the BYEA Journal,* April 1985. The papers are violently opposed to privatization and the scholarship uneven and slanted; but the exercise was useful and illuminating. Incidentally, the Foundation's project with the DSE was identified and developed by me while researching this study.

11. Conversation—Moudud Ahmed, 10/23/86.

12. See PEDS report, op. cit., p. 29, 30, and the notes on the team's debriefing on 5/13/87. By mid-1988, plans were still proceeding for establishing the new bank; but indications are that the government percentage may be more than 30%. Conversation—M. Islam, 7/6/88.

13. WB/Dhaka—Pub. sec., op. cit., p. 12.

14. WB-'88-1, p. vii. The dollar figures are based on an exchange rate of Tk31.25/US$1. It should be noted that the five major Corporations (BJMC, BTMC, BCIC, BSEC and BSFIC) account for 95% of the public enterprise industrial output. ibid, p. 56.

15. "No more subsidy to public sector" *The Bangladesh Observer,* 1/14/87. An exchange rate of Tk28.0/US$1 was used.

16. WB-Bangladesh '85-2, p. 73, 89.

17. WB-'87, p. 66; WB-'88-1, pp. 56-57, 61.

18. Chishty, op. cit., p. 15.

19. WB-'87, p. 87.

20. U.S. Embassy/Dhaka draft cable, sometime in 1984, pp. 6-7. The government has published a lengthy summary of the multi-volume findings of the commission. See *Summary of Recommendations of The National Commission*

on Money, Banking and Credit (Dhaka, Ministry of Finance, Government of Bangladesh, February, 1987).

21. PEDS, op. cit., p. 20 and debriefing on 5/13/87.

22. Much of the material in this section was gleaned from a series of lengthy meetings with Shafiqur Rahman, who was one of the principal designers of IP-'86 and the 51-49 Plan. Numerous other primary and secondary sources and materials were also used to put this section together.

23. PEDS, op, cit., p. 24.

24. See Appendix B, the source for which is Government of Bangladesh, Ministry of Finance: *System For Autonomous Bodies for Reporting and Evaluation* (Dhaka, 1985), as cited in Alamgir, Dr. Muhiuddin Khan: *Public Enterprises and the Financial System in Bangladesh* (Dhaka, September 1986). Unpublished paper by the Managing Director of BSB.

25. WB-Bangladesh '85-2, p. 99.

26. WB-Bangladesh '86-1, p. 123. Of the 144 industrial categories, 125 are now listed as "fee sectors." WB-'88-1, p. 54.

27. ibid, p. 73.

28. ibid, p. 130.

29. ibid, p. 102; PEDS, op. cit., p.6.

8

Conclusions and Recommendations

Conclusions

The conclusions to be drawn from this study can be stated briefly and frankly. Privatization in Bangladesh has been a mixed bag. Statistically, an impressive record has been compiled. Substantively, the results are more difficult to evaluate.

A total of 1,076 public enterprises, 609 of them in the modern industrial sector, have been divested to the private sector; this represents a larger divestiture program than in any other country. The public sector which during the decade of nationalization, controlled over 90 percent of the country's industrial assets, now possesses only 40 percent.

The emergence of the private sector as a major player in the modern industrial sector has not automatically brought prosperity to a troubled, backward, subsistence economy. The economy is still struggling, but there are some encouraging signs, almost all of them emanating from the private sector.

It is difficult to trace, much less gauge, the postprivatization performance of many divested firms. A native unwillingness to share financial information—whether showing profit or loss—combines with the generally unsettled and unstable condition of the Bangladesh economy to thwart the investigator.

In a business community made up of a myriad of medium-sized and ever-changing enterprises, the divested firms have prospered or failed more in relation to the fortunes of their particular industry than because of individual managerial strengths or shortcomings. Privatized firms must be viewed, to a certain extent, as any other private firm, although they may be burdened with residual financial and operational liabilities from their nationalized past with which their counterparts who were private from the start did not have to cope. Some have succeeded, a few have failed, and the rest are limping along. One finds just such a mixture in most developing economies.

In Bangladesh's jumbled, backward economy, there are powerful adverse forces and factors with greater influence in determining an enterprise's fate than its own "performance." Some of these forces and factors arise from the nature of the marketplace in Bangladesh; some stem from the policies, programs, and procedures of the government.

The performance of the collectivity—in this case Bangladesh's private sector—is more significant than the performance of the individual privatized units. Further, the primary focus should be on the privatization of the economy, not on individual privatized state enterprises.

A broader roster of players is engaging in a more varied range of economical activity because of private entrepreneurship. Private investment doubled between 1981 and 1984. Industrial production has increased at twice the rate in the private sector as in the public sector.

The new growth industries—ready-made garments, food processing, light engineering, and pharmaceuticals—have appeared almost exclusively in the private sector, with minimal direct participation by the government. These activities are labor-intensive and mostly export-oriented, two points of priority interest in Bangladesh.

The government's privatization policy has been a key element, perhaps *the* principal stimulus for private sector resurgence. Starting with the cautious moves of 1975, then the "bold stroke" of the NIP-'82 and the IP-'86, privatization has been the symbol of government encouragement of private enterprise.

The transfer of hundreds of enterprises from the public sector has had a profound and lasting influence on industry and commerce at Bangladesh's early stage of economic development. In the country's two leading industries, jute and textiles, the privatized firms have performed better than when they were nationalized and now consistently outperform their counterparts in the public sector. In the ailing jute industry, that may only mean losing less money; but it is a significant indicator nonetheless. Such direct comparisons can be made in other industries, where SOEs complain that they cannot compete with the "flexibility" of private companies, particularly in pricing and marketing.

If there is one overriding conclusion to be drawn from the Bangladesh experience, it is that privatization cannot do the job alone. To be an effective instrument of change, privatization must be integrated with other economic and fiscal programs, and backed up by consistent political will.

With regard to privatization, the Bangladesh government is now in what it calls a "consolidation period," a euphemism indicating that additional major divestitures are not very likely in the next few years (unless the political pendulum swings the other way). For the present, an insecure government will most probably not engage in any bold ventures in privatization, while it generally will continue to encourage private enterprise in building a mixed economy.

Nevertheless, there will be continued, unobtrusive privatization of some state enterprises in ways other than outright divestiture. The government's principal approach in the short range will be the selling of SOE shares through the 51-49 Plan. The government has privately made it clear that it would be willing to sell more than 49 percent under the right circumstances and to make concessions regarding private management of the enterprises to even minority purchasers. This program has its weaknesses; but in the long run, it may have a more significant impact on building a more sophisticated capital market in Bangladesh than its detractors realize.

Given the unstable situation in Bangladesh and the formidable obstacles to sustained growth, predicting economic trends is very risky. Nevertheless, it is not unreasonable to forecast that if no unforeseen economic or political disaster strikes the country, the private sector will play an ever-larger role in the economy. There is no way that substantial and sustained growth can be achieved in Bangladesh's economy with the public sector as the leading player.

As the benefits of increased private activity become more apparent, the chances for additional major privatization moves will become much greater in, perhaps, another three to five years. In the meantime, there will be ample opportunities for selective privatization in addition to buying shares under the 51-49 Plan. For example, large SOEs can be broken up by spinning off sections with greater chances for profitability in the private sector and that do not employ large numbers of workers. Sales and marketing arms would be logical candidates. In other cases, particularly in the agricultural sector, there will be similar opportunities for gradually phasing out cumbersome and inefficient government operations and replacing them with private networks, as has been done so successfully with USAID's fertilizer distribution project.

These examples are merely illustrative. There will be a variety of opportunities. The key will be to ensure that the government plans its economic development more efficiently, fulfills policy goals by better implementation, and keeps alert to identifying industrial areas where it can work cooperatively with private enterprise. If the present ruling group, despite its obvious faults, stays in power, that very continuity will give sound policies (if implemented effectively) a better chance to produce more lasting positive results.

While it may not be possible or even advisable for donor agencies to program forcefully and directly on major privatization initiatives in the near future, the opportunities are infinite for encouraging and assisting the Bangladesh government in promoting private enterprise development. Many of these opportunities will involve privatization of one form or another.

Finally, privatization is a means, not an end in itself. As such the ultimate purpose of privatization is not the unloading of state enterprises, but the privatization of the economy. This, in turn, leads to a more varied, better balanced, and more vibrant economy, with greater benefits to an ever-widening segment of the society.

The following are some recommendations on ways to proceed towards those goals.

Recommendations

These recommendations fall into three groups: those addressed to the Government of Bangladesh, to international donor agencies, and to the local business community. These three sets are not mutually exclusive. They are interdependent and, to be effective, should by implemented in an integrated fashion.

Recommendations for the Government of Bangladesh

It is my firm belief that the Bangladeshis still don't have their act together. Major policy directions and strategies still must be charted out, crucial decisions must be made, and concrete action plans must be designed and implemented. After all, one's house has to be in order before one can get down to specifics. Certain underlying reforms absolutely must be undertaken in Bangladesh before any substantial benefits can be expected from privatization. These reforms include:

- designing and implementing an integrated package of practical policies and programs that clearly demonstrate consistent encouragement and support for private sector development;
- ensuring that the bureaucracy treats the private sector as a valued partner in national economic development, not as an unsavory competitor;
- taking concrete action to streamline procedures, speed up services, and rationalize and liberalize regulations, particularly in regard to imports and financial assistance;
- reforming the tax collection system;
- permitting international donor agencies to deal directly with private sector organizations and companies, with Bangladesh government involvement limited to necessary liaison and monitoring functions;
- curbing the practices of bribe solicitation, influence peddling, and illegal profiteering in both public and private circles, practices that have contributed so heavily to hindering economic progress, weakening the national social fabric and, most important, diverting scarce resources desperately needed for national development.

When measurable gains have been made on these fronts, the following recommendations should be considered for enhancing the contributions that privatization and related initiatives can make toward industrial development, socioeconomic change and modernization.

Recommendation 1. Define privatization goals and objectives. A cabinet-level commission should be appointed to develop a set of precise and practical goals for the government's privatization effort. The commission's report should clearly delineate the purposes of privatization policy and make specific recommendations for implementing it step by step. The report should state exactly what the government expects to achieve through privatization and how it intends to achieve it. The report should avoid eloquent but vague general pronouncements, and should reject the encyclopedic listing of every conceivable item, which has been such a standard feature of previous policy statements. The emphasis should be placed on the practical and attainable. The commission should have the full support of the highest levels of the government and should report its findings within six months.

Recommendation 2. Establish a privatization unit. The government should establish a Privatization/Private Enterprise Development Unit to oversee design and guide implementation of the parallel policies and programs promoting privatization and private sector development.

The proposed unit would provide advice to the highest levels of the government on policy matters related to privatization and private sector development. The unit would also be a principal discussant on the policies and programs relating to the SOE system, and the relation of the SOE system to questions of private sector development in general and privatization in particular. The privatization unit would provide policy guidance and recommend strategies; assist in designing legislation, regulations and programs; monitor performance; and evaluate results.

The unit would oversee the government's policies and programs for SOE divestiture, help ensure inter-ministerial coordination on privatization matters, and play a leading role in organizing and implementing privatization transactions.

The unit would perform a liaison role between the public and private sectors and act as an ombudsman in investigating roadblocks and bureaucratic obstacles to privatization and private sector development. The unit would authorize and supervise policy and administrative research and technical assistance projects related to privatization.

In short, the privatization unit would be a privatization "czar," playing an influential role in developing a varied and vibrant "mixed" economy. The proposed unit should not be confused with the several "disinvestment wings" or "cells" that exist in various ministries for the purpose of supervising the divestiture of SOEs. The proposed unit would function at a higher policy level and have influence over the functioning of the disinvestment wings.

To perform fully its proper function and service to the nation, the privatization unit must be located at the highest possible policy levels of the government and be invested with sufficient power to carry out its mandate. Under ordinary circumstances, the location of the unit should probably be in the Planning Commission; but because of special conditions existing in Bangladesh, this may not be possible or appropriate. If not, the unit should be attached directly to the Office of the President.

Placing the unit in one of the ministries would not be productive, because privatization can be a factor in activities under the jurisdiction of many ministries (Industries, Finance, Commerce, Jute, Textiles, Agriculture, Housing, Transportation, and Health, to mention just a few), and would cause severe turf problems. Under no circumstances should the privatization unit be housed in the Ministry of Finance, where national development is unduly subordinated to immediate fiscal considerations.

Special attention must be given to selecting the right personnel for the unit, particularly its leadership, which should be of unquestioned integrity and stature. The staff must be chosen strictly on the basis of professional credentials and competence. By making the unit a prestigious "elite corps," the government can emulate examples where such units in other developing countries have had resounding success. Building an elite, highly motivated corps was an effective public administration tactic in the colonial days under the Raj.

The unit should not be allowed to deteriorate into an additional layer of government. It should be a policy setter, an expediter, a coordinator, an ombudsman, and a problem solver. The government should make every effort to create an image of the unit as lean, powerful, dedicated, and competent.

Establishing a Privatization/Private Enterprise Development Unit is the top priority recommendation of this study. Experience elsewhere has shown clearly that privatization can be more successful when such a unit is present as a guiding hand. In the case of Bangladesh, the unit would provide policy planning and implementation functions, the lack of which has seriously hampered efforts to date. The unit would also provide donor agencies with a competent and well situated point of entry for influencing policy in constructive, yet discreet ways.

The Planning Commission reported in early 1987 that establishment of a private sector development unit similar to what is suggested here was, in fact, approved in 1983 by the President. It was to be a semi-autonomous unit attached to the Planning Commission. Bureaucratic pressure at the time resulted in the idea being shelved. Conditions warrant bringing it up again. The fact that the general idea has already received the President's endorsement could make resurrection easier, if the proposal is presented correctly.

Recommendation 3. Establish a National Jute Goods Sales Organization. Denationalization of 33 jute mills in 1982 accomplished some positive objectives, but also caused some unforeseen negative results. The desired free market competition degenerated into dog eat dog competition between Bangladeshi and Bangladeshi. This worked to the benefit of international buyers, but to the detriment of the local economy.

While the prices formerly set by the BJMC had been unrealistically high in relation to the cost of competing synthetic fibers, more recent jute prices have been unacceptably low. No one can make money at the present rate.

Cooperation is needed among the public and private mills to present a common front to the international buyers. After that hurdle is passed, legitimate and desirable competition among the Bangladesh mills can be generated through bidding for jute products sales contracts.

A single National Jute Goods Sales Organization (NJGSO) to negotiate *all* international sales contracts on behalf of the entire jute industry would go a long way toward eliminating the destructive price slashing that is crippling an already ailing industry. The NJGSO would be a truly public-private entity, with board members and staff made up of persons from the BJMC, the BJMA, and the Ministry of Jute. The NJGSO would replace existing bodies, which have been singularly ineffective in representing the real interests of the jute industry and the country. The quickest way to launch such an entity would be to spin off the Marketing Division of BJMC and combine it with elements from the BJMA and individual private mills.

To be effective, the NJGSO would operate on a completely commercial basis. A single organization with representatives from all segments of the industry would be in the best position to determine the best free-market price that can be obtained for any order. Through overseas offices, it can better coordinate market analysis and have sufficient power to stimulate the R&D activities so badly needed for quality control and product diversification.

Opposition to setting up a single unit to speak for the industry would be formidable from various vested interests. But the proposed NJGSO would provide a better system than the one present one. Care would have to be taken to avoid the deficiencies and mistakes demonstrated by commodity boards in a number of LDCs (especially former colonies). The NJGSO only superficially resembles a commodity board, but planners should ensure that its mandate is limited to sales and promotion. The NJGSO should not evolve into a jute "czar."

There is a tendency to say, "Ignore jute. It is a dying industry." But the fact remains that jute will continue as Bangladesh's major industry, major foreign exchange earner, and major industrial employer for some time to come. Therefore, every effort must be made to undertake measures that will improve the efficiency and, hopefully, the profitability of the country's most vital industry.

The project for establishing an NJGSO is doubly intriguing in that, if implemented, it would represent the first concrete example of public-private cooperation in a major industrial endeavor. A successful NJGSO would be an important model for other public-private cooperative efforts that are so badly needed in Bangladesh. Therefore, it is essential that the unit be portrayed and operated as a truly joint effort, not a thinly-veiled extension of the official BJMC.

The functions provided by the unit would be beneficial to the 33 mills privatized as the result of NIP-'82. The move would also effectively privatize the government's inept jute marketing arm, replacing it with an entity in which the private sector would have an equal voice. This is constructive privatization, which benefits all parties. The NJGSO would also help to solve a major problem spawned by a poorly planned denationalization program which, while it achieved some beneficial ends, did not anticipate the full implications of the initial, bold action.[1]

Recommendation 4. Perform research and provide technical assistance in the industrial sector related to privatization and private enterprise. Sectoral analyses should be carried out in selected industrial fields, especially those in which the presence of SOEs makes privatization a possibility. Options for various types of privatization should be analyzed, and specific recommendations made. Approaches for encouraging private enterprise activity in those fields should also be a part of this action-oriented research. Also, consultants should be available to provide practical, hands-on technical assistance for particular industries.

Such research and technical assistance could be conducted in any industrial or commercial field with potential for privatization (using the list of industries encouraged in IP-'86), but the following should be given special consideration:

- agri-business, particularly food processing, shrimp raising and processing, tea, tobacco, grain or rice storage and distribution, small tool and equipment manufacture, seeds and milling;
- ship repair;
- rubber products, including recapping;
- small electrical machine manufacture;
- market analysis; and
- light engineering.

Recommendation 5. Resolve the issue of control of the SOE system. The government should resolve the perennial controversy between the line ministries and the sectoral corporations over control of the SOEs.

The dispute should be resolved in favor of the sectoral corporations, and should be combined with parallel administrative reforms to ensure that: (a) SOEs are run on a more businesslike basis, (b) greater SOE managerial autonomy and accountability are encouraged, and (c) bureaucratic interference in SOE operations is lessened.

Recommendation 6. Sell SOE shares. The government should continue, even expand, the plan to sell shares in certain SOEs. The intent should be to eventually sell 100 percent of the shares to private investors. Present political and financial realities, and the unattractiveness of some SOEs as investments, dictate that this be done in gradual stages. Extreme care must be taken to protect the integrity of the share-selling program and to ensure fairness to all potential investors. There will be some SOEs and some functions that should remain in the public sector for reasons of national security, but these should be kept to a minimum.

Recommendation 7. Investigate alternative privatization methods. The advantages and disadvantages of various types of privatization techniques should be carefully investigated to help insure that the appropriate method is used in each case. For example, in one case, optimum results might be best achieved by divestiture, in another case by outright liquidation, or in a third, by spinning off a particular portion or function of an SOE. The suitability of different privatization techniques and approaches should be considered, not only with regard to the privatization of individual enterprises, but also when contemplating privatization of a general function or a particular industry. A combination of methods may be the best approach in the latter case.

Recommendation 8. Continue the privatization of fertilizer distribution. The gradual privatization of fertilizer distribution has proceeded for more than eight years. The program, financed by USAID, has met with considerable success in the retail field, and is now expanding to storage and wholesale levels. The program has become a model emulated in other developing countries, particularly in those where the economy is heavily dependent on agriculture. The Government of Bangladesh is to be complimented for encouraging and sticking with this program, which has been both complex and controversial. The fertilizer industry is of great importance to Bangladesh. The program should be continued, even expanded into other areas of this and other industries.

One of the interesting features of this particular privatization program is that instead of following Bangladesh's usual pattern of divestiture, it has phased down government operations while gradually replacing them with private sector activity.

Recommendation 9. Renegotiate the 1982 divestiture agreements for jute and textile mills. The nonpayment of loans connected with the divestiture of 33 jute mills and 27 textile mills in 1982 has been one of the most troublesome economic problems facing the country in recent years. The varied and adverse effects of this dilemma are well-known and documented, but the time has come to take another look at this unfortunate situation.

There has been fault on both sides. There is no question that the buyers have been derelict in fulfilling the terms of the agreements they signed, particularly their obligation to pay off their loans. Nonpayment of debts has become a national social malaise. The government must be aggressive in regard to collection. Many observers point out, however, that the original terms were unrealistic, even unfair. The buyers had to accept all of the liabilities, and were burdened with impossible interest payments. In some (though not all) cases, the assets were overvalued. The government has made some adjustments already because of further inequities created by necessary devaluation of the currency; but other concessions should be made.[2]

In the best interests of the country, these disputes, which involve the nation's two major industries, must be resolved. Concessions will have to be made on both sides. This will not be easy, not only because of the rigid positions of the two parties, but also because of the great sensitivity of this matter in the eyes of the general public. But the strategic importance of the issues involved makes action and resolution imperative.

Recommendation 10. Realistically valuate SOE assets. The valuation of an SOE's assets is a very complex, technical matter. This is particularly true when a large entity is to be completely divested. Often, however, valuation is as much influenced by political considerations as by accounting factors. For example, government auditors in most developing countries tend to compute the value of the assets on the basis of book value. They use this standard, instead of market value, for fear of being criticized as giving away the country's patrimony to the wealthy or to political cronies. In most cases, however, market value is a far more accurate gauge of actual value. Another factor is that the byzantine systems that most LDC governments employ make honest and accurate valuation very difficult. Many of these systems seem designed for obfuscation, rather than elucidation. What many government auditors and officials fail to consider, and what the government must constantly keep in mind, is that once privatized, the new business should be in a financial position that gives it a fair chance to survive. If the enterprise fails because of too heavy a debt burden, no one gains. Under present conditions in Bangladesh, many of the purchasers of SOEs are faced with unduly heavy debt burdens. If they fall behind on payments, they are not permitted to use the assets of the firm in trying to obtain loans. A downward cycle is inevitable. SOEs should not be sold at fire sale prices, but the negotiated price must reflect realistic value and not endanger the enterprise's viability from the start. The government's objectives for economic development are best served by a thriving private sector. The government should look at the transaction as a way to end losses and therefore should curb the impulse to make a killing on every transaction.

Recommendation 11. Conduct research on labor/employee aspects of privatization. The labor question is one of the most volatile and contentious issues connected with privatization of state enterprises in Bangladesh. Government and business have not come up with satisfactory solutions for the many problems involved, such as comparable fringe benefits, severance packages, retraining programs, employer-employee relations, labor negotiations, employee stock option programs (ESOP), and the like. Research should be undertaken to study these issues and make appropriate recommendations that could be used in negotiations related to privatization transactions.

In a number of countries, developed and underdeveloped, ESOP has been a useful tool for lessening labor's fears and criticisms of privatization. Such plans give workers a stake in the enterprise. Even when their holdings are quite small, being a part owner often changes workers' attitudes toward management and work performance.

Recommendation 12. Educate the public about privatization. One of the biggest weaknesses of privatization programs in most LDCs, including Bangladesh, is that insufficient attention is given to public education and advance notice about privatization moves. More often than not, particular privatization moves are sprung upon the public and workers with little or no notice.

The results of such action are almost always negative. The ruckus over the proposed sale of Rupali Bank shares in early 1987 is a good case in point. Because of no advance notice or consultation, the staff immediately walked off the job. Also, subsequent sale of shares has been slower than the value of the stock would warrant. Both unsatisfactory results could have been avoided with proper preparation.

The government should trust its people and their judgment. The government has an obligation to explain why it is pursuing a certain policy, and to lay out for all parties and to the whole country the benefits of the action. The government may find out to its surprise that transparency of privatization transactions will work to its own benefit. Lacking such a public affairs effort, the government has left the field of influencing public opinion to its opponents.

Recommendation 13. Improve relations between SOEs and the private sector. The government should encourage public sector organizations, whether they be individual SOEs or offices of the bureaucracy, to cooperate with the private sector in promoting economic progress. This can be done when developing markets, both domestic and international, and on individual transactions.

As part of this policy, the government should strive to ensure that favoritism in not shown to SOEs over private enterprises in the allocation of resources, purchasing, sales contracts, and the like. The government must be forceful in changing long-held prejudices within the bureaucracy.

Recommendation 14. Conduct research on privatization and related policy issues. A well-planned and organized program of research should investigate fields of direct relevance to privatization and economic development, with the emphasis on public policy and administration. Such fields include:

- policy formulation and decision making;
- organization for planning;
- relationship of policy and implementation;
- integrated private sector development programs;
- cooperation between public and private sectors;
- valuation of state enterprise assets;
- legal issues involved in privatization;
- regulatory environment, particularly import regulations;
- rationalization of the tax system, reform of both policy and collection;
- dissemination and interpretation of regulations and changes in procedures within the bureaucracy.

The research would be supervised by the privatization unit and would include both Bangladeshi and foreign researchers. All of the research topics listed above are areas in which Bangladesh has been weak. Lack of information in these areas has adversely affected implementation of an effective privatization policy.

Recommendation 15. Observe privatization in other Asian countries. Bangladesh has much to learn about how to plan, organize, and implement a comprehensive privatization program; even though Bangladesh has put through more privatization transactions than any other country. There are several Asian countries that have successfully carried out privatization programs of various types. Small groups of carefully-selected Bangladeshi government and business leaders should visit such countries. The tour group should be evenly balanced between public and private members.

The countries to be visited could include South Korea, Taiwan, Malaysia, Singapore, Thailand, and India. Sri Lanka, Indonesia, Japan, and the Philippines could also be considered. It would probably be the most productive to visit Asian countries. Of course, observation on other continents could be considered, if the conditions were appropriate to Bangladesh's situation and needs.

Each tour should include visits to no more than four countries; and the itinerary and makeup of participants should be designed to emphasize particular aspects of privatization and private sector development. Programs should be intensive and professional, so that the trips do not end up as pleasure junkets. Visits to each country should be arranged well in advance, and set up for stays of four to seven days.

Internships of three to six months should be explored, especially for Bangladeshi civil servants dealing with privatization matters. The privatization unit would be the ideal agency to coordinate the tour programs.

Recommendations for International Donor Agencies

Most of the recommendations in this study are directed at the government of Bangladesh, because it has been, and will continue to be, the primary implementing agency for privatization policies and transactions.

What is to be said to the international donor community is more in the form of general guidance, with a few specific suggestions about how to organize for privatization work. Most, though not all, of the preceding fifteen recommendations would be suitable programming vehicles for the major international donors.

More pertinent and productive programming in private enterprise development could be generated if donor agencies displayed a greater willingness to deal directly with the private sector. But most foreign aid organizations, staffed as they are with civil servants, seem to feel more comfortable programming with government institutions. Most have failed to come to terms with doing business with business. Effective programming in and for the private sector will depend, to a significant extent, on a reversal of that attitude.

Perhaps the most glaring shortcoming of international donors in approaching privatization is their tendency to pay insufficient attention to local circumstances and ways of doing things. There is an inclination, especially among multilateral agencies, to assume a rather olympian posture, dispensing highly technical and generalized solutions based on theories and models from developed countries.

It is often difficult to dispute the pure economic logic of this prescription. Aid-dependent LDCs are in a vulnerable position for arguing, in any case. But one wonders to what extent these generic solutions and ultimata are based on local conditions, needs, aspirations, and capabilities.

Frequently, donors approach privatization in more ideological terms than their clients. The emphasis should be placed more on what will work in a given society, in a given bureaucracy, under the special set of conditions existing in a particular country. Bangladesh is a very poor country, with horrendous economic and development problems. Its special circumstances require tailored solutions, not universal prescriptions.

Developing countries should not use a cultural shield to avoid needed change. But donors must be perceptive, empathetic, and flexible. A little pressure is not necessarily a bad thing. Without some prodding, change may not come. But donors should also guard against intellectual and economic arrogance.

Private sector development would benefit from greater direct involvement of donors with the local business community—actual project involvement, not just social contact. The donors must overcome the resistance the Bangladesh government has shown about direct programming.

Patience is not just a virtue when working in Bangladesh; it is an absolute necessity. One must be content with small gains and limited victories. Donors seeking quick and striking impact from their well-intended efforts are doomed to frustration.

Private consultants are more able to speak their minds than diplomats and aid administrators, who are forced to work under political restraints. Nevertheless, donors must be more frank in dealing with Bangladeshi officials, and must demand more accountability (substantive as well as financial).

Working empathetically does not mean being oblivious to, or glossing over shortcomings. In a sense, greater frankness demonstrates greater respect, though it may ruffle feathers. A recent major donor's review of Bangladesh's civil service, while citing a few obvious problems, generally viewed everything through rose-colored glasses. More to the point, the document made no mention whatsoever of corruption. The report was not merely useless; its failure to investigate or even mention major problems and deficiencies made it downright misleading and dangerous.

The remaining suggestions to donor agencies revolve around organizational preparation for engaging in privatization and private sector programming activity. None of the Dhaka offices of major donors are professionally prepared for extensive programming in these two related fields. Therefore, it is recommended that they seriously consider doing some of the following:

- appoint a privatization/private enterprise officer to take the leading role in planning, coordinating, and monitoring projects in privatization and private enterprise development;
- establish a privatization/private enterprise committee to review all project proposals, planning documents, program materials, etc., to determine if each of the agency's proposed activities have the potential for a private sector component;
- support staff training in enterprise development and privatization through participation in appropriate training programs, conferences, seminars, workshops, and observation tours concerned with privatization and private enterprise development;
- improve liaison and exchange of information within the donor community to ensure better coordination of programming activity in privatization and private enterprise development; and
- expand and deepen agency relations and programming with the private sector through cultivation of contacts with local business leaders, memberships in local business organizations, with the aim of increasing direct programming with the industrial/business community and individual companies.

Recommendations for the Local Business Community

Frequently in Bangladesh, business and government resemble warring camps. Most of the responsibility for both the problem and the solution rests with the government, but there is much that the business community should do to improve the situation.

The business community must put its own house in order. Although business has not, by and large, acted as badly as its popular reputation would indicate, there is no doubt that certain attitudes and practices must change.

Greater appreciation of public service and social responsibility must be engendered. This is a problem in almost every country, but is especially acute in Bangladesh.

Greater willingness to meet obligations must be displayed. At a minimum, the tendency of some to take the view that "profits are mine, losses are the government's," must be discarded.

The several large and influential chambers of commerce can be instruments of self-policing and change. The Federation of Bangladesh Chambers of Commerce and Industry (FBCCI) has the broadest base; the Metropolitan Chamber of Commerce and Industry (MCCI) is the most powerful; and the Dhaka Chamber of Commerce and Industry (DCCI) is perhaps the most practical in terms of engaging in what is normally considered as chamber activities.

As a group, the major chambers are influential bodies that can have a significant impact on the success of privatization initiatives, as well as private sector development in general. They are not at present fulfilling their potential for constructive contribution to private sector development, however. In general, they represent narrow interest groups and promote the agenda of the leadership rather than the general membership. They do not yet offer the broad range of services and activities normally associated with chambers of commerce in the United States.

The chambers of commerce have, however, been the private sector's only spokesmen to the general public and the government. The chambers do have enormous potential for effective promotion of privatization and private sector development. Therefore, the following types of cooperative activities are recommended for the chambers, which would expand and improve their operations:

- The chambers should develop statements of business ethical standards, and introduce measures to police their membership for compliance. An energetic campaign of this type, coupled

with public education activities, could help to improve the poor public image of the business community that has so adversely affected privatization policy.
- Generally, poor management has characterized the performance of many privatized firms. Management and management training need to be professionalized. The chambers are ideally suited to conduct practical management training courses for Bangladesh business firms. In other countries, the business community has sponsored better professional management training than academic institutions (e.g., Taiwan and Malaysia).
- Small and medium-sized businesses are not well represented by current chambers (although the DCCI does a better job at this than the others). Consequently, small and medium-sized enterprises do not look to the current chambers for guidance and help. This is unfortunate, since these smaller enterprises need help the most. The larger firms can take better care of themselves. Also, the interests of the smaller firms are not taken into account in chamber representations to the government. The government wishes to expand the small business sector, feeling, rightly, that the future economic development of Bangladesh is dependent on expanding small business opportunities.

Therefore, it is strongly recommended that a federation of small and medium-sized businesses be formed, either as a separate organization or as a semi-autonomous arm of an existing body. The latter is probably more practical because of the resistance to the idea that would come from the established business community elite.

The proposed small business federation should have a countrywide spread, because the potential is great throughout provincial areas for development of small business. The potential for privatization in agri-business fields is greatest in provincial towns.
- A public-private liaison council should be formed as an informal but continuing forum for discussion of economic development and business issues, including privatization. Similar councils have been effective in other countries. Business leaders meet with government economic officials on a monthly or bi-monthly basis. Continuing contact can help to avoid strident and destructive confrontation in crisis periods. Such a forum can increase two-way flow of information and promote mutual understanding. The present government has not devoted enough attention to meeting with business leaders below the top policy levels.

There are lessons to be learned from Bangladesh's privatization experiment, some positive, some negative. Certain features are unique to the Bangladesh scene, but many are applicable to problems and conditions in other countries. There are common threads that transcend political boundaries, economic situations, or cultural barriers. If thoughtfully analyzed and adapted, Bangladesh's experience can be useful to planners in other developing lands contemplating privatization, while struggling with the complexities of economic development.

Those with interests centering on another country must consider the particular objectives, strategies, circumstances, and action plans of that country. They must also determine what can be extrapolated from the Bangladesh experience and what must be done differently, and why. This was my intent in posing the two sets of questions in the introductory chapter. In the final analysis, the utility of the Bangladesh story will depend on the willingness of other countries to face issues squarely and engage in rigorous self-analysis as they go through their own socioeconomic transitions.

Notes

1. Credit for the idea for a vehicle like the NJGSO should be given to a fine report done by John Kelly and a Price Waterhouse team for the Bangladesh government. Kelly, John, et al: *Review of the Operations of the Bangladesh Jute Mills Corporation* (Dhaka, Price Waterhouse Asia Pacific, July 1985), passim. Especially see a special policy-oriented report Kelly prepared for the government a year later: *Bangladesh Jute Goods Industry: Policies and Actions for Overcoming Existing Problems* (Dhaka, Price Waterhouse Asia Pacific, September 25, 1986).

2. It should be noted that the government took a different stance when it took over private sector enterprises in 1972. At that time, the government's position was that the SOEs should be free from the burden of debts and other liabilities incurred during the war preceding liberation and nationalization. See footnote 62 of Chapter 3 , in which Yusuf was cited, op. cit., p. 165.

Acronyms and Abbreviations

ADB	Asian Development Bank
BADC	Bangladesh Agriculture Development Corporation
BBS	Bangladesh Bureau of Statistics
BCIC	Bangladesh Chemical Industries Corporation
BEA	Bangladesh Economists Association
BFIDC	Bangladesh Forest Industries Development Corporation
BJMA	Bangladesh Jute Mills Association
BJMC	Bangladesh Jute Mills Corporation
BKB	Bangladesh Krishi Bank
BMEDC	Bangladesh Minerals Exploration Development Corporation
BPC	Bangladesh Petroleum Corporation
BSB	Bangladesh Shilpa Bank
BSEC	Bangladesh Steel & Engineering Corporation
BSFIC	Bangladesh Sugar & Food Industries Corporation
BSRS	Bangladesh Shilpa Rin Sangstha (bank)
BTMA	Bangladesh Textile Mills Association
BTMC	Bangladesh Textile Mills Corporation
BYEA	Bangladesh Young Economists Association
CIDA	Canadian International Development Agency
CONOPE	Consulting Committee of Public Enterprises
CRPSC	Committee for Reorganization of Public Statutory Corporations
DCCI	Dhaka Chamber of Commerce and Industry
DFI	development finance institution

179

DGI	Director General of Industries
DPM	Deputy Prime Minister
DSE	Dhaka Stock Exchange
DWT	dead weight tons
ECNEC	Executive Committee of the National Economic Council
EPIDC	East Pakistan Industrial Development Council
ESOP	employee stock option program
FAO	Food and Agriculture Organization
FBCCI	Federation of Bangladesh Chambers of Commerce and Industry
FFYP	first five-year plan
GDP	gross domestic product
GNP	gross national product
HPFB	High-Powered Facilities Board
ICB	Investment Corporation of Bangladesh
IESC	International Executive Service Corps
ILO	International Labor Organization
IP-'86	Industrial Policy of 1986
LDC	less developed country
MCCI	Metropolitan Chamber of Commerce and Industry
MIDAS	Micro Industry Development Assistance Society
MLA	Martial Law Authority
MOC	Ministry of Commerce
MOCI	Ministry of Commerce and Industry
MOF	Ministry of Finance
MOI	Ministry of Industries
MT	metric tons
NCB	nationalized commercial bank
NCID	National Committee for Industrial Development
NGO	non-governmental organization
NIP-'82	New Industrial Policy of 1982
NJGSO	National Jute Goods Sales Organization
NRP	national reserve price
P&L	profit and loss
PC	Planning Commission
PEDS	Private Enterprise Development Studies
PIDC	Pakistan Industrial Development Council
PL480	U.S. Public Law 480
P.O.	presidential order
PVO	private voluntary organization
Rp	rupee
SFYP	second five-year plan
SOE	state-owned enterprise

TFYP   third five-year plan
TIP   Trade and Industry Program
Tk   taka
UN   United Nations
UNDP   United Nations Development Programme
UNIDO   United Nations Industrial Development Organization
USAID   U.S. Agency for International Development
WB   World Bank (actually IBRD or International Bank for
          Reconstruction and Development)
WPIDC   West Pakistan Industrial Development Council

Bibliography

Bangladesh Government Documents and Studies

The Third Five Year Plan, 1985-90 (Planning Commission, Ministry of Planning, Government of the People's Republic of Bangladesh, Dec. 1985).

East Pakistan Act No. VIII of 1985: The Employment of Labor (Standing Orders) Act, 1965 (as modified up to May 31, 1983). Ministry of Law and Land Reforms, Law and Parliamentary Affairs Division, Government of Bangladesh, 1985.

The Industrial Relations Ordinance, 1969. Ordinance No. XXIII of 1969 (as modified up to May 31, 1983). Ministry of Law and Land Reforms, Law and P.A. Division, Government of Bangladesh, 1984.

The Bangladesh Abandoned Property (Control, Management and Disposal) Order, 1972. President's Order No. 16 of 1972 (as modified up to May 31, 1983). Ministry of Law and Land Reforms, Law and P.A. Division, Government of Bangladesh, 1984.

The Bangladesh Bank (Nationalization) Order, 1972. President's Order No. 26 of 1972 (as modified up to July 31, 1982). Ministry of Law and Land Reforms, Law and P.A. Division, Government of Bangladesh, 1982.

The Bangladesh Industrial Enterprises (Nationalization) Order, 1972. President's Order No. 27 of 1972 (as modified up to March 31, 1977). Ministry of Law and Parliamentary Affairs, Government of Bangladesh, 1977.

The Bangladesh Industrial Enterprises (Vested) Order, 1972. Presidential Order No. 27 of 1972 (as modified up to March 31, 1977). Ministry of Law and Parliamentary Affairs, Government of Bangladesh, 1977.

The Transfer of Property Act, Act. IV of 1982 (as modified up to May 31, 1983). Ministry of Law and Land Reforms, Law and Parliamentary Affairs Division, Government of Bangladesh, 1984.

The Companies Act, 1913, Act No. VII of 1913 (as amended up to 1986). (Reprinted by Lahore Law Times Publications, Lahore, 1986).

Revised Investment Policy, Ministry of Industries, Industries Division, Government of Bangladesh, Dec. 7, 1975. (Includes New Investment Policy of July 1974 as an Appendix.)

New Industrial Policy, Ministry of Industry and Commerce, Industries Division, Government of Bangladesh, June 1, 1982.

Industrial Policy—1986, Ministry of Industries, Government of Bangladesh, July 1986.

Formation of a Company in Bangladesh, Ministry of Industries, Department of Industries, Government of Bangladesh, Jan. 1982.

Guide to Investment in Bangladesh, Ministry of Industries, Department of Industries, Government of Bangladesh, Jan. 1982.

Performance of Nationalized Industries, 1974-75, Ministry of Industries, Nationalized Industries Division, Government of Bangladesh, Sept. 29, 1975.

Brief on Mining and Mineral Based Industries in Bangladesh, Bangladesh Mineral Exploration & Development Corporation, Government of Bangladesh, May 1981.

Priority List of Industries for the Years 1974-76 of Industrial Investment Schedule for the First Five-Year Plan 1973-78, Government of Bangladesh, 1974.

Bangladesh Standard Industrial Classification of All Economic Activities 1980 (BSIC-1980), Bangladesh Bureau of Statistics, Statistics Division, Ministry of Planning, Government of Bangladesh, July 31, 1980.

Directory of Selected Industrial Products, Ministry of Industries & Commerce, Department of Industries, Government of Bangladesh, Jan. 2, 1984.

Industrial Investment Schedule for Two Years (1978-1980) for Private Sector, Ministry of Industries, Department of Industries, Government of Bangladesh, Oct. 2, 1978.

Nationalized Industries, Ministry of Industries, Nationalized Industries Division, Government of Bangladesh, July 20, 1974.

Nationalized Industries—Third Quarterly Review for the Period Ending March 31, 1975, Ministry of Industries, Nationalized Industries Division, Government of Bangladesh, May 3, 1975.

Detailed Estimates of Revenue and Receipts, 1986-87, Ministry of Finance, Finance Division, Government of Bangladesh, 1986.

Industrial Development in Bangladesh—Achievements and Potentials (Dhaka, Bangladesh Export Promotion Bureau, 1982?).

Industry, Bangladesh (Dhaka, Bangladesh Export Promotion Bureau, 1983).

Price Waterhouse Asia Pacific: *Review of the Operations of the Bangladesh Jute Mills Corporation.* A report to the Government of Bangladesh, Dhaka, July 1985.

Kelly, John R.: *Bangladesh Jute Goods Industry: Policies and Actions for Overcoming Existing Problems.* A special report by Price Waterhouse Asia Pacific to the Ministry of Jute, Government of Bangladesh, Dhaka, Sept. 25, 1986.

Price Waterhouse Asia Pacific: *Review of the Bangladesh Textile Mills Corporation,* Vol. I—a draft report to the Government of Bangladesh (Dhaka, March 1986).

Bangladesh Census of Manufacturing Industries, Summary Report: 1977-78 (Dhaka, Bangladesh Bureau of Statistics, Mar. 1986).

Bangladesh Census of Manufacturing Industries, Detailed Report: 1981-82 (Dhaka, Bangladesh Bureau of Statistics, Mar. 1986).

Statistical Pocket Book of Bangladesh—1986 (Dhaka, Bangladesh Bureau of Statistics, 1986).

Bangladesh/UNDP Fourth Country Programme (1986-1991), (Dhaka, United Nations Development Programme, June 1986).

United Nation's Development Programme: *Annual Country Programme Review, Bangladesh* (Dhaka, UNDP, Sept. 1986).

Arthur D. Little, Inc.: *Opportunities for Investment in Bangladesh in Fruit, Vegetable, and Spice Processing* (Trade & Industrial Policy Reform Programme, Government of Bangladesh, May 1984).

Summary of Recommendations of The National Commission on Money, Banking and Credit (Dhaka, Ministry of Finance, Government of Bangladesh, Feb. 1987).

Publications of the Trade and Industrial Policy (TIP) Reform Programme:

Engineering Industries in Bangladesh—A Review, a Report by the Industrial Investment Promotion Unit—TIP-IIPU-A-15, June 1985.

The Cotton Spinning Industry in Bangladesh, by Ole David Koht Norbye, Planning and Project Identification Unit—TIP-PPIU.B-8, Jan. 1984.

An Overview of Assistance Policies for Agro-Based Industries, Management Unit—TIP-MU-C, May 1986.

Leather and Leather Products Industries in Bangladesh, Report by the Industrial Investment Promotion Unit and the Development of Potential Export Product Lines Unit—TIP-IIPU-DPEP-C-9, Jan. 1984.

Report on Edible Oils Industry, by S.A. Ather, Effective Protection Study Unit, TIP-EPSU-C-11, April 1985.

Assistance Overview for Chemical and Allied Sectors, Management Unit, TIP-MU-D, Feb. 1986.

Overview of Industrial Investment Incentives, Management Unit, TIP-MU-F, March 1986.

Private Investment in Bangladesh—An Optimistic Appraisal, by Bernard Wasow, Investment Incentive Study Unit, TIP-IISU-F.5, June 1985.

Industrial Planning for the Private Sector, 1973-83, by M.A.H. Khandker, Planning and Project Identification Unit, TIP-PPIU-F.9, Sept. 1984.

An Evaluation of the "One Stop" Service in the Department of Industries, by K.M. Sakhawatullah, Industrial Investment Promotion Unit, TIP-IIPU-F.10, Feb. 1985.

Assistance to Export Development in Bangladesh: An Evaluation, by A. Rab, Planning and Project Identification Unit, TIP-PPIU-G.3, Dec. 17, 1984.

Overview on Policies to Improve Performance Monitoring of Public Sector Enterprises in Bangladesh, by R.D. Mallon, et al, Management Unit, TIP-MU-1, May 1986.

Monitoring the Performance of the Bangladesh Jute Mills Corporation, by R.D. Mallon, Planning and Project Identification Unit, TIP-PPIU-I-1, Dec. 1983.

U.S. Government Documents and Publications

U.S. Agency for International Development: *Country Development Strategy Statement—FY 1986—Bangladesh,* (Washington, D.C., USAID, Jan. 1984).

USAID Country Development Strategy Statement—Bangladesh FY 1983, (Washington, D.C., USAID, Feb. 1981).

USAID Annual Budget Submissions: Bangladesh, FY 1986, FY 1987, FY 1988 (Washington, D.C., USAID). (Note especially "USAID/ Dhaka Privatization Plan" from FY 1988 Budget, June 19, 1986).

U.S. Embassy/Dhaka—draft cable, 2/22/87, dealing with Bangladesh government privatization policy issues, particularly selling of up to 49% of the shares of Rupali Bank, BSB, and BSRS—unclassified.

U.S. Embassy/Dhaka—draft cable, dealing with Bangladesh government privatization policy 1982-84—unclassified, 1984.

U.S. Embassy/Dhaka—cable 0 1406582, Jan. 1987, dealing with Bangladesh economic resources and prospects—unclassified.

Ahmed, Nizam U.: *A Visit to The Bangladesh Textile Mills Association.* A Report to USAID/ECON/Dhaka, July 18, 1984. Mr. Ahmed is a member of the staff of USAID/ECON/Dhaka.

——— : *Improvement in LDC Development Performance: Bangladesh, Country Specific* (A paper presented at the Development Studies Program Course, USC Center, Washington, D.C., Jan. 26, 1986).

Antholt, Charles H. and Wennergren, Boyd E.: *Fertilizer Marketing in Bangladesh: Toward Privatization* (Dhaka, USAID, April 1983).

"Privatization," *Front Lines* (Washington, D.C., USAID, Feb. 1986), a supplement containing 18 short articles.

"Implementing A.I.D. Privatization Objectives," *Policy Determination* (Washington, D.C., USAID, June 16, 1986).

AID and Its Private Sector Initiative Action Brief (Washington, D.C., The President's Task Force on International Private Enterprise, Dec. 1984).

A Review of AID's Experience in Private Sector Development. AID Program Evaluation Report No. 14, by Robert R. Nathan Associates. (Washington, D.C., USAID, April 1985).

Private Enterprise Development: an AID Policy Paper (Washington, D.C., USAID, 1985).

The Private Sector in Bangladesh: USAID and the Local Market Economy (USAID/Dhaka, Feb. 1984).

Background Notes—Bangladesh (Washington, D.C., U.S. Department of State, Bureau of Public Affairs, July 1984).

Investment Climate in Bangladesh (Washington, D.C., U.S. Department of Commerce, International Trade Administration, Dec. 1984).

"Leading Items in U.S. Total Imports to and Exports from Bangladesh 1981-1985," (Washington, D.C., U.S. Department of Commerce, International Trade Administration, Feb. 1986).

Marketing in Bangladesh. Overseas Business Reports (Washington, D.C., U.S. Department of Commerce, International Trade Administration, Oct. 1984).

Study to Determine Procedures Required and Benefits from Allowing Private Sector Firms to Import Fertilizer—draft proposal (Dhaka, USAID, Feb. 1987).

Turner, James: *Approaches to Privatization* (Washington, D.C.,USAID/ S&T, 1986), unpublished draft.

Uniform Urea Ex-Factory Price Policy Study—draft proposal (Dhaka, USAID, Feb. 1987).

"Privatization & the Private Sector: Keys to Third World Development,"
    AID Highlights, Summer 1986 (Washington, D.C., Agency for
    International Development).
Tom Friedkin, Robert Lester, Herbert Blank, & Nizam U. Ahmed:
    Bangladesh Small-Scale Irrigation (Washington, D.C., Agency for
    International Development, April 1983). A.I.D. Project Impact
    Evaluation Report No. 42.
Bangladesh Enterprise Development Project, (Dhaka, USAID, 1986). Project
    #388-0066.
Fertilizer Distribution Improvement II: Project Paper, Project #388-0060
    (Dhaka, USAID, August 1984).
*Foreign Economic Trends and Their Implications for the United States—
    Bangladesh, April 1987* (Washington, D.C., U.S. Department of
    Commerce, International Trade Administration, 1987). Prepared
    by the American Embassy, Dhaka, for the International Markeitng
    Information Series. (Note: issue of April 1986 also consulted.)
"Debt/Equity Swaps," U.S. Department of State cable #186002, drafted
    by AID/PPC/PDPR (Washington, D.C., June 17 1987).
Cowan, L. Gray: *Divestment and Privatization of the Public Sector: Case
    Studies of Five Countries* (Washington, D.C., USAID/PPC/EDD,
    Dec. 1983). Case studies of Jamaica, Kenya, Sudan, Indonesia
    and Bangladesh, with notes on Malaysia.
_____ : *Privatization in South East Asia* (Washington, D.C., USAID/
    PPC/PDPR/EPD, Trip Report, Feb. 1985).
_____ : *Some Practical Issues of Divestment and Privatization Facing LDC
    Governments* (Washington, D.C., USAID/PPC/PDPR/EPD, June
    25, 1985). Reprinted by the Center for Privatization, Washing-
    ton, D.C.
_____ : *Privatization: A Technical Assessment* (Washington, D.C., USAID,
    Sept. 1987), a paper prepared for the Office of Policy Develop-
    ment and Program Review, Bureau for Program and Policy
    Coordination, USAID.
Steinberg, David: *Private Enterprise Development: A Review of AID Ex-
    perience* (Washington, D.C., USAID, July 7, 1982).

Books, Studies, Monographs, and Reports

Alamgir, Muhiuddin Khan: *Development Strategy for Bangladesh* (Dhaka,
    Dhaka University Centre for Social Studies, 1980).
_____ : *Public Enterprises & The Financial System in Bangladesh.* (Unpub-
    lished paper by the Managing Director of Bangladesh Shilpa
    Bank, Dhaka, Sept. 1986).

Ameen, H.H. Mansurul: *A Study of Divestment of Industries in Bangladesh* (in 2 vols.), Vol. I—Main Report (Dhaka, Canadian International Development Agency, March 1987).

Analysis of the Causes of Inflated Loan Liabilities of Denationalised Jute Mills (Dhaka, Metropolitan Chamber of Commerce and Industry, 1986).

Baxter, Craig: *Bangladesh, A New Nation in an Old Setting* (Boulder and London, Westview Press, 1984).

Berg, Elliot: *Changing the Public-Private Mix: A Survey of Some Recent Experience in LDCs* (Fiscal Affairs Dept., International Monetary Fund, Feb. 22, 1983).

_____ : *Divestiture of State-Owned Enterprises in LDCs.* A Consultants' Report prepared at the request of the World Bank (Alexandria, Virginia, Nov. 1985). Draft report. An edited version of this survey report was circulated by the Public Sector Management Unit, Projects Policy Department, World Bank, under the title of *Divestiture in Developing Countries*, July 1986. A further edited version, with Mary M. Shirley as co-author, was published in June 1987 under the same title as #11 in the series of "World Bank Discussion Papers."

Bremer, Jennifer: *Options for Privatizing Agricultural Parastatals in Developing Countries* (Abstract of unpublished paper, Robert R. Nathan Associates, Washington, D.C., 1986).

Capital Market Report. Dhaka Stock Exchange Ltd., Aug. 1986.

Capital Market Report. Dhaka Stock Exchange Ltd., Sept. 1986.

Chafkin, Sol. H., et al: *An Approach to Accelerating Industrial Growth in East Pakistan* (Washington, D.C., American Assistance Corporation, Feb. 1970). A report to USAID/Dhaka.

Chowdhury, Nuimuddin: "Economic Management in Bangladesh, 1975-82," New Series No. 32 of *Research Report Series* (Dhaka, Bangladesh Institute of Development Studies, undated, but circa 1983-84).

_____ : *Towards an Understanding of Entrepreneurship in Early Development: The Case of Cotton Textiles in Bangladesh*, Research Report Series, New Series No. 37 (Dhaka, Bangladesh Institute of Development Studies, Jan. 1985).

Concept papers presented in August 1985 to the Bureau for Private Enterprise, USAID/Washington, D.C., "To Provide Technical Services Related to Privatization of State-owned or State-controlled Enterprises." The three concept papers referred to for the present study were prepared by: Analysis Group, Inc., of Washington, D.C.; Birch & Davis Associates, Inc., of Silver Springs, Maryland; Global Exchange, Inc., of Xenia, Ohio, and Washington, D.C. (in collaboration with Robert R. Nathan Associates), Clare E. Humphrey, Project Director).

Fact Book '84 (Dhaka, Dhaka Stock Exchange Ltd., 1985).

Floyd, Robert H.: *Some Topical Issues Concerning Public Enterprises* (Washington, D.C., Fiscal Affairs Department, International Monetary Fund, July 22, 1983).

Franda, Marcus: *Bangladesh: The First Decade* (New Delhi, South Asian Publishers, Pvt. Ltd., & Universities Field Staff International of Hanover, N.H., 1982).

Haque, M. Shamsul: *Prices Policy, Accounting Methodology & Corporate Financial Liability* (Dhaka, Institute of Business Administration, University of Dhaka, June 1983). Of special use were Chapter 6, "Analysis of Company Accounts: Evidences from the U.K. and Bangladesh," and Chapter 8, "Aggregate Financial Planning, Flow of Funds, Financial Performance and Financing of Public Sector Bodies in Bangladesh."

Hanke, Steve H.: *Privatization and Development* (San Francisco, Institute for Contemporary Studies, 1987), A Publication of the International Center for Economic Growth.

Humphrey, Clare E.: *Preliminary Report With Recommendations for Privatization of the Nepal Tea Development Corporation* (Manila/Kathmandu, Asian Development Bank, Feb. 1988).

_____ : *Divestiture of State Enterprises in Taiwan: A Case Study of an Economy in Transition* (Washington, D.C., USAID, June 1983). (The author condensed and updated the study in January 1987 for the Center for Privatization.)

Lorche, Klaus: *The Privatization Transaction and Its Longer-term Effects: a case study of the textile industry in Bangladesh* (Cambridge, Harvard University Press, April 1988), Harvard Institute for International Development, Center for Business and Government, John F. Kennedy School of Government.

Management Systems International: *Developing Entrepreneurs* (Washington, D.C., 1986).

Mascarenhas, Anthony: *A Legacy of Blood* (London, Hodder & Stoughton, 1986).

Nyrop, Richard F., et al: *Area Handbook for Bangladesh* (Washington, D.C., Foreign Area Studies, American University, 1975). Printed and Distributed through the U.S. Government Printing Office.

Osmani, S.R. and Jahan, Selim: *Pricing and Subsidy Policy for the Public Sector Jute Manufacturing Industry of Bangladesh*, Research Report No. 46 (Dhaka, Bangladesh Institute of Development Studies, Mar. 1986).

Pirie, Madsen: *Privatization: The Facts and The Fallacies* (Published by The Fund for an American Renaissance and The Adam Smith Institute (U.S.A.), Washington, D.C., 1986).

Private Sector in Bangladesh: Its Perspectives and Performance (Dhaka, Metropolitan Chamber of Commerce and Industry, 1986).

Privatization of State-owned Enterprises Technical Assistance Project USAID/Honduras, Task 7 Report—Institutional Configuration, Prepared for USAID by the Center for Privatization, Washington, D.C., June 1986.

Quasem, Md. Abul: *Supply and Distribution of Fertilizers in Bangladesh* (Dhaka, Bangladesh Institute of Development Studies, Jan. 1985).

Rahim, A.M.A: *Current Issues of Bangladesh Economy* (Dhaka, Bangladesh Books International Ltd., 1978). Especially useful were chapters on "Performance of The Banking System, 1971-77," and "A Review of Industrial Investment Policy, 1971-77."

Rahman, Atiq: *Development Strategies and Productivity in Bangladesh* (Dhaka, Bangladesh Institute of Development Studies, Oct. 1985).

Rahman, Sultan Hafeez: *Jute Market Instability: Causes, Nature and Remedial Options,* Research Report No. 47 (Dhaka, Bangladesh Institute of Development Studies, April 1986).

Rakshit, Mridulkanti: *The Law of Vested Property in Bangladesh: A Book on "Conflict of Laws"* (Chittagong, Bangladesh, S.R. Rakshit, 3rd Edition, Oct. 1985).

Rao, V.K.R.V.: *Bangladesh Economy: Problems and Prospects* (Delhi, Vikas Publications, 1972).

Lyell Ritchie, Demos Menegakis, and K.M. Sakhawatullah: *Report on Private Sector Development in Bangladesh* (Washington, D.C., Arthur D. Little, Inc., May 13, 1987). A report for the Private Enterprise Development Study (PEDS) of USAID.

Robbins, Sidney M.: *A Securities Market Development Program for Bangladesh,* A report to the United Nations Development Program, Dhaka, 1983.

Saktiel, David M., et al: *Selected Legal and Regulatory Aspects of Privatization* (Boston, Nutter, McClennen & Fish, 1986).

Salek, Mohammad: *Effect of Environmental Factors on the Operational Effectiveness and Efficiency of Public Enterprises of Bangladesh* (Dhaka, Bangladesh Management Development Centre, 1986). A proposal submitted to USAID/Dhaka on May 4, 1986.

Schaefer, Peter F.: *Philippine Divestiture and Privatization Trust—Concept Memorandum* (Manila, Economic Development Foundation, Dec. 1985). A paper for USAID/Manila.

Shirley, Mary M: *Managing State-Owned Enterprises* (Washington, D.C., World Bank Staff Working Papers #577, Management and Development Series #4, World Bank, 1983).

Shirley, Mary M., et al: *Peru: The Management and Sale of State-owned Enterprises* (Washington, D.C., World Bank and International Finance Corporation, August 27, 1982). Report No. 4088-PE.

Sobhan, Rehman and Ahsan, Ahmad: *Disinvestment & Denationalization: Profile and Performance.* Research Report, New Series No. 38, (Dhaka, Bangladesh Institute of Development Studies, July 1984).

Sobhan, Rehman and Ahmad, Muzaffer: *Public Enterprise in an Intermediate Regime: A Study in the Political Economy of Bangladesh* (Dhaka, Bangladesh Institute of Development Studies, 1980).

Song, Dae Hee: *New Policy Direction of the Korean Public Enterprise Sector As a Source of Growth* (Seoul, Korea Development Institute, Nov. 1983). Working Paper 83-07.

Squire, Lyn: *Employment Policy in Developing Countries: a survey of issues and evidence* (New York/London, Oxford University Press, 1981), A World Bank Research Publication.

Summary of Taxation Rules in Bangladesh, 1986-87 (Dhaka, Metropolitan Chamber of Commerce and Industry, 1986).

Timberg, Thomas A.: *An Essay of Golden Bengal: Contemporary Bangladesh: Assets, Liabilities and Challenges* (unpublished draft manuscript, 1986).

Wennergren, E.B., C.H. Antholt, & M.D. Whitaken: *Agricultural Development in Bangladesh,* (Boulder, Colo., Westview Press, 1984). A Replica Edition.

Wilson, Ernest J., III: *The Privatization Process in Action: Some Lessons from International Experience.* (An address and trip report, Washington, D.C., Center for Privatization, 1986).

World Bank: *Bangladesh: Recent Economic Developments and Selected Development Issues—Summary and Conclusions* (Washington, D.C., South Asia Programs Department, March 18, 1982). Report No. 3768—BD.

_____ : *Bangladesh: Economic and Social Development Prospects,* In four volumes (Washington, D.C., South Asia Programs Department, World Bank, April 2, 1985). Report No. 5409.

_____ : *Bangladesh: Public Sector Industrial Enterprises.* An unpublished working paper of the World Bank Office in Dhaka, 1985.

_____ : *Bangladesh: Industrial Sector.* An unpublished working paper of the World Bank Office in Dhaka, 1986.

_____ : *Bangladesh: Recent Economic Developments and Medium Term Prospects,* In Two Volumes (Washington, D.C., South Asia Programs Department, World Bank, March 17, 1986). Report No. 6049.

_____ : *Bangladesh: Promoting Higher Growth and Human Development* (Washington, D.C., World Bank, 1987), A World Bank Country Study.

_____ : *Bangladesh: Adjustments in the Eighties and Short-term Prospects* (in two volumes), Volume I. "Executive Summary and Main Report" (Washington, D.C., World Bank, Mar. 10, 1988).

_____ : "The Role of Government," Chapter IV of *World Development Report 1987* (Washington, D.C., World Bank, 1987).

Yusuf, Fazlul Hassan: *Nationalization of Industries in Bangladesh* (Dhaka, National Institute of Local Government, Oct. 1985).

Conference Proceedings, Papers, and Speeches

Berg, Elliot: "Overview of Privatization: Role in Economic Growth and Techniques" (A speech given at the International Conference on Privatization, USAID, Washington, D.C., Feb. 17-19, 1986).

International Conference on Privatization, Washington, D.C., U.S. Agency for International Development, Feb. 17-19, 1986. Fourteen background papers were presented at the Conference, of which the following were consulted for the present study:

"An Overview of Privatization and the A.I.D. Experience," by L. Gray Cowan.

"Legal and Tax Considerations in Privatization," by Peter Thomas.

"Privatization of Public Services," by Gabriel Roth.

"Policy Environments and Privatization," by Charles Taylor.

"Public and Private Responsibilities in Privatization," by Dr. Madsen Pirie and Peter Young.

"Strategies Employed in Successful Privatization Efforts: Rx for Privatization," by Steve H. Hanke.

"Deregulation and Privatization of Marketing Boards," by Ian Marceau.

"Development of a Country Privatization Strategy," by Jean de la Giroday.

Papers and Procedures of the BYEA Conference and National Seminar on "Impact of Denationalization of Banks and Industries in Bangladesh," Dhaka Bangladesh Young Economists Association, Nov. 30—Dec. 1, 1984. Reprinted in *The Young Economist, the BYEA Journal,* April 1985. In addition to a recap of the discussion sessions, the following papers were consulted for the present study:

"Death Knell of Jute Industries? Privatization Notwithstanding," by Salahuddin Ahmed.

"Performance of Denationalized Textile Industries in Bangladesh: A Case Study," by M.A. Sattar Bhuyan and M.A. Jabbar.

"A Comparative Evaluation of the Performance of Nationalized vs. Private Sector Industries: an overview of concepts and trend of performance," by Dr. Durgadas Bhattacharjee.

"Performance of Newly Established Private Banks," by Dr. Md. Habibullah.

"Private Banks in Bangladesh—Problems and Prospects," by M. Monwar Hossain.

"Denationalization of Banks: a case study of Pubali and Uttara Banks," by Md. Azizur Rahman.

"Performance of Two Nationalized Commercial Banks: a case study of Sonali and Janata Bank," by M.A. Quiddus.

"Comparative Performance of Nationalized & Denationalized Banks," by Monoranjan Day.

Proceedings and papers presented at the "Conference on Privatization Policies, Methods and Procedures," Sponsored by the Asian Development Bank, held in Manila, Jan. 31-Feb. 1, 1985:

Privatization Policies, Methods and Procedures, by David Heald, Lecturer in Management Studies, University of Glasgow, Scotland.

The Role of Donor Agencies in the Privatization Process, by D.R. Pendse, Economic Advisor, Tata Industries, Bombay.

Privatization: A Viable Policy Option?, by Alan Rufus Waters, Babcock Graduate School of Management, Wake Forest University, U.S.A.

Privatization in Industrialized Countries: The Experience of the United Kingdom, by Mr. David Clement, Director, Corporate Finance Division, Kleinwort, Benson, Ltd., London.

Privatization in Developing Countries: The Experience of Bangladesh, by Shamsul Haque Chishty, Secretary, Ministry of Establishment, Government of Bangladesh.

Privatization in Developing Countries: The Experience of Pakistan, by Zafar Iqbal, Chairman, National Development Finance Corporation, Karachi.

Privatization in Industrialized Countries: The Experience of Japan, by Seizaburo Sato, Department of Social Sciences, School of Liberal Arts, University of Tokyo.

Privatization in Developing Countries: The Experience of the Republic of Korea, by Bon-Ho Koo, Chairman, Financial Federation Committee, Government of the Republic of Korea.

Privatization in Developing Countries: The Experience of Thailand, by Phisit Pakkasem, Deputy Secretary General, National Economic and Social Development Board, Bangkok.

Privatization in Developing Countries: The Experience of Sri Lanka, by Mrs. I. Jayasinghe, Director, Public Enterprises Division, Government of Sri Lanka.

Privatization in Developing Countries: The Experience of Malaysia, by Dato Seri Radin Soenarno Al-Haj, Director General, and Dr. Zainal Aznam Yusof, Director, Economic Planning Unit, Prime Minister's Department, Government of Malaysia.

Sekandar, S.M.: *A Paper on Disinvestment.* He is Director, Development & Member-Secretary, Sub-Committee on Disinvestment. (Dhaka, undated).

Sobhan, Rehman and Ahsan, Ahmad: *Implementation of Projects in the Private Sector in Bangladesh, A Study of DFI-Sponsored Projects.* A paper presented at the 7th Biennial Conference of the Bangladesh Economic Association, held at Jahangirnagar University, Dhaka, Dec. 17-20, 1985.

Murtaza, Md. Ghulam: *Inducing Investment by Multinationals in Bangladesh*, a paper presented at BYEA Seminar on "Role of Multinationals in Bangladesh," held in Dhaka Sept. 19, 1986. This is an extract of a paper prepared by the author while pursuing graduate work at Williams College, U.S.A. in 1984. The author is now Joint Director, Department of Research, Bangladesh Bank.

"Workshop on Review of Sub-contracting Exchange and Linkage Establishment Activities of BSCIC"—materials referred to included "Program" and "Opening Address by BSCIC Chairman Mushfequr Rahman" and "Summary Report" on the Workshop by Fazlul Karim, Financial Analyst, USAID/Dhaka, Sept. 8, 1986.

Alamgir, Dr. Muhiuddin Khan: *Development Banks in Bangladesh, Problems & Policies for Third Five-Year Plan.* Paper presented in the Annual Conference of Bangladesh Economic Association, Jahangirnagar University, Savar, Dhaka, Bangladesh, 1985.

Chowdhury, Tawfique: *Privatization of State Enterprises in Bangladesh, 1976-84* (Seoul, Korea Development Institute, 1987), Case Study III, a paper presented at the KDI/EDI Joint Seminar on Economic Policy Change and Governmental Process in Seoul, Nov. 9-12, 1987.

Islam, Mahfisul and Rahman, Afzalur: *Country Paper on Privatization: Bangladesh's Experience*, a transcript of a presentation at the Seminar on Privatization Strategies and Techniques, sponsored by the International Management Group and the Center for Privatization, in cooperation with The George Washington University International Business Program. The seminar was held in Washington, D.C., June 27-July 7, 1988 for USAID/USIS-sponsored participants.

Articles

"Private sector given greater participation: Industrial Policy provides a new dimension," *The Bangladesh Observer*, June 2, 1982.

"Size of sector corporations to be reduced," *The Bangladesh Observer*, June 2, 1982.

"Bangladeshi owners to get back their jute, textile mills," *The Bangladesh Observer*, June 2, 1982.

"6 sectors in reserved list," *The Bangladesh Observer*, June 2, 1982.

"Text: Industrial, investment policy," *The New Nation*, (Dhaka) June 3, 1982.

Marsden, Keith: "Private Enterprise Boosts Growth," *Chamber News* (Dhaka, Metropolitan Chamber of Commerce and Industry, May 1986). (Reprinted from an unnamed source.) Mr. Marsden is an Advisor at the World Bank.

Rowley, Anthony: "Private Affair in Asia," *Far Eastern Economic Review* (Hongkong, July 25, 1985).

Wilson, Dick: "The Privatization of Asia," *The Banker*, Sept. 1984.

"Privatization: Everybody's Doing It, Differently," *The Economist*, Dec. 21, 1985.

Kaletsky: "Everywhere the state is in retreat," Aug. 2, 1985. Reprint, source not listed.

"Why Malaysia Means Business," *Euromoney*, Feb. 1985.

"Now for Malaysia (Private) Inc.," *Far Eastern Economic Review*, Sept. 15, 1983.

"U.S. Lags Behind in Going Private," *Wall Street Journal*, Feb. 20, 1986.

"Black Africa's Future—Can it go capitalist?," *The Economist*, June 28, 1986.

"New Thrust to Promote Private Initiative in Africa," *DCCI Monthly Review*, Aug. 1986. (The Journal of the Dhaka Chamber of Commerce & Industry).

"Rajiv stresses on private sector to boost India's economy," *Daily Life* (Dhaka) Oct. 11, 1986.

"India in bid to improve public sector enterprises," *DCCI Monthly Review*, Aug. 1986.

Ahmad, Qazi Kholiquzzaman: "The Manufacturing Sector of Bangladesh—An Overview," *The Bangladesh Development Studies*, Vol. VI, No. 4, Autumn 1978.

Baxter, Craig: "Continuing Problems in Bangladesh," *Current History*, Mar. 1986.

Chanda, Nayan: "The March to Democracy," *Far Eastern Economic Review*, Sept. 1, 1983.

Ali, Salamat: "Divide and Rule—Ershad tries to benefit from a split in the opposition," *Far Eastern Economic Review*, July 10, 1986.

Ellis, William S.: "Bangladesh: Hope Nourishes a New Nation," *National Geographic*, Sept. 1972.

Bertocci, Peter J.: "Bangladesh in 1984: A Year of Protracted Turmoil," *Asian Survey*, Feb. 1985.

"Bangladesh in 1985: Resolute Against the Storms," *Asian Survey*, Feb. 1986.

Schroeder, Larry: "Decentralization in Rural Bangladesh," *Asian Survey*, Nov. 1985.

Islam, Syed Serajul: "The State in Bangladesh Under Zia (1975-81)," *Asian Survey*, May 1984.

Rahman, Md. Ataur: "Bangladesh in 1983: Beginnings of the Second Decade," *Asian Survey*, Feb. 1983.

Khasru, Hossain: "More enterprises likely to be disinvested," *Holiday*, (Dhaka) Sept. 19, 1986.

"Another dose of privatization," *Holiday* Oct. 11, 1985.

"536 Industrial Units Disinvested So Far," *The New Nation*, Aug. 5, 1985.

"No More Disinvestment," *The New Nation*, Aug. 26, 1984.

Chowdhury, Nuimuddim: "Public Sector in Some Developing Countries: Its Role, Problems and Prospects," *Journal of Management and Business*, Dhaka, Vol. 10, No. 1, 1984.

Kamaluddin, S.: "A fast-diminishing public presence in Bangladesh," *Far Eastern Economic Review*, July 25, 1985.

Clad, James: "The omnipresent state sector in Malaysia," *Far Eastern Economic Review*, July 25, 1985.

"Attracting foreign investments—four years of progress," *The Bangladesh Times*, Oct. 11, 1986.

"New Industrial Policy Realistic, says Moudud," *The Bangladesh Observer*, Oct. 9, 1986.

"Obstacles for industries," *Holiday*, Sept. 19, 1986.

Quasem, Md. Abul: "New system of Distribution of Fertilizer and Irrigation Equipment: An Analysis," *The Bangladesh Journal of Agricultural Economics*, June 1985.

Das, Shanti Ranjan: "A Comparative Financial Performance of Nationalised Banks in Bangladesh," *Journal of Management and Business and Economics*, Vol. 10, No. 1, 1984.

Haque, M. Shamsul: "Financial Theory and its Implications for Industrial Investment and Financing in Bangladesh," *Journal of Management and Business and Economics*, Vol. 12, No. 1, 1986.

Mohsen, Abul: "Lopsided Insurance," *Holiday*, April 13, 1984.

"Banks Responsible Too," (Editorial) *Holiday*, Sept. 19, 1986.

"Private Insurance Business Allowed," *The Bangladesh Times*, March 29, 1984.

"Two Insurance Ordinances Promulgated," *The Bangladesh Times*, Aug. 27, 1984.

Tareq, Mustafa: "Uttara Bank to float shares," *The New Nation*, March 20, 1984.

"DFIs inflated claims keep dispute alive: BJMA wants implementation of report on loan," *Jute Review*, July 1986. A Publication of the Bangladesh Jute Mills Association.

"BJMA hails the industrial policy," *Jute Review*, July 1986.

"Revamping the Jute Industry," *The Bangladesh Times*, Sept. 23, 1984.

Imam, K.H.: "Public Enterprise in an Intermediate Regime—A Review Article," The Bangladesh Development Studies. A Review of Sobhan and Ahmad's *Public Enterprise in an Intermediate Regime: A Study in the Political Economy of Bangladesh*. Undated.

"Government Begins Jute Procurement,"*DCCI Monthly Review*, Aug. 1986. (The journal of the Dhaka Chamber of Commerce and Industry).

"Progress in Bangladesh means not going backwards," *Economist*, July 20-26, 1985.

"Freeing Constraints on the Economy," a special section in *Economic Impact*, 1986/3, a publication of the U.S. Information Agency, Washington, D.C. The articles included:

Hanke, Steve H.: "The Privatization Option: An Analysis;" "The Reagan Administration's Privatization Program;"

Butler, Stuart M.: "Privatizing Government Services" (which was reprinted in the Sept. 1986 issue of *DCCI Monthly Review*, a monthly publication of the Dhaka Chamber of Commerce and Industry);

Okum, B.Robert: "The Benefits of Deregulation;"

"The Links Between Investment, Intellectual Property and Trade, An Interview with Harvey E. Bale, Jr., Assistant U.S. Trade Representative for Trade Policy and Analysis."

"State owned companies crawl out of the red," *Asian Business* (Bangkok), July 1986.

"15.81 Lakh bales jute purchased so far," *The Bangladesh Observer*, Oct. 20, 1986.

"Malaysia bars corporate holdings by officials," *Far Eastern Economic Review*, Oct. 2, 1986.

"Discipline vital in industries," *The Bangladesh Times*, Oct. 26, 1986.

"Public sector industries to be made holding companies," *The Bangladesh Times*, Oct. 26, 1986.

"Public sector units to be turned into companies," *The Bangladesh Observer*, Oct. 26, 1986.

Robison, Richard and Rodan, Garry: "In defence of state economic intervention," *Far Eastern Economic Review*, Oct. 23, 1986.

"No more special protection for public sector, says Moudud," *The New Nation*, Oct. 26, 1986.

"Industries minister defends privatization policy," *The Tide* (Dhaka), Nov.-Dec. 1984.

"Where the right policies get no credit," *The Economist*, Oct. 18, 1986.

Jute Review, Aug. 1986. (A publication of the Bangladesh Jute Mills Association).

Bremer, Jennifer: "Comparative AIDvantage—The agency's success in spurring private sector development depends on concentrating on programs where it is more effective than the other donors," *Foreign Service Journal* (Washington, D.C.), July/Aug. 1986.

Samad, M.A.: "Privatization of Insurance," *The Bangladesh Observer*, May 24, 1984.

"Draft Insurance Ordinance under scrutiny," *The Bangladesh Observer*, June 21, 1984.

"176 Industrial units disinvested so far," *The Bangladesh Observer*, June 3, 1984.

"Loan recovery to make private sector sluggish," *The Bangladesh Observer*, April 27, 1984.

"Some disinvested units may be taken back," *The Bangladesh Observer*, June 18, 1984.

"Salvaging Sick Industries," *The Bangladesh Observer* (editorial), April 27, 1984.

"Committee to thrash out borrowers' grievances," *The New Nation*, April 26, 1984.

"$140m IDA credit for imports," *The New Nation*, May 11, 1984.

"95 Employees of denationalized jute mills sacked," *The Bangladesh Observer*, April 27, 1984.

Rosario, Louise de: "The private dilemma—China's self-employed want reassurance of state sanction," *Far Eastern Economic Review*, Nov. 20, 1986.

Palmer, Jay D.: "Learning Ways of Bulls & Bears—China's fledgling stock market takes notes from U.S. traders," *Time*, Nov. 24, 1986.

Lamb, David: "It's Time to Stop Blaming the Colonialist Era for All Africa's Ills," *International Herald Tribune*, Nov. 18, 1986.

"Private sector ownership in SBC resented," *The Bangladesh Observer*, Nov. 10, 1986.

"Taka 85 crore earmarked for small industries," *The Bangladesh Observer*, Nov. 10, 1986.

"FBCCI, BAPI memoranda to speaker," *The New Nation*, Nov. 10, 1986.

"Khudra shilpa bank to be set up," *The New Nation*, Nov. 10, 1986.

"Stock Exchange is now buoyant," *Holiday*, Nov. 7, 1986.

Alam, Jaglul: "Anomaly in fertilizer price," *Holiday*, Nov. 7, 1986.

"Jute: private shippers must show stock," *The New Nation*, Nov. 25, 1986.

"3 More insurance companies in private sector likely," *The Bangladesh Observer*, Nov. 25, 1986.

"BSB recovery up, projects decline," *The Bangladesh Observer*, Nov. 25, 1986.

"Misappropriation in Janata Bank branch: 15 held," *The Bangladesh Observer*, Nov. 25, 1986.

"When the government sells out," *The New Nation*, Nov. 13, 1986. (Originally appeared in *US News & World Report*.)

"Capital Market Report, "*Monthly Bulletin of the Dhaka Stock Exchange, Ltd.*," Aug. 1986, Sept. 1986. A two-part article.

"Stock Exchange Review," *Dhaka Stock Exchange, Ltd.*, Jan. 1987.

Fact Book '84, Dhaka Stock Exchange, Ltd.

The Tide—Special Issue, Feb.-Mar.1987:

> "Politics—Past and Present;"
> "We want to maintain a balanced foreign policy"—an exclusive interview with President H.M. Ershad;
> "Industry: a new horizon with delicate issues;"
> The objective of FBCCI;"
> "I did not go to break up the party"—an interview with Moudud Ahmed, Deputy Prime Minister & Minister of Industries;
> "Tax rebation for an investment up to Taka 10 crore;"
> "Banking: trust of responsibility;"
> "Insurance Industry in Bangladesh;"
> "ADP projects are supposed to create the infra-structure;"

Paul, Samuel: "Privatization and the public sector," *Finance & Development*, Dec. 1985.

Kamaluddin, S.: "Projects on Parade," *Far Eastern Economic Review,* Feb. 12, 1987.

"South Asian Economic Scene—II, A World Bank Analysis," *The Bangladesh Observer,* Oct. 9, 1986.

"Disinvestment of NCBs soon likely," *The Bangladesh Observer,* Dec. 20, 1986.

"Faruq, Zahiduzzaman: "Initiative for establishing five more banks in the private sector," *Ittefaq* (Dhaka), Nov. 5, 1986, (A translation by USAID from Bengali).

Montu, Kazi: "Trial begins in Special Tribunal," *The New Nation,* Dec. 18, 1986.

"An episode of dollar and gold," *The New Nation,* Dec. 21, 1986.

"Bangladesh opposition likely to boycott presidential polls," *China Post* (Taipei), Sept. 8, 1986.

Plommer, Leslie: "Love and graft in the world's poorest nation," *Observer* (London), Aug. 31, 1986.

"Disinvestment will continue," *The New Nation,* Aug. 4, 1985.

Kamaluddin, S.: "Progress in private," *Far Eastern Economic Review,* Feb. 17, 1983.

Tareq, Mustafa: "Uttara Bank to float shares," *The New Nation,* Mar. 20, 1987.

"Ties with US," *The Bangladesh Times,* Mar. 2, 1987.

"US plans to crack down on deficits with NICs," *Bangkok Post,* Feb. 26, 1987.

"Conspicuous Consumption," *The Bangladesh Observer,* Feb. 10, 1987.

Kamaluddin, S.: "Bangladesh—Lacking in leadership," *Far Eastern Economic Review,* Feb. 1987.

"Private sector to be made dynamic: Ershad," *Daily News* (Dhaka), Feb. 6, 1987.

"Govt firm to strengthen pvt sector: Moudud," *The Bangladesh Times,* Feb. 18, 1987.

"Foreign investment in private sector Tk147cr in 10 yrs," *The Bangladesh Observer,* Feb. 9, 1987.

"State of Textile Mills," *The New Nation,* Feb. 11, 1987.

"Investment falls, ADP to be cut," *The Bangladesh Observer,* Feb. 3, 1987.

"Largest Indian team for Investors' Forum," *The Bangladesh Observer,* Jan. 14, 1987.

"All foreign investments protected under law," *The Bangladesh Times,* Jan. 22, 1987.

"Foreign investors visit EPZ," *The New Nation,* Jan. 22, 1987.

"Investors Forum begins today," *The Bangladesh Observer,* Jan. 19, 1987.

Quashem, Hassan A.: "Shares ready for public offer," *Holiday*, Jan. 9, 1987.

"Denationalization Lures Wider Base of Investors," *International Herald Tribune*, Feb. 17, 1987.

"Abandoned plants to be made Public Ltd. Cos.," *The Bangladesh Observer*, Apr. 17, 1987.

Talukder, S.I.: "Stabilising the price and production of jute," *The New Nation*, Apr. 11, 1987.

"Abandoned industries to be made public limited cos," *The New Nation*, Apr. 27, 1987.

"Call for strike at industries tomorrow," *The New Nation*, Apr. 27, 1987.

"New Jute Policy on February 28," *The Bangladesh Times*, Feb. 8, 1987.

"Jute market prospect in Europe reviewed," *The Bangladesh Observer*, Feb. 5, 1987.

"Jute policy reviewed," *The New Nation*, Feb. 8, 1987.

"Jute mills disinvested for corruption: Zafar," *The Bangladesh Observer*, Feb. 4, 1987.

"Jute export earnings fall," *The New Nation*, Jan. 27, 1987.

"45 lakh bales of jute production envisaged," *The Bangladesh Observer*, Mar. 3, 1987.

"Nationalised jute mills lose Tk.621 cr," *The Bangladesh Observer*, Feb. 18, 1987.

"Denationalized jute mills lose Tk.621.44 crore," *The Bangladesh Times*, Feb. 18, 1987.

"Nationalised banks lose Tk.26 cr in 10 yrs," *The Bangladesh Observer*, Mar. 3, 1987.

Haque, Dr. M. Shamsul: "Garment And Pharmaceutical Industries," *The Bangladesh Observer*, Feb. 16, 1987.

"UZs to have fisheries, livestock complex," *The Bangladesh Observer*, Feb. 3, 1987.

Kurien, John: "People's Participation in Fisheries," *The Bangladesh Observer*, Feb. 8, 1987.

Hossain, Md. Shahadat: "Inland Fisheries Resources In Bangladesh," *The Bangladesh Observer*, Feb. 5, 1987.

"Joint public-private fishery centre planned," *The Nation* (Bangkok), Feb. 8, 1987.

Hossain, A.K.M. Mosharraf: "Blueprint for tomorrow: Fertilizer industry," *The New Nation*, Feb. 7, 1987.

"70 lakh people unemployed," *The New Nation*, Feb. 10, 1987.

"Tk 90 cr special credit plan for small industries," *The New Nation*, Jan. 7, 1987.

"Plan for overall uplift: Ershad," *The Bangladesh Times*, Feb. 19, 1987.

"Procedure for setting up of joint venture discussed," *The Bangladesh Times*, Feb. 19, 1987.

"Trade deficit with India Tk.935 cr.," *The Bangladesh Observer*, Feb. 3, 1987.

"Trade deficit rises to Tk4,835 cr," *The Bangladesh Times*, Mar. 4, 1987.

"71 nationalised industrial units disinvested," *The Bangladesh Times*, Feb. 9, 1987.

"132 disinvested units failed to pay," *The Bangladesh Times*, Feb. 24, 1987.

"Concern over arrests of 4 industrialists," *The Bangladesh Observer*, Mar. 3, 1987.

Al-Muqtadir, Abul Khair: "Nationalised Privatisation," *The Bangladesh Observer*, Feb. 23, 1987.

"AL urges Govt to stop process of disinvestment," *The Bangladesh Observer*, Feb. 2, 1987.

"AL against process of disinvestment," *The Bangladesh Times*, Apr. 1, 1987.

Khasru, Hossain: "The facts of life," *Holiday*, Jan. 9, 1987.

"Private, public sectors must co-exist," *The Bangladesh Times*, Feb. 6, 1987.

Afzal, Md. Anwarul: "The Public Sector Sickness," *The Bangladesh Observer*, Feb. 8, 1987.

"Public sector units won't be privatised," *The Bangladesh Observer*, Feb. 6, 1987.

"No more subsidy to public sector," *The Bangladesh Observer*, Jan. 14, 1987.

Hossain, Dr. Anwar: (article in 3 parts) (1) "Government and Private Organizations," Feb. 3, 1987; (2) "Government And Private Organizations—II," Feb. 4, 1987; and (3) "Government and Private Organizations—III," Feb. 6, 1987, *The Bangladesh Observer*.

Ahmed, Nizam: "Facilities at EPZ inadequate," *The New Nation*, Jan. 27, 1987.

"High rate of customs duty hinders industrialisation," *The Bangladesh Observer*, Jan. 28, 1987.

"EPZ—A New Horizon For Development," *The Bangladesh Observer*, Feb. 3, 1987.

"Unrecovered loans," *The Bangladesh Times*, Feb. 19, 1987.

"Private sector owe Tk1859 cr to banks," *The Bangladesh Times*, Feb. 16, 1987.

"Highlights" (highlights of summary of recommendations of the report of National Commission on Money, Banking and credit), *The New Nation*, Jan. 22, 1987.

"Fraud, forgery cost banks Taka 22 cr," *The New Nation*, Jan. 22, 1987.

"Rupali Bank to remain in public sector," *The New Nation*, Jan., 22,
     1987.
"Support to road blockade programme,"*The New Nation*, Jan. 27, 1987.
"Bank management, accountability, loan recovery stressed," *The Bang-
     ladesh Times*, Jan. 22, 1987.
The Bangladesh Times—Special Supplement on the Occasion of the An-
     nouncement of Jute Policy 1987-88, Mar. 2, 1987:
     Amed, Sayed: "BJMC: The stronghold of jute industry;"
     Husain, Dr. M.: "Jute research in Bangladesh;
     Imam, T.I.M. Hasan: "Golden fibre: The principal cash crop;"
     Beg, Belal: "Corchorus Capsulris the wonder plant of the Na-
     ture."

Divested Industrial Enterprises

Name and Address	Date of Divestiture (day/month/year)	Divestiture Price (in Tk)
A. FULLY ABANDONED ENTERPRISES (UNDER MANAGEMENT OF SECTOR CORPORATIONS)		
BANGLADESH CHEMICAL INDUSTRIES CORP.		
Orient Tannery Hazaribagh, Dhaka	1/12/76	12,22,222*
Bangladesh Paper Converting Works & Faroukh Industries, Ltd., Demra, Dhaka	16/9/76	71,92,225*
Madras Tannery Hazaribagh, Dhaka	30/11/76	8,02,800*

*The customary Bangladeshi system of "lakhs" (100,000) and "crores" (10 million) is being used in listing monetary amounts. Therefore, an amount listed as 63,72,81,459 = 63 crore, 72 lakh, 81 thousand, 459 (translated to the U.S. system = 637,281,459). For a rough approximation of value today, use Tk33/US$1. Source Ministry of Industries.

Name and Address	Date of Divestiture (day/month/year)	Divestiture Price (in Tk)
Omar Tannery Hazaribagh, Dhaka	29/4/77	9,09,900
Eastern Tannery, Ltd. Kalurghat, Chittagong	18/2/77	12,75,551
Ibrahim Match Works Kalurghat, Chittagong	31/12/76	27,15,000
United Tannery Hazaribagh, Dhaka	30/4/77	5,37,224
Bangladesh Enamel & Aluminum Works, Baizid Bostami Road, Chitt.	16/2/77	73,00,000
S.N.A. Tannery Hazaribagh, Dhaka	9/6/77	14,52,500
Razzak Tannery Ind. Hazaribagh, Dhaka	5/8/77	14,30,275
Agaz Rubber Ind. Tongi Ind. Area Dhaka	26/4/77	56,00,000
Bengal Tannery Co. Hazaribagh, Dhaka	17/6/77	18,55,555
Roushan Tannery Hathazari, Chittagong	9/7/77	8,01,000
Inom Tannery Hazaribagh, Dhaka	4/11/77	25,00,000
North East Tannery Hazaribagh, Dhaka	11/11/77	18,88,885
Bhuishar Bone Mills Sharail, Comilla	13/1/78	8,10,001

Name and Address	Date of Divestiture (day/month/year)	Divestiture Price (in Tk)
Bangladesh National Tannery, Hathazari, Chittagong	24/10/77	15,50,000
Pioneer Tannery Hazaribagh, Dhaka	29/5/78	10,00,537
Modern Bickers & Baffers Mfg. Co. Chandragong, Chittagong	25/4/78	35,00,000
Hafiz Tannery Hazaribagh, Dhaka	29/5/78	27,00,000
Souvenier Tannery & Bone Mills, Kalurghat, Chittagong	31/5/78	13,11,000
Golden Match Works, Ltd., Kalurghat, Chittagong	22/6/78	1,63,00,000
Bengal Rubber Industries, Tejgaon Industrial Area, Dhaka	2/6/78	78,13,146
Rahmania Tannery Hazaribagh, Dhaka	9/5/78	27,17,777
Aziz Match Factory Shopora, Rajshahi	3/8/78	41,77,777
Ferdous Tannery Hazaribagh, Dhaka	8/9/78	40,50,000
National Rubber Ind. Tejgaon I/A, Dhaka	22/9/78	77,00,000

Name and Address	Date of Divestiture (day/month/year)	Divestiture Price (in Tk)
Orient Tannery & Bone Mills, Chandgaon, Chittagong	24/11/78	32,19,774
Sattar Match Factory Korbanigonj Chittagong	20/10/78	80,00,111
Bengal Corporation Hazaribagh, Dhaka	25/6/79	15,52,000
Chattal Match Factory Char Chaktai, Chittagong	31/8/80	11,50,000
Dry Ice & Carbonic Gas Co. & Indo Bangla Corp. Rajbari, Raridpur	13/4/78	15,30,000
Mahtab Tannery Hazaribagh & Mahtab Tannery II Hazaribagh, Dhaka	15/5/79	38,00,000
Resin Complex (Unit No. 2) Fouzderhat Ind. Estate, Chittagong	14/6/79	55,55,850
Kohinoor Rubber Indus. Tejgaon Ind. Area, Dhaka	15/6/79	95,55,555
Asiatic Tannery & Glue Factory, Ltd. Panchlaish, Chittagong	12/11/79	13,09,999
Dilkusha Tannery Hazaribagh, Dhaka	29/10/79	52,30,000

Name and Address	Date of Divestiture (day/month/year)	Divestiture Price (in Tk)
East Bengal Tannery Hazaribagh, Dhaka	15/2/80	47,50,000
Farookh Chemical Ind. Panchalish, Chittagong	13/2/82	63,00,777
Habib Industries Postagola, Dhaka	20/1/83	3,81,00,000
Karim Rubber Ind. Fatulla, Dhaka	27/1/83	5,27,00,000
Star Particle Board Mills, Kuripara, Dhaka	3/2/83	4,00,00,000
Bangladesh Chrome Tannery, Hazaribagh, Dhaka	17/2/83	63,07,777
Kohinoor Detergent Factory, Tongi Ind. Area, Dhaka	15/3/83	2,10,00,000
Bangladesh Paper Products, Ltd. Chittagong	9/4/84	5,32,00,000
Bengal Belting Corp. Nasirabad I/A, Chitt.	15/4/83	4,03,00,000
Crescent Industries Nasirabad Ind. Area, Chittagong	23/3/83	5,26,50,000

BANGLADESH SUGAR AND FOOD INDUSTRIES CORP.

Omar Industries, Ltd. Nasirabad, Chittagong	23/5/77	21,01,000

Name and Address	Date of Divestiture (day/month/year)	Divestiture Price (in Tk)
Adam Ltd., Strand Road, Chittagong & Adam Salt Factory Chittagong	2/4/77	38,82,061
Nawayavek Mills Ltd., Strand Road, Chittagong	25/11/77	38,66,666
People's Tobacco Co., Ltd., Tongi Ind. Area, Dhaka	27/12/77	55,12,500
Noori Mills, Ltd. Khatungonj, Chittagong & Noor Trading Corp. Khatunganj, Chittagong	2/3/78	15,85,200
M.M. Oil Mills Faridabad, Dhaka	24/10/77	33,18,512
Dhaka Tobacco Ind., Ltd., Tongi, Dhaka	21/3/78	80,00,000
Siddiq Oil Mills Nasirabad Ind. Area, Chittagong	3/11/77	28,00,000
Arco Cold Storage, Bhairal, Mymensingh	31/3/78	11,11,000
Dulichand Omraolal Oil Mills, Imamgonj, Dhaka	7/6/78	51,00,000
Golden Bengal Tobacco Co. Ltd., Dhaka	22/6/78	1,63,00,000

Name and Address	Date of Divestiture (day/month/year)	Divestiture Price (in Tk)
Asian Tobacco Co., Ltd., Tejgaon Ind. Area, Dhaka	4/7/78	65,00,000
Daulatpur Cold Storage, Shiromoni Khulna	10/11/78	16,20,000
Crescent Oil Mills Fatulla, Dhaka	15/8/79	40,00,000
Janata Tobacco Co. Tongi Ind. Area, Dhaka & Ismmail Dada Bhai Hatkhola Road, Dhaka	3/3/80	81,11,215
Kohinoor Tobacco Co., Ltd., Tongi, Dhaka	20/3/80	1,27,05,000
Meco Cold Storage, Bhairal Bazar, Mymensingh	23/2/82	11,07,850
Ice Industries, Ltd. Chandpur	23/11/82	45,11,116
Dada, Ltd. (including Hossain Oil Mills & Dada Salt Factory), Chittagong	28/11/82	71,73,080
Babu Oil Mills, Ltd. (incl. Star Metal Ind.), Chittagong	14/12/82	53,00,100
I.K. Industries & Razzak, Ltd., Baizid Bostami Rd., Chitt.	28/2/83	55,50,694

Name and Address	Date of Divestiture (day/month/year)	Divestiture Price (in Tk)
K. Rahman & Co., Ltd. Baizid Bostami Rd., Chittagong	18/7/83	3,77,77,777
Nabisco Bread & Biscuit Factory, Tejgaon Ind. Area, Dhaka	13/6/83	7,00,00,000
Balagamwala Vegetable Products, Ltd. Nasirabad Ind. Area, Chittagong	9/6/83	6,66,26,837
Chittagong Flour Mills, Ltd., Nasirabod I/A, Chittagong	7/4/83	3,76,00,100
Diamond Food Ind., Ltd. (incl. R.A. Mohd.Siddik) Nasirabod, I/A,Chitt.	7/4/83	5,81,13,615
Bangladesh Cold Storage, Ltd., Khulna	19/3/84	5,00,01,000

BANGLADESH STEEL & ENGINEERING CORP.

Kohinoor Aluminum Works Mirpur, Dhaka	11/10/76	13,87,978
Drum Metals, Ltd. Siddirgonj, Dhaka	12/5/77	13,75,000
Mallik, Ind., Ltd. Tejgaon I/A, Dhaka	7/1/77	36,00,000
Chittagong Saw Mill & Engineering Works, Baizid Bostami Rd. Chittagong	4/2/77	30,50,000

Name and Address	Date of Divestiture (day/month/year)	Divestiture Price (in Tk)
Chittagong Saw Mill & Engineering Works Patherghata Chittagong	4/3/77	13,52,000
Noor Industries, Ltd. Narayanganj	27/10/77	19,00,100
Beco Industries, Ltd. Tejgaon I/A, Dhaka	16/1/78	42,00,000
Drum Metals, Ltd. Tejgaon, Dhaka	13/9/77	91,00,000
Sino-Bangladesh Industrial Works Baizid Bostami Rd. Chittagong	20/3/78	41,00,000
Chittagong Pipe Mills, Ltd., Fouzerhat	4/4/78	4,02,00,000
Dhaka Aluminum Works Imamgonj, Dhaka	8/5/78	63,00,000
Bangaldesh Steel Ind. Tejgaon I/A, Dhaka	12/12/78	66,00,000
Domestic Metal Ind. Tejgaon I/A, Dhaka	12/12/78	61,00,600
Tejgaon Engineering Co. Tejgaon I/A, Dhaka	19/1/79	88,00,000
Rahim Metal Ind., Ltd. Tejgaon I/A/, Dhaka	20/2/80	1,67,01,000
Chand Fitting Ltd., Baizid Bostami Rd, Chittagong	14/8/81	55,55,555

Name and Address	Date of Divestiture (day/month/year)	Divestiture Price (in Tk)
Husain Ind., Ltd. Pahartali, Chittagong	22/4/83	71,75,000
Bangladesh Welding Electrodes, Ltd., Sholashar, Chittagong	29/3/83	1,77,77,777
Bengal Metal Ind. Tejgaon I/A/, Dhaka	14/9/83	2,51,00,000
Malik Re-rolling Mills Nasirabad I/A, Chitt.	18/7/83	1,80,88,888
New Era Steel Mills Nasirabad I/A, Chitt. & New Era Metal Ind. Nasirabad I/A/, Chitt.& New Era Trading Co. Nasirabad I/A, Chitt.	27/11/83	2,52,79,970
Mohammadi Iron & Steel Works, Ltd. Nasirabad I/A, Chitt.	24/1/78	4,30,26,000

BANGLADESH TEXTILE MILLS CORP.

Abbasi Thread Mills Sholasahar, Chittagong	9/5/77	46,00,000
Eastern Textile Mills Nasirabad I/A, Chitt. & Zari Tex Ltd. Nasirabad I/A, Chitt.	20/8/80	96,00,000

BANGLADESH FREEDOM FIGHTERS WELFARE TRUST

Hamedia Oil Mills Nasirabad I/A, Chitt.	6/11/81	46,51,000

Name and Address	Date of Divestiture (day/month/year)	Divestiture Price (in Tk)
Bengal National Tanneries Sher-e-Bangla Rd., Dhaka	12/5/83	29,55,555
National Tannery Hazaribagh, Dhaka	28/6/83	73,33,733
Jatrik Publications Gulistan Bldg., Dhaka	7/3/84	6,10,000
Madina Tannery Hathazari, Chittagong	3/4/84	90,00,001

BANGLADESH FOREST INDUSTRIES DEVELOPMENT CORP.

United Bobbin Factory Narayangonj, Dhaka	4/6/79	13,50,153
Integrated Timber Industrial Unit Mohigonj, Rangpur	8/6/79	15,13,515
Rahimi Industries, Ltd. Kalurghat I/A, Chitt.	11/9/79	29,70,851

BANGLADESH JUTE MILLS CORP.

Hamidia Jute Mills, Ltd. Comilla	1/1/79	2,71,75,555
N.A. Malek Jute Mills Demra, Dhaka	27/4/79	2,67,55,762
Sonar Bangla Jute Mills Kaliganj, Dhaka	1/2/80	1,31,00,000
Trans Ocean Fibres Processor (Bd.), Ltd. Shiromoni, Khulna	11/3/81	60,00,000

Name and Address	Date of Divestiture (day/month/year)	Divestiture Price (in Tk)

B. PARTIALLY ABANDONED ENTERPRISES

BANGLADESH STEEL AND ENGINEERING CORP.

Masood Raza & Co., Ltd., Dhaka	1/9/79	0
East Bengal Trading & Commercial Corp. Limited, Chittagong	1/9/77	9,86,843
Rahman Metal Ind., Dhaka	21/4/79	0
National Iron & Steel Industries, Ltd. Chittagong (54% divested 46% held by govt.)	13/12/79	0
General Iron & Steel Co., Chittagong	21/1/80	35,10,000
Prince Iron & Steel Ind., Dhaka	8/4/84	2,25,320
G.M. Steele Limited Chittagong (70% divested 30% held by gov't.)	2/4/84	74,98,560
Qureshi Steel Ltd. Khulna (53% divested 47% held by gov't.)	29/3/84	24,44,955
Khulna Industrial & Trading Corp., Ltd., Khulna	30/3/84	8,20,000

Name and Address	Date of Divestiture (day/month/year)	Divestiture Price (in Tk)
BANGLADESH SUGAR AND FOOD INDUSTRIES CORP.		
Rahman Oil Mills Dhaka	23/11/77	0
Rahatin Industries Ltd. Rangpur	17/11/78	10,82,444
Argosy Conserves Dhaka	15/10/80	6,75,761
Noorani Group of Industries, Bogra	13/6/78	0
Bay Fishing Corp., Ltd. Chittagong	21/11/83	50,50,253
Eastern Fisheries, Ltd. Chittagong	22/3/84	5,00,000
Fish Exports, Ltd. Khulna	17/2/84	1,07,48,000
Hasni Vanaspati Mfg. Co., Ltd., Chittagong	8/4/84	70,43,600
Ahmedi Oil Mills, Ltd. Chittagong	8/4/84	11,46,200
Al-Mustafa Industries Ltd., Chittagong	8/4/84	33,69,000
Arco Industries, Ltd. Chittagong (88% divested 12% held by gov't.)	1/7/78	0
Mirpur Ceramic Works Dhaka (70% divested 30% held by gov't.)	1/1/79	0

Name and Address	Date of Divestiture (day/month/year)	Divestiture Price (in Tk)
Bangladesh Paper Mills Dhaka (1/3 divested 2/3 held by gov't.)	10/4/79	9,50,386
Bangladesh Glass Works Dhaka (89% divested 11% held by gov't.)	10/8/77	0
Bangladesh Tannery Dhaka	1/6/83	5,00,485
National Ceramic Industries, Dhaka	29/2/84	2,30,90,450
Albert David (Bd) Ltd. Dhaka	7/4/84	13,78,07,100
Bella Artifitex, Ltd. Dhaka (61% divested 9% held by gov't.)	28/5/84	9,18,570

BANGLADESH TEXTILE MILLS CORP.

Dhaka Dyeing & Mfg. Co. Dhaka	28/1/77	0
Metex Cotton, Ltd. Dhaka	3/10/77	0
Jess Blanket Mfg. Co. Dhaka	9/5/77	0
Alauddin Taiwa Textile Mills, Dhaka	7/2/77	0

Name and Address	Date of Divestiture (day/month/year)	Divestiture Price (in Tk)
Ahmed Silk Mills, Ltd. Dhaka	4/2/77	0
Mohammadi Calendering & Printing Works, Dhaka	27/2/80	0
BANGLADESH JUTE MILLS CORP.		
Sarwar Jute Mills, Ltd. Dhaka	3/5/78	0
Hossain Jute Mills, Ltd. Dhaka	21/6/78	0
New Dhaka Industries, Ltd., Dhaka	28/12/77	0

C. FULLY ABANDONED ENTERPRISES (UNDER MANAGEMENT OF DIRECTOR GENERAL OF INDUSTRIES)

Kalim Art Printers & Good Luck Corp. Tejgaon I/A, Dhaka	22/6/74	17,77,777
Hafiz Brothers Tongi I/A, Dhaka	23/10//74	6,63,000
Bectro Chemical Labs. Tejgaon I/A, Dhaka	30/10/74	1,60,089
Ittefaq Foundry & Workshop Tejgaon I/A, Dhaka	3/1/75	20,30,000
Bengal Process Ind. Postogola, Dhaka	26/2/75	3,68,600

Name and Address	Date of Divestiture (day/month/year)	Divestiture Price (in Tk)
Sabi Hosiery Faridabad, Dhaka	7/3/75	12,00,000
National Wire Nails Ind. Tejgaon I/A, Dhaka	15/3/75	6,25,104
Amania Hotel and Restaurant Nowabpur Rd, Dhaka	20/5/75	1,00,000
Zilani Flour Mills Rankin St., Dhaka	18/6/75	35,000
C.I. Corporation Demra, Dhaka	6/6/75	4,00,000
National Oil Mills Gandaria, Dhaka	17/6/75	10,00,000
Noor Engineering Works BCC Road, Dhaka	25/7/75	76,000
Haji Engineering Works Aramnitola, Dhaka	24/6/75	1,40,000
Peeracha & Co. Motijheel C.A., Dhaka	26/5/77	1,50,501
Steelman Industries Baitul Mukarram, Dhaka	30//7/77	3,05,000
Fazal Rubber & Khulna Rubber Ind. Mirpur, Dhaka	16/3/77	3,50,000
Overseas Agencies Tejgaon I/A, Dhaka	10/12/75	5,50,100
Shafique Press Bangla Bazaar, Dhaka	21/1/76	6,06,006

Name and Address	Date of Divestiture (day/month/year)	Divestiture Price (in Tk)
Punjab Iron Safe Works Tejgaon I/A, Dhaka	8/5/75	6,11,111
Kabir & Sons Toyenbee Circular R. Dhaka	5/7/77	20,200
Dhaka Oil Mills, Ltd. Faridabad, Dhaka	3/6/77	21,11,299
Eastern Rubber Ind. Tejgaon I/A, Dhaka	7/10/77	7,00,000
Globe Mantle Ind. Tejgaon I/A, Dhaka	10/7/75	6,00,000
Dhaka Cork Ind. Faridabad, Dhaka	30/9/74	3,00,000
Bengal Industries & Trading Co. Tejgaon I/A, Dhaka	24/12/74	5,00,000
Bangladesh Flour Mill Posta, Dhaka	27/6/74	1,01,110
Abdul Gaffar Zip Eastern, Demra, Dhaka	20/11/74	1,25,000
Amin Industries, Ltd. K.M. Alam Lane, Dhaka	23/11/74	10,01,777
United Box Factory Sowari, Ghat, Dhaka	30/1/75	50,000
Flatinum Ice Factory Postogola, Dhaka	1/2/75	8,05,000
Mubarak Engineering Ind., Tongi I/A, Dhaka	28/2/75	2,01,103

Name and Address	Date of Divestiture (day/month/year)	Divestiture Price (in Tk)
Jan Lace & General Mill Tejgaon I/A, Dhaka	18/3/75	16,25,000
Neon Makers Setmasjid Rd., Dhaka	2/5/75	23,000
Bangladesh United Rubber Ind., Tongi I/A, Dhaka	11/6/75	4,07,000
Bangladesh Ind. Corp. Tejgaon I/A, Dhaka	14/5/75	5,05,000
Young Press Kailash Ghosh, Dhaka	6/5/75	6,00,000
Masuma Hosiery B. Das Rd., Dhaka	29/5/75	3,15,000
Yakub Industries Demra, Dhaka	29/7/75	5,00,000
City Engineering Co. Joykali Mondir Rd. Dhaka	15/11/78	22,201
Dhaka Metal Ind. M.N. Das Rd., Dhaka	26/4/75	2,05,100
Salam Industries Siddirgonj, Dhaka	8/7/75	9,00,000
National Thread Works Nasirabad I/A, Chitt.	17/4/75	9,00,009
M.N. Sadak Silk Mill BSCIC I/E, Chitt.	6/9/74	10,00,000
Al-Amin Mills Chandpur, Comilla	29/7/74	2,25,000

Name and Address	Date of Divestiture (day/month/year)	Divestiture Price (in Tk)
Bangladesh Engg. Co. Pathantoly, Chitt.	10/9/74	4,02,000
Kashem Oil Mills Nasirabad I/A, Chitt.	12/4/75	6,00,000
Chittagong Electric Mfg. Co., Nasirabad, Chittagong	4/4/75	17,10,000
Asam Bengal Hosiery Bandar, Narayangonj, Dhaka	30/5/75	6,01,000
Kaiser Industrial Corp. Tejgaon I/A, Dhaka	21/6/75	10,00,000
Eastern Engg. Agencies N. Gonj, Dhaka	2/12/75	15,07,000
Wali Textile Mills Pahartoli, Chitt.	5/9/74	11,25,000
Bangladesh Rolling & General Mills, Baizid Bostami Rd., Chitt.	10/4/74	13,01,101
Kash Industries Chowkbazar, Chitt.	23/6/75	10,00,000
Mohammodi Iron Safe Products, Baizid Bostami Rd., Chitt.	8/4/75	15,52,527
Eastern Jute Products Nasirabad I/A, Chitt.	18/7/75	11,00,000
Daud Sultan & Co. Tejgaon I/A, Dhaka	23/5/75	3,00,005

Name and Address	Date of Divestiture (day/month/year)	Divestiture Price (in Tk)
Shfiq Flour Mills Posta, Dhaka	3/6/75	1,56,100
Majur Rubber Ind. Tongi I/A, Dhaka	12/6/75	1,95,000
Karsaz Engg. Works Nowabpur Rd., Dhaka	8/5/75	40,501
Timbrex (Bd), Ltd. Tejgaon I/A, Dhaka	14/7/75	3,85,000
Mian & Co. Tejgaon I/A, Dhaka	5/6/75	2,80,000
Aftak Flour Mills Water Works Rd., Dhaka	8/5/75	2,00,000
Crescent Wooden Spool Mfg. Co., Nawab Salmullah Rd. N. Gonj, Dhaka	2/3/74	3,60,000
United Engg. Ind. Tipu Sultan Rd., Dhaka	1/3/74	3,00,000
Barisal Traders Urdu Rd., Dhaka	1/4/74	1,71,200
A.B. Polythone (Khawaja Box Factory) Urdu Rd., Dhaka	25/6/74	71,700
Shaikh Flour Mill Chandrighat, Dhaka	13/4/74	1,50,000
Mecca Oil, Dal & Flour Mill Bara Katra, Dhaka	26/6/74	1,55,119

Name and Address	Date of Divestiture (day/month/year)	Divestiture Price (in Tk)
Dhaka Bobbin & Wood Products Tongi I/A, Dhaka	2/10/75	4,49,000
Diamond Rubber & Plastic Ind. Fatullah, Dhaka	13/8/77	5,32,000
Farouk Chemical Ind. Tejgaon I/A, Dhaka	27/8/74	13,54,000
Baby Ice Cream Co. Nowabkatra, Dhaka	24/11/75	6,10,000
Lacknow Star Factory Mitford Rd., Dhaka	8/12/78	85,000
Friends Optical Services Patuatully, Dhaka	12/6/79	1,04,351
Amin Metal Works K.M. Azam Lane, Dhaka	18/1/75	unknown
Bengal Hosiery Mill Narayanganj	1/1/75	unknown
Friends Rubber Ind. Posta, Dhaka	16/11/78	unknown
Ali Automobiles Motijheel C/A, Dhaka	11/12/74	1,77,777
Guilder Automatic Dry Cleaners Victoria Park, Dhaka	22/9/75	1,10,000
Baby Flour Mills BCC Road, Dhaka	6/11/75	70,125

Name and Address	Date of Divestiture (day/month/year)	Divestiture Price (in Tk)
East Bengal Flour Mill Narayanganj	1975	1,40,000
Mohammadi Oil Mills Narayanganj	23/10/74	41,000
Majid Flour Mills Kazi Reazuddin Rd. Dhaka	24/11/75	80,000
Fazli Films Nowabpur, Dhaka	1975	41,000
Desh Bandhu Chula Karkhana, Aga Sadak Rd. Dhaka	20/6/75	45,100
Crown Hosiery Mills Narayanganj	2/6/75	2,75,000
Ark Knitting Mills Narayanganj	5/10/79	3,00,000
Arman Steam Calander Narayanganj	1975	32,020
Omar Brothers Dhaka	1975	6,110
Eblic Ltd. Baizid Bostami Rd. Chittagong	26/6/75	3,80,000
Ansari Flour Mills Tajhat, Rangpur	8/12/75	75,959
North Bengal Oil Mill Santahar Rd., Bogra	3/12/79	4,00,000

Name and Address	Date of Divestiture (day/month/year)	Divestiture Price (in Tk)
S.P. Trading Co. BSCIC I/A, Comilla	30/11/78	14,02,457
Ibrahim Rice & Husking Mills, Bogra	13/5/77	41,333
Adam Salt Factory Chandpur	4/4/75	3,41,000
Abdur Razak Salt Factory Chandpur	4/4/75	3,15,000
Kohinoor Optical Ind. BSCIC I/A, Comilla	24/11/82	1,03,550
Bangladesh Cocoanut Co. Nowapara, Jessore	13/9/77	1,20,000
S.A. Sakur & Co. Natore, Rajshahi	3/2/77	2,79,521
Iqbal Saw Mill Alu Patty, Rajshahi	1/8/75	35,700
Pak Flour Mills Zadab Lahiri, Mymensingh	6/8/75	5,100
United Engineers Dhupadighi, Sylhet	28/8/75	28,00,000
Apollo Engg. Works Mirabazar, Sylhet	23/3/74	79,100
Noorahi Atta & Flour Mill, Kazir Bzr., Sylhet	21/1/74	21,200
S.E. Jan Oil Mills Kalighat, Sylhet	20/4/74	33,200

Name and Address	Date of Divestiture (day/month/year)	Divestiture Price (in Tk)
Workshop of Abdul Haq Kalighat, Sylhet	20/3/74	57,500
Tawakhal Husking Mill Dinajpur	12/12/75	4,17,997
Mohamad Ali Glass Factory, Dinajpur	1979	55,000
Diamond Flour Mills BSCIC I/A, Barisal	6/6/77	2,25,025
Star Art Press Jubilee Rd., Chitt.	12/4/75	4,60,000
Begum Rice & Oil Mills Dinajpur	17/2/75	2,61,000
Solam Nabi & Co. Dinajpur	27/1/75	1,00,500
Ali Husain Biscuit & Bread Factory Dinajpur	12/3/75	18,000
Rahman Rice & Oil Mills Dinajpur	17/2/75	1,51,000
Kohinoor Husking Mills Dinajpur	28/2/75	22,100
Mozid Iraq Husking Mills, Dinajpur	14/6/75	48,000
S.A. Malik Atta and Dal Mills, Dinajpur	18/3/75	46,000
Soleiman Rice Mill Dinajpur	18/4/75	1,31,031

Name and Address	Date of Divestiture (day/month/year)	Divestiture Price (in Tk)
Bismillah Ind. Dinajpur	3/5/78	27,200
Pak Rice Mills Dinajpur	7/2/75	71,000
Rahman Flour & Husking Mill, Dinajpur	3/5/78	41,000
Khan Rice & Atta Mills Dinajpur	17/7/75	10,000
Union Soap & Chemical Works, Dinajpur	14/3/77	90,000
Hasan Dal, Oil & Leather Factory Dinajpur	1/11/74	70,000
Khawaja Soap Factory Dinajpur	1//11/74	36,000
Star Husking Mills Dinajpur	1/11/74	9,100
Seba Husking Mills Dinajpur	1/11/74	8,100
Motor Welding Works Dinajpur	27/2/75	5,000
Saiful Haq Husking Mills, Dinajpur	27/2/75	6,400
Huda Husking Mills Dinajpur	1975	9,000
Fazal Malli Husking Mills #1, Dinajpur	1975	4,000

Name and Address	Date of Divestiture (day/month/year)	Divestiture Price (in Tk)
Fazal Malli Husking Mills #2, Dinajpur	1975	10,000
Mizam Mallik Husking Mills, Dinajpur	1975	8,000
Alauddin Husking Mill Dinajpur	1975	9,000
Shamin Rice & Atta Mill Dinajpur	1975	4,000
Shamin Printing Press Dinajpur	1975	19,700
Husbun Nessa Husking Mill, Dinajpur	1975	6,500
Seraj Aluminum Works Dewanhat, Chittagong	2/4/75	3,87,000
Steelman Engg. Works Dewanhat, Chittagong	23/6/75	30,000
Market Report Press Chand Mia Rd., Chitt.	11/4/75	65,000
Khoker Steel Ind. Dhaka Trunk Rd., Chitt.	2/10/79	3,05,000
Zenith Ltd. Shalashahar, Chitt.	24/6/77	2,81,000
Eastern Engg. Works Nasirabad, Chittagong	26/7/77	8,10,000
Premier Oil Co. Chittagong	4/1/79	8,01,000

Name and Address	Date of Divestiture (day/month/year)	Divestiture Price (in Tk)
Saleh Industries Serajdowlah Rd., Chitt.	26/6/75	5,20,000
Muradabad Ware House Dewamgonj. Chittagong	28/5/75	2,51,000
Eastern Plastic Ind. Noyeen Khan Magar Chittagong	23/6/78	20,200
Reliance Timber Works Kalirghat, Chittagong	11/7/78	18,000
Karim Roller & Flour Mills, Chittagong	23/10/75	48,004
Bangladesh Metal Ind. Leve Lane, Chittagong	12/9/75	70,250
Progati Press Sir Iqbal Rd., Khulna	25/6/75	2,00,225
Bengal Oil, Dal & Haroon Saw Mills, Khulna	30/12/75	3,87,500
Abdullah Bros. Engg. Works, Khulna	15/3/73	2,20,000
Kohinoor Oil & Dal Mills K.D. Ghose Rd., Khulna	25/5/75	2,50,000
Warzi Printing Works P.C. Roy Rd., Khulna	7/12/79	2,05,100
Ameer Engg. Works Upper Jessore Rd. Khulna	1974	1,02,000
Royal Atta Mill Sher-e-Bangla Rd., Khulna	30/5/74	23,391

Name and Address	Date of Divestiture (day/month/year)	Divestiture Price (in Tk)
Siddique Flour Mills Daulatpur, Khulna	29/5/74	15,000
Gowsia Husking & Flour Mill, Dinajpur	17/3/75	18,750
Ramna Oil Mill Sendar, Narayanganj	14/7/81	1,55,555
Central Offset Press Dhaka	8/3/72	1,55,000
Steel King Baitul Mukarram, Dhaka	8/3/72	8,00,121
C.I. Corporation Dhaka	24/5/72	2,250
New Dhaka Handloom Factory Shantibag, Dhaka	13/12/77	13,50,500
Bangladesh Knitting Mills, Narayanganj	22/7/78	6,70,000
Feroz Textile Mills Fatullah, Dhaka	8/12/78	16,06,051
Mohajir Soap Works Tejgaon I/A, Dhaka	9/5/79	60,00,000
Corn Flour Mills Demra, Dhaka	7/1/79	1,06,00,000
Spintex Agencies Jatrabari, Dhaka	8/5/78	1,85,000
United Plastic & Rubber Ind. Fatullah, Dhaka	1/3/79	17,50,000

Name and Address	Date of Divestiture (day/month/year)	Divestiture Price (in Tk)
Noor Industries BSCIC I/A, Barisal	25/11/78	3,56,197
Rupkhate Cinema Comilla	25/10/79	31,15,000
Bangladesh Rope Works North Kotalli, Chitt.	2/12/77	48,00,500
Al Modina Printing Press, Chittagong	17/2/78	1,26,611
Millat Board Mills Pahartali, Chitt.	27/7/78	3,08,000
National Radio Products Asadgonj, Chitt.	25/3/78	17,00,707
M.A. Jan Co. Mujib Rd., Chittagong	15/12/78	1,00,250
Dessa Extractions Fouzdarhat, Chitt.	12/5/78	20,00,000
Sitara Iron & Steel Ind., Baizid Bostami Rd. Chittagong	27/11/79	8,05,000
Yousuf Oil Mill Shar-e-Bangla, Khulna	16/11/77	10,10,110
Bangladesh Oil Mills Sephlia, Khulna	23/10/78	4,02,000
Shakhara Fish Freezing Satkhira, Khulna	23/12/76	81,500
Khulna Ice Co. Belphulia, Khulna	15/1/79	55,54,757

Name and Address	Date of Divestiture (day/month/year)	Divestiture Price (in Tk)
Sultan Ice & Cold Storage Faridabad, Dhaka	25/3/80	18,50,000
Fazal Industries Nasirabad I/A, Chitt.	9/4/80	17,01,105
Khawaja Hosiery Mill Narayanganj	4/3/82	4,01,102
Oriental Cinema Rangpur	6/4/81	25,00,000
Bawany Waterproofing & Shabashah Trading Co. Nasirabad I/A, Chitt.	6/5/81	21,00,000
Al-Hamd Industries Satkhira, Khula	3/3/81	2,31,001
Salubari Oil Mill Dinajpur	28/10/80	16,00,001
Ali's Laboratories Eora Hagh Bazaar, Dhaka	6/11/81	10,00,001
Jahan Killer (Bd) Ltd. Dhaka	20/6/78	50,000
Karnaphuli Mills (Eastern) Ltd. & Bengal Embroidery Mill Fatulla, Dhaka	10/6/81	50,40,560
Dhaka Glass Works Faridabad, Dhaka	25/3/80	22,00,000
Welliany Trading Co. Brahmanbaria, Comilla	1980	100

Name and Address	Date of Divestiture (day/month/year)	Divestiture Price (in Tk)
Central Offset Press Tejgaon I/A, Dhaka	1980	100
Nas Helal Press Chittagong	5/2/82	100
Tajmahal Plastic Ind. Dhaka	17/5/79	5,200
Silver Oil Mills Chittagong	7/12/79	2,37,500
Zilani Saw Mills Chittagong	7/12/79	3,91,000
Flour Mill Chandmari Rd., Chitt.	2/7/80	7,700
Bengal Coir Rope Mfg. Co. Jessore	28/3/79	41,000
Chittagong Timber Works A.S. Das Lane, Chitt.	2/7/80	1,80,000
Sabu Salt Factory Chandpur	29/8/78	65,250
Star Engg. & Flour Mills, Mymensingh	26/9/79	7,100
Haji Atta & Oil Mills Bonarpara, Rangpur	5/3/79	21,000
Bengal Soap Factory Gaibandha, Rangpur	5/3/79	15,000
Ramna Atta & Dal Mills Gaibandha, Rangpur	5/3/79	4,101

Name and Address	Date of Divestiture (day/month/year)	Divestiture Price (in Tk)
Islam Flour Mills Station Rd., Rangpur	5/3/79	10,510
Star Flour Mills Mymensingh	26/9/79	2,100
Bahar Flour Mills Mymensingh	26/9/79	1,700
Mohajir Flour Mills Mymensingh	26/9/79	5,600
Aleem Dal Mills Jessore Rd., Khulna	26/10/81	21,100
Aziz Metal Works Tejgaon I/A, Dhaka	24/10/82	5,50,000
National Ice Factory Mymensingh	31/1/83	10,25,100
Aftab Khan Saw Mills Station Rd., Jamalpur	21/7/82	40,500
Golden Ice Cream Fac. Syedpur, Rangpur	6/9/82	10,050
Shaidi Oil Mills Rajshahi	18/6/82	36,000
Aftab Ahmed Oil Mills Station Rd., Pabna	18/1/83	3,65,200
Sharahi Hotel Serajgonj, Pabna	18/1/83	4,05,500
Premier Polythane Ind. Agasadek Rd., Dhaka	19/1/83	2,28,808

Name and Address	Date of Divestiture (day/month/year)	Divestiture Price (in Tk)
Zamindar Tobacco Co. Begum Bazaar, Dhaka	31/1/83	10,001
Arag Salt Factory Chandpur	20/6/76	10,600
National Flour Mill Adamjee Nagar, Dhaka	9/7/84	75,000
Bangladesh United Traders Nasirabad I/A, Chitt.	Dec. 1983	26,01,000
Vulcan Pictures Nowabpur Rd. Dhaka	1975	25,250
Star Roller Flour Mills BSCIC I/A, Barisal	3/3/83	6,25,000
Shakoor Oil Mill Rajgonj, Comilla	27/8/82	2,51,000
J.S. Hosiery BSCIC I/A, Pabna	16/11/83	51,500
Ayrunachal Oil Mills Serajgonj, Pabna	31/10/83	35,100
Mustari Begum Flour Mill #1, Jamalpur	3/10/83	5,000
Litho Art Press Dhaka	18/2/81	100

D. PARTIALLY ABANDONED ENTERPRISES (UNDER MANAGEMENT OF DIRECTOR GENERAL OF INDUSTRIES)

Name and Address	Date of Divestiture (day/month/year)	Divestiture Price (in Tk)
Anwar Textile Mills Tejgaon I/A, Dhaka	11/3/75	3,03,750

Name and Address	Date of Divestiture (day/month/year)	Divestiture Price (in Tk)
Hotel Nizami Liakat Ave., Dhaka	4/11/75	50,000
Hakim Engg. Works, Ltd. Baizid Bostami, Chitt.	5/10/74	8,525
Asbestos Products Tejgaon I/A, Dhaka	31/12/74	2,05,832
Atlas Engg. & Ship Builders, Narayanganj	25/5/79	53,665
Khurshed Industrial Corp. Tejgaon I/A, Dhaka	12/6/81	20,00,000
Yusuf Mills Jessore	15/9/80	1,00,557
Bangladesh Enterprise, Ltd., Tejgaon I/A, Dhaka	27/5/81	7,51,387
Kashem Metal Works Brahmanbaria, Comilla	8/9/81	20,000
Megregur Salfar (Bd), Ltd., Dhaka	1981	2,70,000
Bengal Steel Works, Ltd. Tejgaon I/A, Dhaka	11/8/81	7,71,597
Sunshine Cables & Rubber Works Tongi I/A, Dhaka	29/3/80	22,40,000
Farooq Services Chittagong	7/1/82	80,000
G.M.G. Industrial Corp. Dhaka	19/5/83	unknown

Name and Address	Date of Divestiture (day/month/year)	Divestiture Price (in Tk)
Suihari rice & Oil Mill Dinajpur	19/3/84	unknown

E. FULLY VESTED (FORMER "ENEMY PROPERTY") INDUSTRIAL ENTERPRISES

Name and Address	Date of Divestiture (day/month/year)	Divestiture Price (in Tk)
South Sylhet Grinding Mill, Sreemongal, Sylhet	10/4/70	51,000
Rice Mill of Sohanlal Bazle, Nilphamary	25/5/70	27,125
Dhanwat Rice Mill Birampur, Dinajpur	24/10/70	1,91,000
Gunin Ice Factory Kawarchar, Barisal	20/8/70	1,40,000
Amar Talkies Parbotipur, Dinajpur	19/11/70	1,51,000
Banga Luxmi Mill Panchbibi, Bogra	25/12/73	75,151
Kushtia Sugarcane Mill Kushtia	26/6/74	45,577
East Bengal Co. Chandpur	29/1/71	95,000
Moha Luxmi Rice Mill Bedarganj, Rangpur	26/5/70	1,50,000
Malpani Rice Mill Dinajpur	31/3/70	1,55,000
Gualnondo Ice Factory Rajbari, Faridpur	15/11/70	7,95,000

Name and Address	Date of Divestiture (day/month/year)	Divestiture Price (in Tk)
Padma Ice Factory Rajbari, Faridpur	15/11/70	2,31,000
Bengal Burma Rice Trading & Rice Mill Chandpur	8/9/70	2,00,000
Kamala Rice Mill Kalkini, Faridpur	14/3/75	20,600
Sen Agarwala & Co. Kushtia	3/4/75	9,000
Sree Shankar Rice Mill Pulhat, Dinajpur	9/2/75	8,52,500
Sree Mohabir Rice & Oil Mill, Fulbari, Dinajpur	9/2/75	5,22,350
Bhawanipur Rice Mill Bhawanipur, Dinajpur	9/2/75	1,11,500
Sree Ratan Rice Mill Pulhat, Dinajpur	9/2/75	7,75,940
E.B. Silicate Mfg. Works, Ltd., Narayangonj	4/7/75	10,000
Baizanath Prosad Mahadeo Prosad Dal Mill Ranibazar, Rajshahi	17/11/75	2,05,000
B.G. (Bangla) Rice Mill #2, Ruhea, Dinajpur	31/10/75	1,71,000
Harikrishn Rice Mill Chirirbandar, Dinajpur	28/1/76	2,65,707
Azad Oil Mill Daulatgonj, Comilla	6/12/75	17,000

Name and Address	Date of Divestiture (day/month/year)	Divestiture Price (in Tk)
Sree Mahabali Rice & Dal Mill, Pabna	5/1/78	1,70,000
Nursingh Rice Mill Pulhat, Dinajpur	17/9/68	46,000
Sree Durga Rice, Dal & Flour Mill, Bogra	24/3/76	3,00,000
Sree Sankar Rice Mill Fulbari, Dinajpur	24/12/76	4,50,000
River View Rice Mill Chirirbandar, Dinajpur	30/4/75	4,85,000
Sree Mohabir No. Bengal Mill, Pabna	4/2/76	3,71,000
Sree Durga Mill Mirkadim, Dhaka	17/6/76	13,05,551
Khetawat Oil Mill Rupsa, Khulna	1/3/76	9,27,000
Pulhat Rice Mill Pulhat, Dinajpur	8/7/77	2,55,000
Luxmi Rice, Atta & Oil Mill, Lalmonirhat	20/7/77	1,44,000
Indo-Bangla Pharmaceutical Works, Barisal	16/12/77	6,51,000
Mohabir Rice & Oil Mill Saidpur, Nilpharmary	24/3/78	unknown
Tatarkandi Ice Factory Kuliarchar, Kishoregonj	10/12/78	72,000

Name and Address	Date of Divestiture (day/month/year)	Divestiture Price (in Tk)
B.G. Bangla Rice Mill #1 Ruhea, Thakurgaon	6/11/78	5,67,000
Luxmi Rice Mill Cemetery Rd., Khulna	3/11/78	2,31,010
Bangla Hilli Rice Mill Hilli, Dinajpur	7/11/78	3,00,000
Arag Oushadhalaya Pyaridas Rd., Dhaka	8/5/79	14,05,555
Ayurvedia Pharmacy Armanian St., Dhaka	15/1/81	35,00,000
Jessore Oil Mill Jessore	18/4/80	2,550
Robson Rice Mill Bhoysewar, Faridpur	2/7/81	8,600
Shakti Oushadhalaya Shamibagh Rd., Dhaka	24/8/81	2,37,00,000
H.N. Poddar & Co. Boyra, Khulna	28/9/81	70,10,000
Chowdhiram Kushalchand Nilpamary	25/2/82	47,500

F. PARTLY VESTED (FORMER ENEMY PROPERTY) INDUSTRIAL ENTERPRISES

Khactawat Aluminum Works Talora, Bogra (40% shares)	12/11/75	1,38,613

Name and Address	Date of Divestiture (day/month/year)	Divestiture Price (in Tk)
Luxmi Rice & Oil Mill Domar, Nilpamary (7 annas share)	6/10/76	36,102
Comilla Laboratories Comilla (200 shares)	21/3/78	4,332
Zenith Laboratories Feni (50% shares)	14/9/79	5,643
Swoika Oil Mills Imamgonj, Dhaka (90 shares)	24/10/80	56,250
Badargonj Rice Mill Badargonj, Rangpur (5.5 annas share)	3/5/81	1,46,446

G. MISCELLANEOUS (UNITS THAT DID NOT MATCH BETWEEN TWO MINISTRY OF INDUSTRIES LISTS AND FOR WHICH DATES OF DIVESTITURE NOT KNOWN)

Name and Address	Date	Price
Javed Tannery Hazaribagh, Dhaka	1984?	15,10,500
Arag Ltd. Strand Rd., Chittigong	unknown	1,26,80,241
Bangladesh Cold Storage Mirkadim, Munshigonj	unknown	1,23,45,633
Omar Sons Ltd. Tejgaon I/A, Dhaka	1979?	1,61,50,000
Bangladesh Fabric Co. Nabigonj, Narayanganj	unknown	1,74,00,000

Name and Address	Date of Divestiture (day/month/year)	Divestiture Price (in Tk)
Parbatipur Rice & Oil Mill, Partbatipur Dinajpur (movable assets only	unknown	2,38,888
A.B. Das Engg. Works Firingee Bazar, Chitt.	unknown	70,000
A.B. Das Saw Mill Firingee Bazar, Chitt.	unknown	80,000
Gour Oil Mill Chowmohuni, Noakali	unknown	1,90,000
Barisal Ice Assn. Chamarpatty, Barisal	unknown	3,10,000
Hussain Electric Ind. & Group of Industries Purana Paltan, Dhaka	unknown	5,50,000
Taj Wire Nail Ind. Tejgaon I/A, Dhaka	unknown	4,00,000
Verzinia Tobacco Ltd. Bogra Jamil Soap Works Ltd. Bogra Jamiluddin Ltd. Bogra Azizuddin Industries Chittigong Hill Tracts Tobacconi (Bd) Ltd. Dhaka National Tobacco Ltd. Rangpur Aslam Bhai & Iqbal Bhai Bogra	unknown	2,37,89,012

Name and Address	Date of Divestiture (day/month/year)	Divestiture Price (in Tk)
Progressive Industries Sylhet	unknown	3,10,000
Aftab Khan Flour Mills Jamalpur	unknown	2,40,000
Islamabad Sewing Thread Chowkbazar, Chitt.	unknown	50,555
Suihari Rice & Oil Mills Dinajpur	unknown	27,13,325
Rahmania Popular Bread & Biscuit Factory Sutrapur, Dhaka	unknown	10,01,101
Shamim Industries Block-D, Rd. #2, ?	unknown	5,10,500
Shabana Talkies Ruhia, Thakurgaon	unknown	1,67,067
Atlas Industries Kazi Reazuddin Rd. Dhaka	unknown	3,75,000
Mustari Begum Flour Mill, Jamalpur	unknown	2,500
Mozhul Industries Amin Jute Mill, Chitt.	unknown	87,547
Zakaria Roller Flour Mill, P.O. Double Mooring, Chittagong	unknown	2,20,000
Rahim Flour Mills Chittagong	unknown	20,000

Name and Address	Date of Divestiture (day/month/year)	Divestiture Price (in Tk)
Hotel Afgania West Mecot Rd. Khulna	unknown	6,53,900
Ispahani Marshall Ltd. Chittagong (85% sold 15% held by gov't.)	unknown	29,15,220
Bangladesh Tyres Ltd. Fatuallay, Dhaka	unknown	25,000

H. TEXTILE MILLS TRANSFERRED TO BANGLADESHI SPONSORS

Ashraf Textile Mills Tongi, Dhaka	30/11/82
Al-Haj Textile Mills Iswardi, Pabna	12/12/82
Asiatic Cotton Mills Chittagong	5/12/82
Asfar Cotton Mills Savar, Dhaka	6/3/83
Bogra Cotton Spinning Mills, Bogra	14/12/82
Chittagong Textile Mills Chittagong	6/12/82
Chand Textile Mills Dhaka	8/12/82
Chand Textile (Spinning) Mills, Dhaka	8/12/82

Name and Address	Date of Divestiture (day/month/year)	Divestiture Price (in Tk)
Gawsia Cotton Spinning Mills, Murapara, Dhaka	5/12/82	
Halima Textile Mills Comilla	14/12/82	
Ibrahim Cotton Mills Chittagong	30/11/82	
Jaba Textile Mills Dhaka	5/12/82	
Jalil Textile Mills Chittagong	5/12/82	
Mainamati Textile Mills Comilla	2/12/82	
Muslin Cotton Mills Kaliganj, Dhaka	12/12/82	
Serajgonj Spinning & Cotton Mills Serajgonj, Pabna	30/11/82	
Mowla Textile Mills Dhaka	5/1/83	
Quashem Cotton Mills Tongi, Dhaka	1/2/83	
Raz Textile Mills Noapara, Jessore	13/2/83	
Calico Cotton Mills Pabna	28/2/83	
Haibibur Rahman Textile Mills, Comilla	9/3/83	

Name and Address	Date of Divestiture (day/month/year)	Divestiture Price (in Tk)
Goalundo Textile Mills Faridpur	3/4/83	
Kushtia Textile Mills Kushtia	6/3/83	

Incomplete & Inoperative Mills

Tamizuddin Textile Mills Conapara, Dhaka	19/1/83	
Rupali Noor Textile Mills Hasnabad, Dhaka	13/2/83	
Cotton Textile Crafts Ltd., Dhaka	14/2/83	
Pahartali Textile & Hosiery Mills Chittagong	26/5/84	

I. JUTE MILLS TRANSFERRED TO BANGLADESHI SPONSORS

[Source *Quarterly Jute Goods Statistics*, a publication of the Bangladesh Jute Mills Corporation, Apr.-June 1985-86, pp. 22-23. These are the mills now under the Bangladesh Jute Mills Association (BJMA).]

Allied Jute Mills Kanchan, Dhaka	30/11/82	
Alijan Jute Mills Narsinghdi, Dhaka	30/11/82	
Ajax Jute Mills Mirerdanga, Daulatpur	9/12/82	
A.R. Howlader Jute Mills Madaripur, Fairdpur	12/12/82	

Name and Address	Date of Divestiture (day/month/year)	Divestiture Price (in Tk)
Ashraf Jute Mills Kanchan, Dhaka	9/1/83	
A.K. Khan Jute Mills North Kattali, Chitt.	31/1/83	
Alhaj Jute Mills Sarishabari, Jamalpur	30/12/82	
Anowara Jute Mills Barabkunda, Chittagong	12/12/82	
Afil Jute Mills Atra, Khulna	30/11/82	
Broad Burlap Industries Betka, Dhaka	30/11/82	
Cooperative Jute Mills Ghorashal, Dhaka	30/11/82	
Chittagong Jute Mfg. Co. Kallurghat, Chittagong	15/2/84	
Dhaka Jute Mills Faridabad, Dhaka	30/11/82	
Delta Jute Mills Chaumuhani, Noakhali	30/1/83	
Fauji Chakal Ghorashal, Dhaka	25/9/83	
Gawsi Jute Mills Murapara, Dhaka	23/1//83	
Janata Jute Mills Ghorashal, Dhaka	9/1/83	

Name and Address	Date of Divestiture (day/month/year)	Divestiture Price (in Tk)
Jabbar Jute Mills Bhairab Bazar Mymensingh	27/2/84	
Kohinoor Jute Mills Gouripur, Dhaka	15/12/82	
M. Rahman Jute Mills Barb Kunda, Chittagong	15/1/83	
Mashriqui Jute Mills Kanchan, Dhaka	30/11/82	
Moshen Jute Mills Siromoni, Khulna	9/12/82	
National Jute Mills Ghorashel, Dhaka	25/6/83	
Noapara Jute Mills Noapara, Jessore	9/12/82	
N. Askari Jute Mills Kanchan, Dhaka	31/7/85	
Pubali Jute Mills Ghorashal, Dhaka	2/2/83	
Quasem Jute Mills Sitallpur, Chittagong	29/12/82	
Sattar Jute Mills Kanchan, Dhaka	30/11/82	
Sonali Jute Mills Mirerdanga, Khulna	6/1/83	
S.K.M. Jute Mills Barabkunda, Chittagong	30/11/82	

Name and Address	Date of Divestiture (day/month/year)	Divestiture Price (in Tk)
Sultana Jute Mills Kumira, Chittagong	30/11/82	
Star Alkaid Jute Mills Chandpur, Comilla	13/1/83	
Taj Jute Backing Co. Demra, Dhaka	27/5/85	
Victory Jute Products No. Kattali, Chittagong	15/2/84	
W. Rahman Jute Mills Chandpur, Comilla	19/1/83	

APPENDIX B

State-Owned Enterprises

BANGLADESH TEXTILE MILLS
    CORP.
Amin Textiles, Ltd.
Barisal Textile
Bengal Textile Mills, Ltd.
Chisty Textile Mills, Ltd.
Dinajpur Textile Mills, Ltd.
Darwani Textile
Dost Textile Mills, Ltd.
Eagle Star Textile Mills, Ltd.
Fine Cotton Mills, Ltd.
Kokil Textile Mills, Ltd.
Kohinoor Spinning Mills, Ltd.
Kishoregonj Textile
Monoo Textiles
Madaripur Textile
Noakhali Textile
Orient Textile Mills, Ltd.
Quaderia Textile Mills, Ltd.
R.R. Textile Mills, Ltd.

Rajshahi Textile
Rangamati Textile
Satraq Textile Mills, Ltd.
Sylhet Textile
Tangail Cotton Mills, Ltd.
Ahmed Bawany Textile Mills
Bangladesh Textile Mills, Ltd.
Chittaranjan Cotton Mills
Dhaka Cotton Mills, Ltd.
Khulna Textile Mills, Ltd.
Luxminarayan Cotton Mills
Meghna Textile
National Cotton Mills, Ltd.
Olympia Textile Mills, Ltd.
Sharmin Textile Mills, Ltd.
Sundarban Textile
Zeenat Textile Mills, Ltd.
Pylon Industries, Ltd.
Karilin Silk Mills, Ltd.
Valika Woolen Mills, Ltd.

Source: Government of Bangladesh, Ministry of Finance: *System For Autonomous Bodies for Reporting and Evaluation* (Dhaka, 1985), as cited in Alamgir, Dr. Muhiuddin Khan: *Public Enterprises and the Financial System in Bangladesh* (Dhaka, Sept. 1986).]

Zofine Fabrics, Ltd.
Magura Textile Mills
Kurigram Textile Mills
Paruma Textile Mills, Ltd.
Elahi Textile Mills, Ltd.
Rupali Nylon, Ltd.
N.H. Textile Mills, Ltd.
Rahman Textile Mills, Ltd.
Panchbibi Textile Mills
Hafiz Textile Mills

BANGLADESH JUTE MILLS
    CORP.
Adamjee Jute Mills
Associated Bagging
Bangladesh Jute Mills
Bawa Jute Mills
Karim Jute Mills
Latif Bawany Jute Mills
Munwar Jute Mills
Mymensingh Jute Mills
Nabarun Jute Mills
Nishat Jute Mills
Taj Jute Backing Co.
U.M.C. Jute Mills
Bangladesh Fabrics Co.
Aleem Jute Mills
Carpeting Jute Mills
Crescent Jute Mills
Daulatpur Jute Mills
Eastern Jute Mills
Jessore Jute Industries
Peoples Jute Mills
Platinum Jubilee Jute Mills
Purbachal Jute Mills
Star Jute Mills
Rajshahi Jute Mills
Quami Jute Mills
Amin Jute Mills
Gul-Ahmed Jute Mills
Hafiz Jute Mills
Karnafuli Jute Mills
M.M. Jute Mills

R.R. Jute Mills
Bagdad-Dhaka Carpet Factory
Furat-Karnafuli Carpet Factory
Jute Plastic Plant
Galfra Habib

BANGLADESH SUGAR AND
    FOOD INDUSTRIES CORP.
Rajshahi Sugar Mills, Ltd.
Kushtia Sugar Mills, Ltd.
Rangpur Sugar Mills, Ltd.
Thakurgaon Sugar Mills, Ltd.
North Bengal Sugar Mills, Ltd.
Carew & Co. (BD), Ltd.
Zeal Bangla Sugar Mills, Ltd.
Mobarakganj Sugar Mills, Ltd.
Shampur Sugar Mills, Ltd.
Panchgarh Sugar Mills, Ltd.
Kaliachapra Sugar Mills, Ltd.
Faridpur Sugar Mills, Ltd.
Setabganj Sugar Mills, Ltd.
Deshbandhu Sugar Mills, Ltd.
Joypurhat Sugar Mills, Ltd.
Natore Sugar Mills
Dhaka Vegetable Oil Industries,
    Ltd.
Rice Bran Oil Extraction Plant

BANGLADESH STEEL AND
    ENGINEERING CORP.
Engineering Industries, Ltd.
Eastern Cables
Eastern Tubes, Ltd.
Gazi Wires, Ltd.
General Electric Manufacturing
    Co., Ltd.
Metalex Corporation, Ltd.
Bangladesh Diesel Plant
Bangladesh Machine Tools
    Factory
Bangladesh Can Co., Ltd.
Prantik Traders
Quality Iron & Steel Co., Ltd.

Dockyard & Engineering Works, Ltd.
Khulna Shipyard, Ltd.
Chittagong Steel Mills, Ltd.
Atlas Bangladesh, Ltd.
Pragoti Industries, Ltd.
Dhaka Steel Works, Ltd.
National Tubes, Ltd.
Dhaka Radio Electronic Co., Ltd.
Fecto Industries, Ltd.
Meher Industries (BD), Ltd.
Bangladesh Cycle Industries, Ltd.
Bangladesh Blade Factory
Chittagong Dry Dock & HSS
Renwick, Tajneswar & Co., Ltd.

BANGLADESH CHEMICAL INDUSTRIES CORP.
Zia Fertilizer Co., Ltd.
Urea Fertilizer Factory, Ltd.
Natural Gas Fertilizer Factory, Ltd.
Triple Super Phosphate Complex, Ltd.
Khulna Newsprint Mills, Ltd.
Karnaphuli Paper Mills, Ltd.
North Bengal Paper Mills, Ltd.
Sylhet Pulp & Paper Mills, Ltd.
Karnaphuli Rayon & Chemicals Ltd.
Khulna Hard Board Mills, Ltd.
Bangladesh Insulator & Sanitary Ware Factory, Ltd.
Chhatak Cement Co., Ltd.
Chittagong Cement Clinker Grinding
Chittagong Chemical Complex

Usmania Glass Sheet Factory, Ltd.
Kohinoor Chemical Co., Ltd.
Kohinoor Battery Manufacturing Co., Ltd.
Lira Industrial Enterprise, Ltd.
Ujala Match Factory, Ltd.
Polash Urea Fertilizer Factory
Dhaka Match Factory
Dhaka Match Works
Eagle Box & Carton Manufacturing Co., Ltd.

BANGLADESH FOREST INDUSTRIES DEVELOPMENT CORP.
Karnaphuli Valley Timber Extraction, Kaptai
Expanded Rubber Planting, Processing Project, Dhaka
Lumber Processing Complex and Saw Mill
Industrial Estate, Kaptai
Sangoo-Matamuhuri Projects, Chittagong
FIDCO Furniture Complex, Chittagong
Cabinet Manufacturing Plant, Dhaka
Cabinet Manufacturing Plant, Chittagong
Cabinet Manufacturing Plant, Khulna
Particle Board & Veneering Plant
Wood Treating Plant, Chittagong
Wood Treating Plant - 2nd Expansion, Chittagong
Wood Treating Plant, Khulna
National Tea Company Ltd.

BANGLADESH OIL, GAS &
MINERALS CORP.
Takerghat Limestone Mining
Project
Bijoypur White Clay Mining
Project
Joypurhat Limestone Mine &
Cement Project
Jamalganj Coal Mine
Madhyapara Hard Rock
Mining Project
Bagali Bazar Limestone
Bangladesh Gas Fields Co.,
Ltd.
Sylhet Gas Fields, Ltd.
Amin Oil Field
Kailash Tilla Gas Field Project
Kamta Gas Fields Project
Bakhrabad Gas System, Ltd.
Titas Gas Transmission and
Distribution, Ltd.
Jalalabad Gas Transmission
and Distribution System

BANGLADESH FISHERIES
DEVELOPMENT CORP.
Fish Processing Scheme, Cox's
Bazar
Boat Building Complex,
Chittagong
Fish Net Factory, Comilla
Marketing and Distribution,
Pagla
Wholesale Fish Market,
Rajshahi
Fish Processing Plant, Mongla
Fish Landing and Marketing,
Khepupara
Fish Landing and Marketing,
Pathagata
Wholesale Fish Market, Cox's
Bazar

Fish Harbor Complex,
Chittagong
Wholesale Fish Market,
Khulna

BANGLADESH FREEDOM
FIGHTERS' WELFARE
TRUST
Paruma (E), Ltd.
Bux Rubber Co., Ltd.
Eastern Chemical Industries
Metal Packages, Ltd.
United Tobacco Co., Ltd.
Tabani Beverage Co.
Mimi Chocolate, Ltd.
Hyesons Group of Industries
Model Engineering Works
Hardeo Glass Works
Buxly Paints, Ltd.
Sirco Soap & Chemical
Industries, Ltd.
Gulistan Film Corp.
Chow-Chin-Chow Restaurant
Durbar Advertising and
Publication
Purnima Filling and Service
Station
Electronics and Film
Equipment
Multiple Juice Concentrate
Plant

BANGLADESH PARJATAN
CORP.
Duty Free Shop
Khulna Project (Hotel Section)
Ruchita Restaurant, Bar
Sakura Restaurant, Bar
Mary Anderson Restaurant
Chittagong Project Hotel
Cox's Bazar Project Hotel
Rangamati Project Motel

Rajshahi Project Hotel
Bogra Project
Sylhet Project
Nagarbari Project Restaurant
Cox's Bazar Youth Hostel
Bangladesh Tours and Travels

BANGLADESH SMALL AND
   COTTAGE INDUSTRIES
   CORP.
Bangladesh Handicraft
   Marketing Corp.

BANGLADESH PETROLEUM
   CORP.
Bangladesh Petroleum Corp.
Burmah Eastern, Ltd.
Jamuna Oil Co., Ltd.
Meghna Petroleum, Ltd.
Eastern Refinery, Ltd.
Eastern Lubricant Blenders,
   Ltd.
Standard Asiatic Oil Co., Ltd.
Asphaltic Bitumen Plant
Liquefied Petroleum Gas, Ltd.

BOARD OF MANAGEMENT OF
   BANGLADESH
   GOVERNMENT
   SERVANT'S
   BENEVOLENT FUND
Board of Management of
   Bangladesh Government
   Servant's
Benevolent Fund
Board of Trustees, Bangladesh
   Government's Group
Insurance Fund
Board of Trustees, Bangladesh
   Government's (former
   central)
Servant's Benevolent & Group
   Insurance Fund

CIVIL AVIATION AUTHORITY
Bangladesh Services, Ltd.
   (Hotel Sheraton)
Hotel Sonargaon

BANGLADESH ROAD
   TRANSPORT CORP.
Bus Division
Truck Division

BANKS AND FINANCIAL
   INSTITUTIONS
Bangladesh Bank
Sonali Bank
Agrani Bank
Janata Bank
Rupali Bank
Bangladesh Krishi Bank
Grameen Bank
Bangladesh Shilpa Bank
Bangladesh Shilpa Rin
   Sangstha
Bangladesh House Building
   Finance Corp.
Investment Corporation of
   Bangladesh
Investment Advisory Centre of
   Bangladesh
Jiban Bima Corp.
Sadhran Bima Corp.

MISCELLANEOUS
Telephone Shilpa Sangstha,
   Ltd.
Bangladesh Cable Shilpa, Ltd.
Bangladesh Power
   Development Board
Chittagong Water Supply and
   Sewerage Authority
Dhaka Water Supply and
   Sewerage Authority
Chittagong Development
   Authority

Dhaka Improvement Trust
Khulna Development
Authority
Rajshahi Town Development
Authority
Dhaka Divisional
Development Board
Rajshai Divisional
Development Board
Khulna Divisional
Development Board
Chittagong Divisional
Development Board
Chittagong Hill Tracts
Development Board
Offshore Island Development
Board (Barisal)
Haor Development Board
Bangladesh Jute Corp.

Trading Corporation of
Bangladesh
Bangladesh Consumer
Supplies Co.
Bangladesh Warehouse Corp.
Karnaphuli Shipping, Ltd.
Bangladesh Shipping Corp.
Bangladesh Inland Water
Transport Corp.
Chittagong Port Authority
Port of Chalna Authority
Bangladesh Biman Corp.
Bangladesh Railway
Bangladesh Telegraph and
Telephone Board
Bangladesh Plantation
Employees Provident Fund
Bangladesh Industrial
Technical Assistance Centre

APPENDIX C

Survey Questionnaire for Privatized Enterprises

Note: All information will be (a) kept completely confidential, (b) used only for study and research, and (c) used to identify problems and solutions relating to privatization

ORGANIZATIONAL INFORMATION

Name of Enterprise _____

Address_____ Telephone _____

Previous Enterprise Name or Structure (with approximate dates) _____

Legal Status of Enterprise: Proprietary_____ , Partnership_____ , Ltd. Co. _____

Year Established _____ , Date Nationalized _____ , Date Privatized _____

Nature of Business: Manufacturing ____ , Commercial ____ , Wholesale _____ ,
Retail_____ , Domestic Trading _____ , Export Trading _____ ,
Transportation ____ , Construction ____ , Agribusiness ____ ,
Food Processing ____ , Jute ____ , Textiles ____ , Garments ____ ,
Steel/Metals _____ , Engineering _____ , Chemicals ____ ,
Service (specify) _____ , Other (specify) _____

Principal Products or Services _____

Names of Principal Officers (and titles) _____

Names of Principal Shareholders _____
_____

OPERATIONAL INFORMATION

Compensation if any, when taken over by government _____
What percent of enterprise was considered "abandoned" property? _____

Price negotiated when purchased from government _____
Percentage of sale price paid off to date _____
Percentage ownership of enterprise _____ ; Government retains _____ percent

Liabilities accepted when purchased from government
Only liabilities that existed when taken over by government _____
Total liabilities existing when divested and purchased _____
Other liabilities (specify) _____
Liabilities (type and %) paid off to date _____

General condition (and age) of major equipment and facilities when purchased
from government _____

Major equipment added by government during time nationalized (cost & type)
_____

Major equipment or renovations added since purchase from government
(cost and type) _____

Production (in units)—percentage increase (+) or decrease (–) since purchase from
government** _____

Production (costs)—percentage increase or decrease since purchase from
government** _____

Sales—percentage increase or decrease since purchase from government** _____
_____

Profit (or loss) before taxes—percentage change (+ or –) since purchase from
government** _____

Number of employees	When Nationalized	When purchased from government	Present
Officers	_____	_____	_____
Staff	_____	_____	_____
Permanent Workers	_____	_____	_____
Bodli Workers	_____	_____	_____
Casual Workers	_____	_____	_____
Total:	_____	_____	_____

Value of shares (if applicable)—percentage increase or decrease in value since purchase from government** _____

Amount invested in enterprise since purchase from government _____
    Source of funds: Own funds _____ , family _____ , friends _____ ,
                DFI _____ , bank _____ , Other (specify) _____

General comments on future plans for modernization, expansion or reduction of company _____
_____
_____
_____
_____
_____

General comments on government policies, programs, and procedures that have affected your business (positively or negatively), including any suggestions for changes _____
_____
_____
_____
_____
_____

Note: ** = Actual figures would be appreciated in answering questions marked with the asterisk (**). At the optimum, we would appreciate figures for 2-3 years before nationalization, (b) 2-3 years just before disinvestment and purchase from government, and (c) annual figures since purchase from government. At the minimum, we would appreciate percentages.

AGAIN, BE ASSURED — ALL INFORMATION WILL BE KEPT
COMPLETELY CONFIDENTIAL

Terms and Conditions for Transfer of Ownership of Privatized Jute Mills

Government of the People's Republic of Bangladesh
Ministry of Industries & Commerce
Jute Division
Adamjee Court
115-120 Motijheel Commercial Area, Dacca - 2.

No. JD/UC/TJM-1/82/   Dated: 27/9/82

DATED*

Whereas the following industrial enterprises were Nationalised under the Bangladesh Industrial Enterprises (Nationalisation) Order, 1972 (P.O. 27 of 1972) and all shares in each of these Industrial Enterprises vested in Government;

And whereas the Government has decided to transfer all the shares of the aforesaid industrial enterprises;

Now, therefore, in pursuance of the second proviso to clause (2) of Article 4 of the said Order, the Government is pleased to make an offer to the persons entitled to receive payment of compensation under Article 9 of the said Order to sell, on the terms and conditions specified below, shares of the said industrial enterprises in propor-

*As cited in the Chishty, Shamsul Haque: *Privatization in Developing Countries: The Experience of Bangladesh* (Manila, ADB Conference on Privatization, Jan./ Feb. 1985).

tion to their respective shareholdings in such industrial enterprises as on the date of nationalisation.

Name of the Industrial Enterprises:

1. Broad Burlap Industries Ltd.
2. Mohsen Jute Mills Ltd.
3. S.K.M. Jute Mills Ltd.
4. Sultana Jute Mills Ltd.
5. Mashrique Jute Mills Ltd.
6. Dacca Jute Mills Ltd.
7. Allied Jute Mills Ltd.
8. Noapara Jute Mills Ltd.
9. Afil Jute Mills Ltd.
10. Ajax Jute Mills Ltd.
11. Alhaj Jute Mills Ltd.
12. A.R. Howladar Jute Mills Ltd.
13. Alijan Jute mills Ltd.
14. Co-operative Jute Mills Ltd.
15. Delta Jute Mills Ltd.
16. Kohinoor Jute Mills Ltd.
17. Maqbular Rahman Jute Mills Ltd.
18. Pubali Jute Mills Ltd.
19. Sattar Jute Mills Ltd.
20. W. Rahman Jute Mills Ltd.
21. Anowara Jute Mills Ltd
22. A.K. Khan Jute Mills Ltd.
23. Aleem Jute Mills Ltd.
24. National Jute Mills Ltd.
25. Star Alkaid Jute Mills Ltd.
26. Sonali Jute Mills Ltd.
27. Ashraf Jute Mills Ltd.
28. Janata Jute Mills ltd.
29. Quasem Jute Mills Ltd.
30. Gawais Jute Mills Ltd.

In addition to the above, some more Bangladeshi managed enterprises are under scrutiny for transfer.

Terms and Conditions Under Which the Transfer is Proposed

1. The Bangladeshi shareholders whose names appeared in the share register of the company on the date of nationalisation and are

entitled will be offered such number of shares as were held by them on that date. The price charged for each such share will be the same as worked out at the time of payment of compensation.

2. In cases where the Bangladeshi shareholders held less than 51% of the shares, they will be required to buy additional shares to enable them to acquire controlling shares of 51% or more, before transfer of management can take place. While they will be charged the same price per share as worked out for payment of compensation for the shares held by them on the date of nationalisation, the additional shares will be sold on the basis or revaluation.

3. The former Bangladeshi shareholders will have to pay in cash for the shares held by them on the date of nationalisation and now offered for sale to them. If for any reason some of them cannot pay cash for the entire value of these shares, they will be allowed to pay 51% of the total value of the shares in cash as a lump sum payment and the balance amount will be paid within a period not exceeding 12 months from the date of acceptance of the offer. Such shareholders will furnish adequate guarantee for the unpaid balance.

4. The former Bangladeshi shareholders will be offered to buy all the shares of the company, in addition to those held by them on the date of nationalisation. If some of the shareholders are unable to pay in cash the full value of these additional shares at a time, they will be allowed to pay in cash 10% of the full value of the shares and the balance within a period not exceeding 5 (five) years in 10 (ten) half-yearly installments. Number of actual shares transferred will correspond to the payments received. If they do not exercise the option, those shares may be sold to other private parties. If sufficient response is not received from private buyers, Government may sell the balance shares to financial institutions like BSB, BSRS, ICB, Insurance Companies, etc. provided that if any of the financing institutions held any shares in the mills prior to nationalisation, then those shares may be transferred to them on the same basis as transfers to the original Bangladeshi shareholders.

5. If after offer of shares mentioned herein before the Government still holds shares in the capital of a company, the Government will have the right to nominate Director(s) in proportion to its shareholding interest in the company.

6. The former Bangladeshi shareholders who will buy shares from the Government, will not be allowed to sell these shares within the period of encumbrancy without prior approval of the Government.

7. If the Bangladeshi shareholders default in discharging their liabilities to the Government, they will be liable to pay on the defaulted installments a penal interest @ 2% (two percent) above the contracted rate.

8. Before handing over management of the mills, the Government under P.O. 27 will notify the formation of the first Board of Directors of the concerned mills. This Board will be a temporary one and it will function for a period not exceeding one year or till a new Board is elected in accordance with the Articles of Association, whichever is earlier.

9. All assets and liabilities of the companies existing on the date of transfer will continue to be the assets and liabilities of the denationalised companies.

10. The denationalised companies will take over the liabilities to BSB, BSRS, Commercial Banks, foreign creditors, etc. on the same terms and conditions as exist at present between the borrower and the lender.

11. BJMC's loan from Bangladesh Bank and Commercial Banks against Government undertaking or BJMC's debentures utilised for denationalised companies will be passed on to them on the same terms and conditions.

12. Any contract made or understanding arrived at by the mills or on their behalf by the Corporation either for sale or purchase including claims will be honoured by the new management of the denationalised companies.

13. For co-ordination of export sales, a Pricing Committee composed of representatives of BJMC, denationalised companies and Bangladesh Bank will be set up in the proportion 3:2:1.

14. All sales under barter/tender to foreign Government and local sales to Government/Sector Corporation will continue to be negotiated by the BJMC and allocated to the concerned mills on the basis of loomage. Common expenses in connection with such sales (including CBC) and allied functions will be shared proportionately by BJMC and denationalised mills. Details will be worked out by the Pricing Committee.

15. Repayment of Government investments (excluding the amount paid as subsidy) in the Jute Mills proposed for transfer will be the responsibility of the denationalised companies, part of this amount was in the form of capital infusion for equity support which did not carry any interest. These liabilities will be repaid by the companies to the Government in 12 years in respect of composite

mills and 15 years in respect of broad loom units, the rate of interest remaining the same as at the time of initial investment by the Government.

16. In order to give relief to these mills under the new management, a moratorium on the repayment of Government investment for a period of 2 years will be given from the date of transfer within the overall repayment period stipulated in para 15 above.

17. The denationalised companies will take over all officers, staff and workers in employment in the enterprises on the date of transfer along with liabilities of service benefits. They will also take over an agreed number of officers and staff from BJMC Head Office and Zonal Offices, likely to be declared surplus after transfer of these mills to denationalised companies. There will be no termination or retrenchment for one year from the date of transfer.

18. If the company—

(i) persistently defaults in discharging its liabilities to the Government, Krishi Bank, Bangladesh Shilpa Bank, Bangladesh Shilpa Rin Sangstha, Commercial Banks and foreign creditors in accordance with the terms and conditions of the agreements with them as adopted by the company; or

(ii) does not faithfully and diligently discharge its liabilities in respect of the loans of Bangladesh Jute Mills Corporation taken from Bangladesh Bank and Commercial Banks against Government undertakings and now adopted by the company as its own liabilities; or

(iii) does not observe and perform the terms and conditions of finances obtained by debentures issues by Bangladesh Jute Mills Corporation and utilised by the Company and now passed on the company for observance and performance; or

(iv) does not operate the Mills for any reason which is not beyond its control;

the Government will have the right to intervene in the affairs of the Company.

Applications (in duplicate) in the following form, from persons willing to buy the shares must reach within 21 days of the publication of this notice to Joint Secretary In-Charge of the Implementation Cell for transfer of Jute Mills, Jute Division, Adamjee Court, Motijheel Commercial Area, Dacca.

FORM OF APPLICATION FOR SHARES OF

_____ LIMITED.

1. Name of the applicant:
2. Present address of the applicant:
3. Permanent address of the applicant;
4. Citizenship of the applicant (Documentary proof in support of Bangladeshi citizenship to be enclosed):
5. Total number of shares issued, subscribed and paid up:
6. Number of shares applied for:
7. Total number of shares originally held:
8. Distinctive number of such shares:
9. Face value and paid up value of each share:
10. Present status of the shares—

    (a) Whether in the possession of the applicant or deposited with the "Compensation Cell" of the Ministry of Industries & Commerce:
    (b) If placed as security with any Bank or Financial Institution as Collateral, names thereof:

11. Whether any compensation under Article 9 of P.O. 27 of 1972 has been received for the shares, if so state total amount:
12. Whether shares claimed as heirs/successors of original share-holders (if succession certificate obtained, attested copy to be enclosed).

I _____ do hereby declare that
(Name of the applicant)
the particulars furnished in the application are correct and for any incorrect particulars, it shall stand cancelled. I further declare that I shall abide by the terms and conditions of the transfer of shares prescribed by the Government.

_____
(Signature of the applicant)

By Order of the
Chief Martial Law Administrator

(M.A. Waheed)
Joint Secretary

Index

Abandoned enterprises, 33, 41(n33), 137
  commercial sector, 29, 41(n35), 50–51
  divestiture of, 33, 50, 57, 62(n51), 66,
    71
  looting of, 28, 29, 50–51
ADB. *See* Asian Development Bank
Agriculture, 91
  and British colonial rule, 20
  GDP percent, 41(n43), 54
  importance to economy of, 11, 105,
    142
  inelasticity of, 4, 63, 78
  during Pakistan period, 22, 28
  private investment in, 54, 60(n34)
  privatization of, 156, 162
  and world economy, 35
  See also Fertilizer industry
Ahmed, Moudud, 82, 96–97(n57), 138, 151
Akberali family, 38–39
Asia Foundation, 149
Asian Development Bank (ADB), 149, 152
Awami League, 29, 35, 40(n29), 42(n41),
    44(n60)
  class makeup of, 34
  opposition to privatization, 68, 83, 90,
    137
Azam, Shafiul, 47, 48, 58, 59(n4), 92(n3),
    136, 145
  and New Industrial Policy—1982, 64,
    70, 74

BADC. *See* Bangladesh Agricultural
    Development Corporation
Bangladesh Agricultural Development
    Corporation (BADC), 128, 156
Bangladesh Chemical Industries
    Corporation (BCIC), 53, 76, 87–88,
    120, 121, 152
Bangladesh Jute Mills Association
    (BJMA), 73
Bangladesh Jute Mills Corporation
    (BJMC), 53, 55, 76, 139, 167
Bangladesh Re-Rolling Mills, Ltd., 38–39
Bangladesh Shilpa Bank (BSB), 48, 55,
    72–73, 87–88, 152
Bangladesh Shilpa Rin Sangstha (BSRS),
    72–73, 87–88, 152
Bangladesh Steel and Engineering
    Corporation (BSEC), 53, 76, 120, 121
Bangladesh Sugar and Food Industries
    Corporation (BSFIC), 53, 76, 120,
    121
Bangladesh Textile Mills Corporation
    (BTMC), 53, 55, 75–76
Banking. *See* Financial sector
BCIC. *See* Bangladesh Chemical
    Industries Corporation
Bengal, East. *See* British colonial rule
Berg, Elliot, 3, 56, 91
BJMA. *See* Bangladesh Jute Mills
    Association

BJMC. *See* Bangladesh Jute Mills
Corporation
Black market, 77, 95(n41), 105–106, 108
government responses to, 91, 106
and India trade, 22
and Mujib nationalization policy, 34,
37
and private investment, 42(n45), 106,
119
and private sector performance, 91,
123, 127
British colonial rule, 4, 19, 20–21, 142
BSB. *See* Bangladesh Shilpa Bank
BSEC. *See* Bangladesh Steel and
Engineering Corporation
BSFIC. *See* Bangladesh Sugar and Food
Industries Corporation
BSRS. *See* Bangladesh Shilpa Rin
Sangstha
BTMC. *See* Bangladesh Textile Mills
Corporation
Bureaucracy
Bengalis in, 26, 28
corruption in, 106–107, 111,
131–132(n6)
and foreign donor agencies, 164
inefficiency of, 12, 17, 67, 70, 106–107,
136, 144–145, 151, 164
loss of prestige, 145
management expertise in, 11
resistance to privatization in, 12, 14,
69, 144, 146, 164
and sectoral Corporations, 31–32,
41–42(n37), 168–169
Business community, 100–106
attitude toward government, 112, 145,
176
Bengali role in, 20–21, 23–24, 25–27,
28, 29, 100, 119
chambers of commerce, 14, 104–105,
176–177
commercial nature of, 5, 11, 52,
93(n13), 134(n43), 142
ethnic minority role in, 11, 20, 23
family business pattern in, 101, 142
interest in industrial sector, 52–53, 77,
101–102
lack of resources in, 24, 25
during Pakistan period, 24, 25, 100
public mistrust of, 10, 11, 29, 102–103,
107

recommendations for, 176–177
See also Management expertise;
Private sector

Calcutta, 4, 21–22, 35
Chambers of commerce, 14, 104–105,
176–177
China, People's Republic of, 112
Chishty, Shamsul Haque, 32, 64, 70,
92(n7), 126, 136
Civil service. *See* Bureaucracy
Civil war, effects on economy of, 25, 28,
35, 50
Colonialism, 10. *See also* British colonial
rule
Commercial sector, 11
abandoned enterprises, 29, 41(n35),
50–51
corruption in, 50, 51
divestiture in, 50–52, 59–60(n17),
60(n18)
GDP percent (Mujib), 41(n34)
importance to economy of, 105
and industrial sector, 52–53, 77,
101–102
management expertise in, 5
during Pakistan period, 24, 26
Committee for Reorganization of Public
Statutory Corporations (CRPSC),
74–75
Contract management, 17, 74, 156
Corporations, sectoral, 36, 41(n36), 49,
53–54, 60(n28)
class makeup of, 62(n50)
conflict with bureaucracy, 31–32,
41–42(n37), 168–169
divestitures by, 57–58, 66, 73
Corruption, 12, 164
in bureaucracy, 106–107, 111,
131–132(n6)
in commercial sector, 50, 51
and divestiture, 104
in labor movement, 116
during Mujib period, 29, 34, 38
in state-owned enterprises, 12, 34, 38,
51, 68, 107
See also Loan repayment problem
Cotton textiles. *See* Textile industry
CRPSC. *See* Committee for
Reorganization of Public Statutory
Corporations

Debt-equity conversion, 18, 75
Development Finance Institutions (DFIs), 18, 24, 55, 89, 90, 152
DFIs. *See* Development Finance Institutions
DGI. *See* Director General of Industries
Dhaka Stock Exchange (DSE), 48–49, 55, 86, 88, 149, 154
Director General of Industries (DGI), 107
Disinvestment, 44–45(n71). *See also* Divestiture; Privatization
Divestiture, 3, 8
  of abandoned enterprises, 33, 50, 57, 62(n51), 66, 71
  of commercial sector, 50–52, 59–60(n17), 60(n18)
  effects on private sector, 161
  and ethnic minority control, 25
  evaluation of applicants, 123, 129, 134(n43), 153
  financing for, 18, 42(n45), 110, 123, 131(n1)
  government policies, 109–110, 112
  Indian-owned enterprises, 38, 44(n70), 50, 56–57
  inherited liabilities, 18, 44(n62), 72, 94(n22), 99, 131(n1), 161, 170, 178(n2)
  legal basis for, 46, 62(n51)
  during Mujib period, 30, 33, 38, 44(n70), 50, 91
  negotiations, 70–73, 94(n22), 140
  New Industrial Policy—1982, 66–67, 70–74, 78, 91
  during Pakistan period, 25
  prevalence of, 3
  pricing, 15, 71, 72, 103–104, 123, 140, 170–171
  public opinion, 25
  of small businesses, 30, 33, 49, 57
  suitability of enterprises for, 15, 17, 129, 151, 153, 155
  in Taiwan, 143
  See also Personnel issues; Privatization; State-owned enterprises
Divestiture, partial. *See* Share-selling
Donors. *See* Foreign donor agencies
DSE. *See* Dhaka Stock Exchange

East Pakistan Industrial Development Corporation (EPIDC). *See* Pakistan Industrial Development Corporation

Employee Stock Option Program (ESOP), 18, 87, 90, 115–116, 153–154, 171
EPIDC. *See* Pakistan Industrial Development Corporation
Ershad, Hussain Muhammad, 59(n4), 64, 70, 73, 91, 93(n8), 139, 155
ESOP. *See* Employee Stock Option Program
Exports
  government encouragement of, 20, 22–23, 48, 65
  growth in, 119
  jute, 5, 25, 54, 77, 104, 126, 167
  See also Black market; Commercial sector

Fertilizer industry, 24, 84, 135(n45)
  privatization of, 8, 127–129, 149, 155, 158(n8), 169–170
  share-selling, 97(n62)
51-49 Plan. *See* Share-selling
Financial sector, 11, 22, 24, 105
  nationalization of, 29, 30, 54–55
Foreign donor agencies, 142, 163
  and bureaucracy, 164
  preference for state-owned enterprises, 148–149, 174
  pressure for privatization by, 2–3, 13, 83–84
  and privatization financing, 18, 143
  recommendations for, 173–175
  See also names of specific organizations
Foreign investment
  assembly vs. manufacturing enterprises, 94(n15), 148
  and debt-equity conversion, 75
  joint ventures with private sector, 66, 148
  and labor movement, 148
  limitations on, 34
  and low productivity, 117, 147
  during Mujib period, 34, 38, 41(n34)
  New Industrial Policy encouragement of, 66, 67–68, 152
  Revised Investment Policy, 48
  and state-owned enterprises, 11
Foreign models for privatization, 2, 12, 64, 97(n69), 130, 138, 173
  assembly vs. manufacturing, 93–94(n15), 117–118, 148
  choice of enterprises for divestiture, 15

economic planning, 141
management expertise, 101
marginalization, 84, 134(n44), 143
Taiwan, 141–144, 157(n5)

Government role in economy, 13, 78, 146,
    155
    under British colonial rule, 21
    economic planning, 140–141
    during Pakistan period, 22
    privatization unit, 165–166, 173
    recommendations for, 163–173
    regulatory environment, 18, 91, 98,
        108–109, 112, 125
    research and development, 140, 168
    responses to black market, 91, 106
    support for private sector, 8–9, 18,
        106, 145–146
    See also Bureaucracy; State-owned
        enterprises

Hindu-Muslim rivalry, 20–21. See also
    Non-Bengali control of business

ICB. See Investment Corporation of
    Bangladesh
ILO. See International Labor
    Organization
IMF. See International Monetary Fund
India
    East Pakistan, trade with, 22
    Indian-owned enterprises, 38, 44(n70),
        50, 56–57
    jute industry, 40(n21)
    See also Black market
Industrial development, 78, 161
    Industrial Policy—1986, 85–91
    New Industrial Policy—1982, 63–74
    New Investment Policy, July 1974, 48
    during Pakistan period, 22–24
    Revised Investment Policy, Dec. 1975,
        47–49, 59(nn 12, 14)
    See also Industrial sector;
        Privatization; Private sector
Industrial Policy—1986 (IP-'86), 85–91,
    97(n60)
Industrial sector
    assembly vs. manufacturing, 67,
        93–94(n15), 117–118, 148
    commercial sector interest in, 52–53,
        77, 101–102

financing for, 24, 54–55
image of, 102
importance to economy of, 105, 114
increase in, 5, 119
nationalization of, during Mujib
    period, 29–39
    during Pakistan period, 23–24, 25, 26,
        27–28
performance of, 91
public-private mix, 27, 76
statistics, 5, 24, 27, 31, 53, 76, 77, 78
See also Fertilizer industry; Jute
    industry; Private sector;
    Privatization; Sugar industry;
    Textile industry
Informal economy, 95(n41), 118,
    134(n43). See also Black market
International Labor Organization (ILO),
    117, 149
International Monetary Fund (IMF), 84
Investment. See Foreign investment;
    Private investment
Investment Corporation of Bangladesh
    (ICB), 48
IP-'86. See Industrial Policy—1986
Islam, 4. See also Hindu-Muslim rivalry

Janata Bank, 96
Joint ventures (public-private), 18, 28, 32,
    72
    agribusiness, 156
    Industrial Policy—1986, 85, 97(n60)
    New Industrial Policy—1982, 65, 66
    public opinion, 108
    Revised Investment Policy (1975),
        47–48
Jute industry, 52, 54
    and black market, 91
    under British colonial rule, 20
    corruption in, 104
    foreign buyers, 139, 166
    Industrial Policy—1986, 85
    loan repayment problem, 72–73, 90,
        104, 139, 170
    management expertise in, 101
    nationalization of, 31, 32, 34, 36, 37, 39
    national sales organization, 166–168
    New Industrial Policy privatization,
        65, 66–67, 69, 70–73, 78
    during Pakistan period, 22, 25, 26, 27,
        126

performance of, 91, 119, 123, 124–126, 133(n31), 161
personnel reduction in, 114, 115, 116
private-public competition within, 56, 61(n46), 146
privatization of, 49, 57, 58, 114, 139
reduced demand, 5, 35, 77, 115

Labor movement, 94(n16)
corruption in, 116
Employee Stock Option Program (ESOP), 18, 87, 90, 115–116, 153–154, 171
and foreign investment, 148
resistance to privatization by, 14, 68–69, 73, 83, 90, 96(n53), 113–117, 132(n12)
Liquidation, 16, 169. *See also* Marginalization
Loan repayment problem, 77, 78, 95–96(n42), 119, 147
government response to, 89–90, 104
and government support for state-owned enterprises, 55, 125
and inherited liabilities, 72, 170
and New Industrial Policy, 72–73
during Pakistan period, 24

Management expertise
and assembly vs. manufacturing, 94(n15)
among Bengalis, 24, 25, 28, 29, 119
in bureaucracy, 11
business community training, 177
in commercial sector, 5
increase in, 77, 99, 100–101
in private sector, 12–13, 35–36, 123, 124, 127, 134(n43)
shortage of, 28, 29, 35–36, 100–101, 117, 119, 142
in state-owned enterprises, 38, 151
Manufacturing sector. *See* Industrial sector
Marginalization, 16, 134(n44), 143, 162–163
fertilizer industry, 84, 127–128, 155, 163, 170
Martial Law Authority (MLA), 46, 83
Micro-enterprise Industrial Development Assistance Society (MIDAS), 158(n8)

MIDAS. *See* Micro-enterprise Industrial Development Assistance Society
MLA. *See* Martial Law Authority
Mujib. *See* Rahman, Sheikh Mujibur

Nationalization
of abandoned enterprises, 33, 41(n33), 50, 51, 137
and colonialism, 10
of financial sector, 29, 30, 54–55
ideological motivations for, 36, 46–47, 137
and management expertise, 101
motivations for, 10–11
during Mujib period, 29–39, 41(nn 35, 36), 44(n60)
private sector role in, 32–34, 35, 37–38
public support for, 14, 29, 32–33, 40–41(n32)
shareholder compensation, 50, 59(n12)
See also State-owned enterprises
National security, 11, 17, 169
New Industrial Policy—1982 (NIP-'82), 65–74, 78, 85, 93(n11), 101, 124
and private investment, 65, 66, 105
state-owned enterprises reform, 74–77
NIP-'82. *See* New Industrial Policy—1982
Non-Bengali control of business, 11, 20, 23–24, 25, 26. *See also* Abandoned enterprises

Pakistan, East, 4, 19, 21–28, 35, 126
Pakistan Industrial Development Corporation (PIDC), 22–23, 24, 25, 30, 52, 68, 91, 148
bureaucratic attitude toward, 32
nostalgia for, 154–155
public-private joint ventures, 97(n60)
Permanent Settlement Act, 1793, 20
Personnel issues, 14, 116–117, 122–123, 154, 171
and divestiture agreements, 73, 114–115
and labor opposition to divestiture, 68–69, 113
and performance, 98, 123, 132(n17)
PIDC. *See* Pakistan Industrial Development Corporation
Planning Commission, 31, 33, 35, 47, 79, 137, 140–141
recommendations, 165, 166

Political instability, 4, 35
    and private investment, 11, 78
    and resistance to privatization, 25, 39
President's Order (P.O.) No. 27, 29, 30,
    31, 37, 40(n29), 49
Private investment, 18
    in agriculture, 54, 60(n34)
    and black market, 42(n45), 106, 119
    and financing roadblocks, 55, 110
    free zone policy, 67, 85
    increase in, 52–53, 91, 119, 156, 161
    Industrial Policy—1986, 105
    limitations on, 34
    during Mujib period, 34, 37
    and New Industrial Policy—1982, 66,
        67, 105
    New Investment Policy (July 1974), 48
    and political instability, 11, 78
    Revised Investment Policy (Dec.
        1975), 47–49, 59(nn 12, 14), 65
    in small business, 33–34
    tax incentives, 48
    under Zia government, 52
    See also Foreign investment; Joint
        ventures (public-private); Private
        sector; Privatization
Private sector
    financing for, 24–25, 55
    government consultation regarding
        privatization with, 64–65
    government support for, 8–9, 18, 106,
        145–146
    informal economy, 95(n41), 118
    management expertise, 12–13, 35–36,
        123, 124
    during Mujib period, 32–34, 36, 37–38,
        42(n46)
    and nationalization, 32–34, 35, 37–38
    during Pakistan period, 22, 23, 27–28
    role in economy of, 37, 52–53, 156, 162
    size of, 27, 60(n27), 62(n51), 105, 130,
        156, 162
    See also Black market; Business
        community; Private investment;
        Private sector performance;
        Privatization
Private sector performance, 55–56, 77,
    98–130, 160–161
    and black market, 91, 123, 127
    and bureaucracy, 106–108, 110–111

Canadian International Development
    Agency study, 121–123
    competition with state-owned
        enterprises, 56, 61(n46), 151, 208
    context of, 98–100
    and government policy, 108–110,
        111–112, 122, 123, 125
    and inherited liabilities, 99, 131(n1), 161
    and labor movement, 113–117
    and low productivity, 99, 117–118, 123
    and poor management, 123, 124, 127,
        134(n43)
    profit and loss, 118–127
Privatization, 1–2, 55–56, 61(n48), 79–82,
    138
    of agriculture, 8, 127–129, 149, 155,
        156, 158(n8), 162, 169–170
    alternative methods of, 15–16, 169
    break-up method, 16, 143, 155–156,
        162, 169
    contract management, 17, 74, 156
    donor pressure toward, 2–3, 13, 83–84
    franchising, 17, 156
    ideological motivations for, 13, 174
    importance of planning for, 5–6, 8,
        9–10, 14, 92, 136, 139, 143, 157,
        164–166, 172–173
    increase in, 1–2
    Industrial Policy—1986, 85–91
    legal basis for, 89
    liquidation, 16, 169
    motivations for, 8, 14, 69–70, 92
    New Industrial Policy—1982, 65–77, 85
    overview of, 7–18
    personnel issues, 14, 154
    political influences on, 8, 152–153
    public opinion, 10, 14, 39, 68–69,
        82–83, 90, 108, 147
    public relations for, 16–17, 87,
        172–173
    and social injustice, 10, 14, 89
    of whole economy, 8, 92, 98–99, 105
    See also Divestiture; Foreign models
        for privatization; Joint ventures
        (public-private); Marginalization;
        Private investment; Private sector;
        Share-selling
Public Enterprise (Management and
    Coordination) Ordinance of 1986,
    90

Public sector. *See* Bureaucracy;
  Government role in economy; Joint
  ventures (public-private); Public
  sector performance; State-owned
  enterprises
Public sector performance, 5, 36, 55–56,
  75–76, 77, 90, 111, 133(n31)
  and bureaucracy, 12, 17, 41–42(n37),
    151
  and contradictory motivations, 11–12
  and corruption, 12, 38, 51, 68
  and privatization, 39, 63–64, 137

Quiet liquidation. *See* Marginalization

Rahman, Shafiqur, 58, 64, 70, 73, 74,
  92–93(n7), 97(n60), 153
Rahman, Sheikh Mujibur, 19, 28–39,
  43(n51), 55, 91, 141
Rahman, Zaiur, 46–58, 59(nn 4, 5), 91,
  94(n16)
Revised Investment Policy (Dec. 1975),
  47–49, 59(n12)
Rupali Bank, 83, 88, 152, 171–172

Share-selling, 16, 85–89, 96(n53), 97(n62),
  152–155, 162
  Employment Stock Option Program
    (ESOP), 18, 87, 90, 115–116,
    153–154, 171
  public opinion, 66, 87, 88
  recommendations, 169
  in Taiwan, 143
Small business, 78
  Bengali management of, 26
  divestiture of, 30, 33, 49, 57
  foreign aid for, 158(n8)
  government support for, 24, 48, 65
  lack of chamber of commerce
    representation, 104–105, 177
  loan repayment, 24
  during Mujib period, 30, 33–34
  during Pakistan period, 24, 26, 27, 28
  private investment in, 33–34
  Small Industries Bank, 149–150
Smuggling. *See* Black market
Sobhan, Rehman, 25, 26–27, 33, 42(n41),
  119–121, 137, 157(n2)
Socialism. *See* Nationalization; State-
  owned enterprises

SOEs. *See* State-owned enterprises
Soviet Union, 43(n51)
State-owned enterprises (SOEs)
  administration of, 31–32, 35, 41(n36),
    53–54, 59–60(n17), 60(nn 28, 31),
    151, 168–169
  commercial sector, 51
  competition with private sector, 56,
    61(n46), 151, 208
  corruption in, 12, 34, 38, 51, 68, 107
  financial sector, 29, 30, 54–55
  financing for, 54–55
  government policies favoring,
    44(n62), 109, 122, 123, 125, 155, 172
  and industrial development, 63–64
  leasing, 17
  liability forgiveness, 44(n62), 178(n2)
  management expertise in, 38, 151
  management information system
    (MIS), 68
  number of, 27, 30, 41(n33), 52–53,
    60(n27), 76
  during Pakistan period, 22, 23, 27–28
  private sector role in, 32–34, 35, 172
  and social injustice, 46–47
  suitability for divestiture, 15, 17, 129,
    151, 153, 155
  See also Divestiture; Privatization;
    Public sector performance; Share-
    selling; State-owned enterprises
    reform
State-owned enterprises reform, 17,
  150–151
  debt-equity conversion, 18, 75
  foreign donor pressure for, 84
  and joint ventures, 86
  New Industrial Policy—1982, 65, 67,
    68, 74–77
  Public Enterprise (Management and
    Coordination) Ordinance of 1986,
    90
Stock market, 48–49, 55, 86, 88, 90, 149,
  154
Sugar industry, 53
  nationalization of, 31, 32, 34, 35, 37
  during Pakistan period, 24, 25, 27
  performance of, 120
  privatization of, 65
  public-private mix in, 76
  See also Public sector performance

Taiwan. *See* Foreign models for
    privatization
Taxes, 23, 48, 123, 147
Textile industry, 52, 91
    and black market, 123
    under British colonial rule, 20
    Industrial Policy—1986, 85
    loan repayment problem, 72–73, 170
    management expertise in, 101
    nationalization of, 31, 32, 34, 36, 37,
      39
    New Industrial Policy privatization,
      65, 66–67, 69, 70–73, 78
    during Pakistan period, 24, 25–26, 27
    performance of, 119, 123, 126–127,
      162
    personnel reduction in, 114, 115, 116
    privatization of, 38, 49, 57, 58, 114,
      134(n41)
Trade. *See* Commercial sector
Traditional societies, 19, 142
    factionalism in, 4, 13
    role of business communities in, 10,
      11, 13–14

UNDP. *See* United Nations Development
    Program
Unemployment, 37, 68–69, 77, 113–114, 116
United Kingdom. *See* British colonial rule
United Nations, 149, 158(n9)
United Nations Development Program
    (UNDP), 74, 149
U.S. Agency for International
    Development (USAID), 75, 83–84,
    127–129, 149, 169
USAID. *See* U.S. Agency for International
    Development
Unofficial economy. *See* Black market

War, effects on economy of, 25, 28, 35,
    39(n7), 50, 142
World Bank
    on loan repayment, 90, 104
    state-owned enterprises, reform of,
      74, 75, 76, 78, 149, 151
    support for privatization, 83–84, 149
World economy, influence of, 35, 125

Zia. *See* Rahman, Zaiur

About the Author

A recognized authority on privatization, Clare Humphrey has been involved in Asian affairs and the process of national development for thirty years. Nineteen of those years were spent as an officer of The Asia Foundation, where he held various senior positions, including Director of the Southeast Asia Division, Director of Management and Economic Development Programs, and resident representative in Cambodia and Taiwan.

As an independent consultant for the past decade, Mr. Humphrey has directed major privatization projects in Pakistan, Nepal, Indonesia, Taiwan, and Bangladesh and has been involved in privatization and private sector development activities in over a dozen other Asian and African countries.

Besides privatization, Mr. Humphrey specializes in policy implications of development strategies, problems arising from the process of social change and modernization, and the role of culture in development.

His early career was spent in industry as a Territory Manager for U.S. Royal Tires in Los Angeles. A native Californian, Mr. Humphrey earned his M.A. from the School of International Relations at the University of Southern California and a B.A. from the University of California, Berkeley. He presently resides in the Washington, D.C., area.